EMPLOYMENT LAW

HUGH COLLINS

OXFORD
UNIVERSITY PRESS

OXFORD

UNIVERSITY PRESS

Great Clarendon Street, Oxford OX2 6DP

Oxford University Press is a department of the University of Oxford.
It furthers the University's objective of excellence in research, scholarship,
and education by publishing worldwide in

Oxford New York

Auckland Bangkok Buenos Aires Cape Town Chennai
Dar es Salaam Delhi Hong Kong Istanbul Karachi Kolkata
Kuala Lumpur Madrid Melbourne Mexico City Mumbai Nairobi
São Paulo Shanghai Taipei Tokyo Toronto

Oxford is a registered trade mark of Oxford University Press
in the UK and in certain other countries

Published in the United States
by Oxford University Press Inc., New York

British Library Cataloguing in Publication Data

Data available

Library of Congress Cataloging in Publication Data

Data available

ISBN 0–19–876386–7

1 3 5 7 9 10 8 6 4 2

Typeset in Ehrhardt
by RefineCatch Limited, Bungay, Suffolk
Printed in Great Britain by
Biddles Ltd., Guildford and King's Lynn

Preface

As this is a short book, it has taken a long time to write. Three editorial teams for this series have patiently awaited the outcome, whilst I have tried to discipline the prolific legislative progeny of the same number of British Prime Ministers. In response to my disclosure of what I had been trying to write, a barrister recently confided in me over traditional festive mulled wine and mince pies that he had always steered clear of employment law, because it is the most complicated and transient branch of law. That sobering though accurate indictment of the subject perhaps excuses some of my dilatoriness, yet it also explains the attraction of the intellectual challenge that has held my attention.

The task has been to give the reader a picture of the whole subject, which explains in an accessible way how the many layers of legal sources regulate a central institution of modern society—the employment relationship—whilst striving to give a perspective on the subject that will have a longer shelf-life than the next major legislative intervention, which, if past performance supplies any guide, will be before the printer's ink on this book is dry. To achieve that goal, I have eschewed, albeit reluctantly and with special exceptions for the tastiest morsels, much of the traditional fare of British labour law, and replaced it with a concept of employment law that is founded on what seem to me to comprise the key themes in the evolving and increasingly dominant European Community initiatives in this field: social inclusion, competitiveness, and citizenship.

During the long gestation period for this book, I have incurred too many intellectual debts to recall and to account for. Students and colleagues from many countries have contributed to my appreciation of the subject, especially my collaborators in other writings, Keith Ewing and Aileen McColgan. But I have the sense, though they may not feel entirely comfortable with this attribution of paternity, that my teachers, Mark Freedland and Paul Davies, and their teachers in turn, Lord Wedderburn and Otto Kahn-Freund, always exerted the greatest influence on the evolution of my thinking. As is usually the case, I can with greater certainty gratefully acknowledge a maternal influence, that of my colleagues, Nicola Lacey, Emily Jackson, Elizabeth Barmes, and Claire Kilpatrick, who cast their friendly but critical eyes over a penultimate draft of what follows. My special thanks to them, for they persuaded me that it was time to deliver.

London School of Economics
New Year's Day, 2003

Contents

Preface   v
Table of Cases   xi
Table of Legislation and Statutory Material   xix
Table of European Legislation   xxiv

PART I Aims and Techniques of Employment Law   1

1. 'Labour is not a Commodity'   3
    1   The contract of employment   6
    2   The shifting objectives of employment law   14
    3   An emerging European model   21

2. Regulating the Workplace   27
    1   Compliance, reflexivity, and procedural regulation   28
    2   Regulating contracts   33
    3   The case for mandatory regulation   42
    4   Globalization and levels of regulation   45

PART II Social Inclusion   51

3. Opportunity and Discrimination   53
    1   Proving discrimination   56
    2   Justifying discrimination   62
    3   Eradicating discrimination   73

4. Work and Life   76
    1   A living wage   79
    2   Equal pay   86
    3   Flexible hours   90
    4   The role of government   94

PART III Competitiveness   97

5. Co-operation   99
    1   Mutual trust and confidence   103

2   Adaptation   106
3   Formality   107
4   Grievances   109
5   Human capital   110
6   Flexibility and fairness   114

6. **Partnership**   116
1   Promoting collective bargaining   120
2   Consultation mechanisms   126
3   Stakeholder organizations   130
4   Industrial democracy   132

7. **Competition and Industrial Action**   135
1   Migration   136
2   State aid   139
3   Industrial action   140
4   Contractual restraints on competition   150

8. **Discipline and Dismissal**   157
1   Contractual protection   159
2   Collective self-regulation   167
3   Mandatory regulation   169
4   The standard of fairness   173
5   The problem of compliance   176

9. **Economic Security**   181
1   Contractual allocation of risk   184
2   Safeguarding deferred pay   186
3   Economic dismissals   187
4   Transfers of businesses   196
5   Corporate insolvency   201

PART IV Citizenship   205

10. **Civil Liberties at Work**   207
1   Rights talk   207
2   The European Convention on Human Rights   210
3   Privacy   214
4   Freedom of expression   224

11. **Social Rights** 232
   1   Health and safety 235
   2   The right to organize 240
   3   The right to strike 244
   4   Rights and citizenship 249

12. **Shelf-life** 250

   Index 255

Table of Cases

Abrahamsson v Fogelqvist (C407/98) [2000] E.C.R. I-5539; [2002]
    I.C.R. 932; [2000] I.R.L.R. 732, ECJ (5th Chamber) 66
Adarand Constructors Inc v Pena 115 S Ct 2097 (1995) 67
Ahmad v Inner London Education Authority [1978] Q.B. 36; [1977] 3
    W.L.R. 396; [1978] 1 All E.R. 574; [1977] I.C.R. 490; 75 L.G.R. 753,
    CA 213, 214
Ahmad v United Kingdom (8160/78) (1982) 4 E.H.R.R. 126, Eur Comm
    HR 93
Ahmed v United Kingdom (22954/93) [1999] I.R.L.R. 188; (2000) 29
    E.H.R.R. 1; 5 B.H.R.C. 111; (1999) 1 L.G.L.R. 94; [1998] H.R.C.D.
    823, ECHR 226
Amalgamated Food Employees Union v Logan Valley Plaza 391 US 308
    (1968) 230
American Cyanamid Co v Ethicon Ltd [1975] A.C. 396; [1975] 2 W.L.R.
    316; [1975] 1 All E.R. 504; [1975] F.S.R. 101; [1975] R.P.C. 513; 119
    S.J. 136, HL 142
Associated Newspapers Ltd v Wilson 1995] 2 A.C. 454; [1995] 2 W.L.R.
    354; [1995] 2 All E.R. 100, HL 233–234
Attorney General v Blake [2001] 1 A.C. 268; [2000] 3 W.L.R. 625; [2000]
    4 All E.R. 385; [2000] 2 All E.R. (Comm) 487; [2001] I.R.L.R. 36, HL
   152

Bilka-Kaufhaus GmbH v Weber von Hartz (C170/84) [1986] E.C.R.
    1607; [1986] 2 C.M.L.R. 701; [1987] I.C.R. 110; [1986] I.R.L.R. 317,
    ECJ 67
Bladon v ALM Medical Services Ltd [2002] EWCA Civ 1085; [2002]
    I.C.R. 1444, CA 228
Boys Markets Inc. v Retail Clerks Union, Local 770, 398 US 235 (1970)
   149
British Aerospace Plc v Green [1995] I.C.R. 1006; [1995] I.R.L.R. 433,
    CA 192
Brown v Amalgamated Union of Engineering Workers (Engineering
    Section) [1976] I.C.R. 147; (1975) 119 S.J. 709 240
Bullock v Alice Ottley School [1993] I.C.R. 138; [1992] I.R.L.R. 564; 91
    L.G.R. 32, CA 69

Carrington v Therm-A-Stor Ltd [1983] 1 W.L.R. 138; [1983] 1 All E.R.
796; [1983] I.C.R. 208, CA 123
Clymo v Wandsworth LBC [1989] 2 C.M.L.R. 577; [1989] I.C.R. 250;
[1989] I.R.L.R. 241, EAT 93
Connick v Myers 461 US 138, 103 S Ct 1684 (SCUS, 1983) 229
Cort v Bristol Myers Co. 385 Mass 300, 431 NE ad 908 S Ct of Mass
(1982) 221
Courtaulds Northern Textiles v Andrew [1979] I.R.L.R. 84, EAT 106
Credit Suisse First Boston (Europe) Ltd v Lister [1999] 1 C.M.L.R. 710;
[1999] I.C.R. 794; [1998] I.R.L.R. 700; (1998) 95(44) L.S.G. 35; (1998)
142 S.J.L.B. 269, CA 198
Cresswell v Inland Revenue Commissioners [1984] 2 All E.R. 713; [1984]
I.R.L.R. 190; (1984) 81 L.S.G. 1843, Ch D 112
Crofter Hand Woven Harris Tweed Co Ltd v Veitch [1942] A.C. 435;
[1942] 1 All E.R. 147; 1943 S.L.T. 2, HL 144
Cutter v Powell (1795) 6 Term Rep. 320; [1775–1802] All ER Rep 159 160

Dines v Initial Health Care Services Ltd [1995] I.C.R. 11; [1994]
I.R.L.R. 336, CA 200

E O C v Secretary of State for Employment [1995] 1 A.C. 1; [1994] 2
W.L.R. 409; [1994] 1 All E.R. 910, HL 74
ECM (Vehicle Delivery Services) Ltd v Cox [1999] 4 All E.R. 669; [2000]
1 C.M.L.R. 224; [1999] I.C.R. 1162; [1999] I.R.L.R. 559, CA 200
Edwards v Halliwell [1950] 2 All E.R. 1064; [1950] W.N. 537; 94 S.J. 803,
CA 241
Enderby v Frenchay HA (C127/92) [1994] 1 All E.R. 495; [1993] E.C.R.
I-5535; [1994] 1 C.M.L.R. 8; [1994] I.C.R. 112; [1993] I.R.L.R. 591,
ECJ (1st Chamber) 88–90

Foley v Interactive Data Corporation 47 Cal. 3d 654, 765 P 2d 373, S Ct
Cal (1988) 229
Fortune v National Cash Register Co. 364 NE 2d 1251 S Judicial Ct of
Mass (1977) 162
French v Barclays Bank Plc [1998] I.R.L.R. 646, CA 105, 163
French Republic v Commission (C241/94) [1996] ECR I-4551, ECJ 140

Grant v South West Trains Ltd (C249/96) [1998] All E.R. (EC) 193;
[1998] E.C.R. I-621; [1998] 1 C.M.L.R. 993; [1998] C.E.C. 263; [1998]
I.C.R. 449, ECJ 57
Grigoriades v Greece (24348/94) (1999) 27 E.H.R.R. 464; 4 B.H.R.C. 43;
[1998] H.R.C.D. 103, ECHR 229

Gunton v Richmond upon Thames LBC [1981] Ch. 448; [1980] 3
W.L.R. 714; [1980] 3 All E.R. 577; [1980] I.C.R. 755; [1980] I.R.L.R.
321; 79 L.G.R. 241; 124 S.J. 792, CA 166

Halford v United Kingdom (20605/92) [1997] I.R.L.R. 471; (1997) 24
E.H.R.R. 523; 3 B.H.R.C. 31, ECHR 216, 217
Hampson v Department of Education and Science [1990] 2 All E.R. 25;
[1989] I.C.R. 179; [1989] I.R.L.R. 69; (1989) 86(13) L.S.G. 43; (1989)
133 S.J. 151, CA 69
Hatton v Sutherland [2002] EWCA Civ 76; [2002] 2 All E.R. 1; [2002]
I.C.R. 613, CA 239
Hayward v Cammell Laird Shipbuilders Ltd (No.2) [1988] A.C. 894;
[1988] 2 W.L.R. 1134; [1988] 2 All E.R. 257, HL 87
Herbert Clayton & Jack Waller Ltd v Oliver [1930] A.C. 209; [1930] All
E.R. Rep. 414, HL 113
Hivac Ltd v Park Royal Scientific Instruments Ltd [1946] Ch. 169, CA
....151
Hodgson v NALGO [1972] 1 W.L.R. 130; [1972] 1 All E.R. 15; (1971)
116 S.J. 56, Ch D 240
Hollister v National Farmers Union [1979] I.C.R. 542; [1979] I.R.L.R.
238, CA 193
Hudgens v NLRB 424 US 507 (1976) 230

Ipswich Taylor's (1614) 11 Co Rep 53 53
Irani v Southampton and South West Hampshire HA [1985] I.C.R. 590;
[1985] I.R.L.R. 203; (1985) 82 L.S.G. 1167, Ch D 165

Jet Courier Service v Mulei 771 P 2d 484 S Ct Colorado (1989) 153
Johnson v Unisys Ltd [2001] UKHL 13; [2001] 2 W.L.R. 1076; [2001] 2
All E.R. 801; [2001] I.C.R. 480; [2001] I.R.L.R. 279; [2001] Emp. L.R.
469, HL 162, 164
Johnstone v Bloomsbury HA [1992] Q.B. 333; [1991] 2 W.L.R. 1362;
[1991] 2 All E.R. 293, CA 36

Kara v United Kingdom No. 36528/97, 22 Oct. 1998 223
Kelley v Johnson 425 US 238 (1976) 223
King v Great Britain China Centre [1992] I.C.R. 516; [1991] I.R.L.R.
513, CA 58
Kirsammer-Hack v Sidal (C189/91) [1993] E.C.R. I-6185; [1994]
I.R.L.R. 185, ECJ 139
Kreil v Germany (C285/98) [2000] E.C.R. I-69; [2002] 1 C.M.L.R. 36,
ECJ 63

Lambeth LBC v Commission for Racial Equality [1990] I.C.R. 768;
 [1990] I.R.L.R. 231, CA 64
Laws v London Chronicle (Indicator Newspapers) [1959] 1 W.L.R. 698;
 [1959] 2 All E.R. 285; 93 I.L.T. 213; 103 S.J. 462; 103 S.J. 470, CA 161
Lesney Products & Co v Nolan [1977] I.C.R. 235; [1977] I.R.L.R. 77;
 (1976) 12 I.T.R. 6, CA 193
Lewis v Motorworld Garages [1986] I.C.R. 157; [1985] I.R.L.R. 465, CA
105
Lingens v Austria (No.2) (A/103) (1986) 8 E.H.R.R. 407, ECHR 224
Lister v Romford Ice and Cold Storage Co Ltd [1957] A.C. 555; [1957] 2
 W.L.R. 158; [1957] 1 All E.R. 125; [1956] 2 Lloyd's Rep. 505; 121 J.P.
 98; 101 S.J. 106, HL 103
Lommers v Minister van Landbouw Natuurbeheer en Visserij (C476/99)
 [2002] I.R.L.R. 430, ECJ 70
London Underground Ltd v Edwards (No.2) ...[1999] I.C.R. 494; [1998]
 I.R.L.R. 364; (1998) 95(26) L.S.G. 32; (1998) 148 N.L.J. 905; (1998)
 142 S.J.L.B. 182, CA 62, 72, 93
Lumley v Gye (1853) 2 El. & Bl. 216 145

Mahmoud v Bank of Credit and Commerce International SA (In
 Liquidation); BCCI SA, Re [1998] A.C. 20; [1997] 3 W.L.R. 95; [1997]
 3 All E.R. 1, HL 35, 104
Mallone v BPB Industries Ltd [2002] EWCA Civ 126; [2002] I.C.R.
 1045; [2002] I.R.L.R. 452; [2002] Emp. L.R. 919, CA 107
Manchester University v Jones [1993] I.C.R. 474; [1993] I.R.L.R. 218;
 (1993) 137 S.J.L.B. 14, CA 69
Mandolidis v Elkins Industries Inc. 246 SE 2d 907 (1978) 238
Marschall v Land Nordrhein-Westfalen (C-409/95) [1997] All E.R.
 (E.C.) 865; [1997] E.C.R. I-6363; [1998] 1 C.M.L.R. 547; [1998]
 C.E.C. 152; [2001] I.C.R. 45; [1998] I.R.L.R. 39, ECJ 66
Marshall v Southampton and South West Hampshire AHA (No.1)
 (C152/84) [1986] Q.B. 401; [1986] 2 W.L.R. 780; [1986] 2 All E.R.
 584; [1986] E.C.R. 723, ECJ 57
Mathewson v RB Wilson Dental Laboratory [1989] I.R.L.R. 512, EAT
 ....175, 222
McClaren v Home Office [1990] I.C.R. 824; [1990] I.R.L.R. 338; (1990) 2
 Admin. L.R. 652; [1990] C.O.D. 257; (1990) 87(17) L.S.G. 31; (1990)
 134 S.J. 908, CA 166
McMeechan v Secretary of State for Employment [1997] I.C.R. 549;
 [1997] I.R.L.R. 353, CA 42

Middlebrook Mushrooms v Transport and General Workers Union
[1993] I.C.R. 612; [1993] I.R.L.R. 232, CA 231

Miles v Wakefield MDC [1987] A.C. 539; [1987] 2 W.L.R. 795; [1987] 1
All E.R. 1089; [1987] I.C.R. 368, HL 160

Mirror Group Newspapers Ltd v Gunning [1986] 1 W.L.R. 546; [1986] 1
All E.R. 385; [1986] I.C.R. 145, CA 41

Monge v Beebe Rubber Co. 114 NH 130, 316A 2d 549 S Ct New
Hampshire (1974) 162

Murray v Foyle Meats Ltd [2000] 1 A.C. 51; [1999] 3 W.L.R. 356; [1999]
3 All E.R. 769; [1999] N.I. 291; [1999] I.C.R. 827; [1999] I.R.L.R. 562,
HL (NI) 193

NLRB v Gissel Packing Co., 395 US 575, S Ct US 124

NWL Ltd v Woods (The Nawala) (No.2) [1979] 1 W.L.R. 1294; [1979] 3
All E.R. 614; [1980] 1 Lloyd's Rep. 1; [1979] I.C.R. 867; [1979]
I.R.L.R. 478; 123 S.J. 751, HL 142

Nagle v Fielden [1966] 2 Q.B. 633; [1966] 2 W.L.R. 1027; [1966] 1 All
E.R. 689; 110 S.J. 286, CA 53

National Union of Mineworkers (Kent Area) v Gormley, The *Times*,
October 21, 1977, CA 241

Nerva v RL&G Ltd [1997] I.C.R. 11; [1996] I.R.L.R. 461; (1996) 93(23)
L.S.G. 35; (1996) 140 S.J.L.B. 140, CA 207

Nerva v United Kingdom (42295/98) [2002] I.R.L.R. 815; (2003) 36
E.H.R.R. 4; 13 B.H.R.C. 246, ECHR 207

Nethermere (St Neots) Ltd v Taverna [1984] I.C.R. 612; [1984] I.R.L.R.
240; (1984) 81 L.S.G. 2147; (1984) 134 N.L.J. 544, CA 38

Niemitz v Germany (1992) 16 E.H.R.R 7, ECHR 217

North Riding Garages v Butterwick [1967] 2 Q.B. 56; [1967] 2
W.L.R. 571; [1967] 1 All E.R. 644; 1 K.I.R. 782; 111 S.J. 72, DC
....188

Office Angels v Rainer-Thomas [1991] I.R.L.R. 214, CA 154

O'Kelly v Trusthouse Forte Plc [1984] Q.B. 90; [1983] 3 W.L.R.
605; [1983] 3 All E.R. 456; [1983] I.C.R. 728; [1983] I.R.L.R.
369, CA 40

Oy Liikenne AB v Liskojarvi (C172/99) [2001] All E.R. (EC) 544; [2001]
E.C.R. I-745; [2001] 3 C.M.L.R. 37; [2002] I.C.R. 155; [2001]
I.R.L.R. 171; [2001] Emp. L.R. 235, ECJ (6th Chamber) 200

Parkins v Sodexho Ltd [2002] I.R.L.R. 109, EAT 227

Pickering v Board of Education 391 US 563 (1968) 214

Polkey v AE Dayton Services Ltd [1988] A.C. 344; [1987] 3 W.L.R.
   1153; [1987] 3 All E.R. 974; [1988] I.C.R. 142; [1987] I.R.L.R. 503,
   HL 175
Porter v American Optical Corp. 641 F 2d 1128, 5th Circ. (1981) 238
Post Office v Foley; Midland Bank Plc v Madden [2001] 1 All E.R. 550;
   [2000] I.C.R. 1283; [2000] I.R.L.R. 827, CA 158, 159, 173, 174

R. v Commission for Racial Equality ex p. Prestige Group plc [1984] 1
   W.L.R. 335; [1984] I.C.R. 473; [1984] I.R.L.R. 166; (1984) 81 L.S.G.
   134; (1984) 128 S.J. 131, HL 74
R. v Secretary of State for Employment ex p. Seymour–Smith (No.1)
   [1995] I.C.R. 88; [1997] 1 W.L.R. 473; [1997] 2 All E.R. 273; [1997] 2
   C.M.L.R. 904; [1997] I.C.R. 371; [1997] I.R.L.R. 315; (1997) 147
   N.L.J. 414, HL 62
Radford v National Society of Operative Printers Graphical & Media
   Personnel [1972] I.C.R. 484; 116 S.J. 695, Ch D 240
Ratcliffe v North Yorkshire CC [1995] 3 All E.R. 597; [1995] I.C.R. 833;
   [1995] I.R.L.R. 439, HL 89
Regents of University of California v Bakke 438 US 265, 98 S Ct 2733
   (1978) 67
Rekvenyi v Hungary (25390/94) (2000) 30 E.H.R.R. 519; 6 B.H.R.C.
   554, ECHR 226
Ridge v Baldwin (No.1) [1964] A.C. 40; [1963] 2 W.L.R. 935; [1963]
   2 All E.R. 66; 127 J.P. 251; 127 J.P. 295; 61 L.G.R. 369; 37 A.L.J.
   140, HL 166
Roger Bullivant Ltd v Ellis [1987] I.C.R. 464; [1987] I.R.L.R. 491; [1987]
   F.S.R. 172, CA 153
Rookes v Barnard (No.1) [1964] A.C. 1129; [1964] 2 W.L.R. 269; [1964] 1
   All E.R. 367; [1964] 1 Lloyd's Rep. 28; 108 S.J. 93, HL 145

Safeway Stores Plc v Burrell [1997] I.C.R. 523; [1997] I.R.L.R. 200,
   EAT 193
Scally v Southern Health and Social Services Board [1992] 1 A.C.
   294; [1991] 3 W.L.R. 778; [1991] 4 All E.R. 563; [1991] I.C.R. 771;
   [1991] I.R.L.R. 522; (1991) 141 N.L.J. 1482; (1991) 135 S.J. 172,
   HL 108
Secretary of State for Employment v Associated Society of Locomotive
   Engineers and Firemen (No.2) [1972] 2 Q.B. 455; [1972] 2 W.L.R.
   1370; [1972] 2 All E.R. 949; [1972] I.C.R. 19, CA 99
Sirdar v The Army Board and Secretary of State for Defence (C273/97)

[1999] All E.R. (EC) 928; [1999] E.C.R. I-7403; [1999] 3 C.M.L.R.
559; [1999] C.E.C. 554; [2000] I.C.R. 130; [2000] I.R.L.R. 47; 7
B.H.R.C. 459, ECJ 63

Smith v Safeway Plc [1996] I.C.R. 868; [1996] I.R.L.R. 456, CA 223

Squibb United Kingdom Staff Association v Certification Officer [1979]
1 W.L.R. 523; [1979] 2 All E.R. 452; [1979] I.C.R. 235; [1979] I.R.L.R.
75; 123 S.J. 352, CA 122

Steel v United Kingdom (1999) 28 E.H.R.R. 603; 5 B.H.R.C. 339; [1998]
Crim. L.R. 893; [1998] H.R.C.D. 872, ECHR 231

Stenhouse Australia v Phillips [1974] A.C. 391; [1974] 2 W.L.R. 134;
[1974] 1 All E.R. 117; [1974] 1 Lloyd's Rep. 1; (1973) 117 S.J. 875, PC
(Aus) 154

Swain v Denso Marston Ltd [2000] I.C.R. 1079; [2000] P.I.Q.R. P129,
CA 238

Sybron Corp v Rochem Ltd [1984] Ch. 112; [1983] 3 W.L.R. 713; [1983]
2 All E.R. 707; [1983] I.C.R. 801; [1983] I.R.L.R. 253; (1983) 127 S.J.
391, CA 152

Taylor v National Union of Mineworkers (Derbyshire Area) (Injunction)
[1985] I.R.L.R. 99, HC 241

Taylor v Secretary of State for Scotland [2000] 3 All E.R. 90; 2000 S.C.
(H.L.) 139; 2000 S.L.T. 708; [2000] I.C.R. 595; [2000] I.R.L.R. 502;
2000 G.W.D. 17-686, HL 164

Teamsters Local 695 v Vogt Inc. 354 US 284 (1957) 230

Thornhill v Alabama 310 US 88 (1940) 230

Tottenham Green Under Fives Centre v Marshall (No.2) [1991] I.C.R.
320; [1991] I.R.L.R. 162, EAT 64

UNISON v United Kingdom (Admissibility) (53574/99) [2002] I.R.L.R.
497, ECHR 245

Union Royale Belge des Societes de Football Association (ASBL) v
Bosman (C415/93) [1996] All E.R. (EC) 97; [1995] E.C.R. I-4921;
[1996] 1 C.M.L.R. 645; [1996] C.E.C. 38, ECJ 138

United Bank v Akhtar [1989] I.R.L.R. 507, EAT 107

University College London Hospitals NHS Trust v UNISON [1999]
I.C.R. 204; [1999] I.R.L.R. 31; (1998) 95(41) L.S.G. 45; (1998) 142
S.J.L.B. 270, CA 146

Vogt v Germany (A/323) (1996) 21 E.H.R.R. 205; [1996] E.L.R. 232,
ECHR 225

WA Goold (Pearmak) Ltd v McConnell [1995] I.R.L.R. 516, EAT ...109
William Hill Organisation Ltd v Tucker [1999] I.C.R. 291; [1998]
    I.R.L.R. 313; (1998) 95(20) L.S.G. 33; (1998) 142 S.J.L.B. 140,
    CA 155
Williams v Compair Maxam [1982] I.C.R. 156; [1982] I.R.L.R. 83, EAT
   191
Wilson v Racher [1974] I.C.R. 428; [1974] I.R.L.R. 114; (1974) 16 K.I.R.
    212, CA 161
Wilson v St Helens Borough Council [1999] 2 A.C. 52; [1998] 3 W.L.R.
    1070; [1998] 4 All E.R. 609; [1999] 1 C.M.L.R. 918; [1998] I.C.R.
    1141, HL 198
Wilson and National Union of Journalists v United Kingdom [2002]
    I.R.L.R. 568, ECHR 234, 235, 240, 244
Wiluszynski v Tower Hamlets LBC [1989] I.C.R. 493; [1989] I.R.L.R.
    259; 88 L.G.R. 14; (1989) 133 S.J. 628, CA 160
Woods v WM Car Services (Peterborough) Ltd [1982] Com. L.R. 208;
    [1982] I.C.R. 693; [1982] I.R.L.R. 413, CA 181

Young, James and Webster v United Kingdom (A/44) [1982] E.C.C. 264;
    [1981] I.R.L.R. 408; (1982) 4 E.H.R.R. 38, ECHR 243

Table of Legislation

UK Statutes

Agricultural Wages Act 1948 (c.47) 83

Companies Act 1985 (c.6)
  s.309 130

Contracts (Applicable Law) Act 1990 (c.36) 138

Data Protection Act 1998 (c.29)
  s.4(3) 218
  Sched.3 218

Disability Discrimination Act 1995
  s.1 71
  s.6 71

Employment Act 2002 (c.22)
  ss 29–33 110
  s.30 167
  s.31 175
  s.38 108
  s.47 94

Employment Protection Act 1975 (c.71) 121
  s.1(2) 20

Employment Relations Act 1999 (c.26) 121
  s.21 42

Employment Rights Act 1996 (c.18)
  Pt VIII 92
  s.1 108
  s.13 171
  ss 17–22 172
  ss.47A–47L 227
  s.47B 227
  s.57A 92

s.63A 92, 112
s.63B 112
s.80F 94
s.81(2)(b) 193
s.86 ....167, 185, 233
s.94 157
s.95(1) 185
s.100 227
s.102 227
s.103 227
s.103A 227
s.112 178
s.113 178
s.116 178

Health and Safety at Work etc. Act 1974 (c.37) 30, 127
Human Rights Act 1998 (c.42) 93, 210, 213, 225

Incitement to Disaffection Act 1934 (c.56) 248
Industrial Relations Act 1971 (c.72) 99, 121

Jobseekers Act 1995 (c.18)
  s.14 247

National Minimum Wage Act 1998 (c.39) 27, 80

Patents Act 1977 (c.37) 114
Pensions Act 1995 (c.26) 187
  Pt I 186

Pension Schemes Act 1993 (c.48)
  s.13 187
  s.14 187
  ss 145–151A 187

Police Act 1996 (c.16)
  s.91 248

Race Relations Act 1976 (c.74)
  s.5(2)(d) 64
  s.49 74
  s.50 74
  s.71 59
  s.71A–71E 59

Race Relations (Amendment) Act 2000 (c.34)
  s.2(1) 59

Regulation of Investigatory Powers Act 2000 (c.23) 216

Sex Discrimination Act 1975 (c.65) 56
  s.7(2)(e) 64

Social Security Contributions and Benefits Act 1992 (c.4)
  Pt XI 237
  s.126 247

"Ten Hours Act" 1847 16
Trade Boards Act 1909 82
Trade Disputes Act 1906 (c.47) 18
Trade Union Act 1913 (c.30) 19
Trade Union and Labour Relations (Consolidation) Act 1992
  s.5 122
  s.11 140
  s.22 142
  ss 24–45D 241
  ss 71–96 19
  ss 46–61 241
  ss 64–67 242
  s.137 243
  s.146 ....233, 243
  s.152 243
  ss 174–177 242
  s.179 ....149, 247
  s.180 ....149, 247
  s.181 125
  s.188 127
  s.193 194
  s.194 194
  s.200 148
  s.212A 169
  s.219 145
  s.220(1) 230
  s.221 142
  s.223 246
  ss 228–235 149
  s.224 148

s.234A 245
s.238 246
s.238A 246
s.244 146
Sched.A1 121

Truck Act 1896 (c.44) 171

Wages Councils Act 1945 (c.17) 82
Wages Councils Act 1979 (c.12)
s.1(2) 82
s.5 83
s.6 83

Statutory Instruments

ACAS Arbitration Scheme (England and Wales) Order (SI 2001/1185)
....169

Fair Employment and Treatment (Northern Ireland) Order (SI 1998/
3162) 74, 225

Health and Safety (Consultation with Employees) Regulations (SI 1996/
1513) 30, 127

Local Government Officers (Political Restrictions) Regulations (SI 1990/
851) 226

Maternity and Parental Leave etc. Regulations (SI 1999/3312) 92

National Minimum Wage Regulations (SI 1999/584) 84

Part-time Workers (Prevention of Less Favourable Treatment)
Regulations (SI 2000/1551) 94

Safety Representatives and Safety Committees Regulations (SI 1977/
500) 30, 127

Trade Union Recognition (Method of Collective Bargaining) Order (SI
2000/1300) 125
Transfer of Undertakings (Protection of Employment) Regulations (SI
1981/1794) 127, 197

Transnational Information and Consultation of Employees Regulations
(SI 1999/3323) 129

Working Time Regulations (SI 1998/1833) 91, 128

US Statutes

Civil Rights Act 1964 53
Civil Rights Act 1991
  s.105 69

Employee Polygraph Protection Act 1988 (29 USC)
  s.2001 220

Fair Labor Standards Act 1938 (29 USC)
  s.201 91

National Labor Relations Act 1935 (29 USC) 121
  s.157 19

Norris–La Guardia Act 1932 (29 USC)
  s.101 143

Worker Adjustment and Retraining Notification Act 1988 (29 USC)
  s.2101 195

Table of European Legislation

Treaties and Conventions

Charter of Fundamental Rights of the European Union 2000 .....25, 126, 232, 233, 253
    Arts 125–130 47

Charter of Fundamental Rights of the European Union 2002 249
    Art.12 54
    Art.13 54

European Community Treaty 1957
    Art.39 ....137, 138
    Art.87 139
    Art.136 21
    Art.137 46
    Art.139 47
    Art.141 87
    Art.141(4) 66

European Convention for the Protection of Human Rights and
    Fundamental Freedoms 1950 ....232, 234, 235
    Art.1 207
    Art.6 211
    Art.8 ....211, 212, 216
    Art.9 ....93, 212, 213
    Art.10 212
    Art.10(2) 224
    Art.11 212

European Social Charter 1961 ....232, 233, 235, 244
    Protocol 233

ILO Convention 87 1944 244

Rome Convention 1980 138

Termination of Employment Convention 233

Directives

Dir.77/187 Acquired Rights Directive
Art.1(b) 199

Dir.80/987 on the Protection of Employees in the Event of their
Insolvency 201

Dir.89/48 on Mutual Recognition of Higher Education Diplomas 138

Dir.89/391 Framework Directive 127
Art.11 30

Dir.91/553 108

Dir.92/85 Pregnancy Directive 92

Dir.93/104 Working Time Directive 91

Dir.94/23 Young Workers Directive 48

Dir.94/45 European Works Council Directive 127

Dir.95/46 Data Processing Directive 218

Dir.96/34 Framework Agreement on Parental Leave Directive 92

Dir.96/71 139

Dir.98/49 on the Fair Treatment of Part Time Workers 94

Dir.98/50 Acquired Rights Directive 198, 203
Art.4(1) 196

Dir.98/59 Collective Redundancies Directive 127, 190

Dir.98/391 on the Duty of Employers to Ensure the Safety and
Health of Workers 236

Dir.99/7 185

Dir.2000/43
Art.5 66

Dir.2000/78 Equal Opportunities in Employment Directive 93, 214, 221
Art.7 66

Dir.2001/23 Consolidated Acquired Rights Directive 127

Dir.2002/14 127

Regulations

Reg. 1612/68 137
Reg. 1408/71 137

Part I

Aims and Techniques of Employment Law

I

'Labour is not a Commodity'

This cry—'labour is not a commodity'—echoes down the centuries. Radicals, socialists, trade unionists, and right-wing economists have proclaimed it. To this day it is the motto of the International Labour Organization (ILO), the arm of the United Nations whose aim is to establish protective standards for every working person. Despite this impressive list of endorsements, the slogan presents us with a paradox. It asserts as a truth what seems to be false.

Employers buy labour rather like other commodities. The owner of a factory purchases the premises, raw materials, machinery, and labour, and combines these factors of production to produce goods. A business does not own the worker in the same way as it owns the plant, machinery, and raw materials. As a separate legal person, the worker is free to take a job or not, subject of course to what Marx called 'the dull compulsion of economic necessity'. Without that freedom, workers would be slaves. Yet the employer certainly buys or hires the worker's labour for a period of time or for a piece of work to be completed. Workers sell their labour power—their time, effort, and skill—in return for a wage. As with other market transactions dealing in commodities, the legal expression of this relation between employer and employee is a type of contract. The contract of employment, like other contracts, confers legally enforceable rights and obligations. It seems that labour is in fact regarded much like a commodity in a market society and its laws.

Yet the slogan also draws our attention to distinctive features of the employment relation that render it unlike other market transactions. Workers are people, not things. As such, they deserve to be treated with respect. By agreeing to work for another, employees do not consent to be treated like chattels or slaves. They expect to be treated fairly and with reasonable care for their safety. Moreover, the opportunity to work in return for a wage has greater significance for the employee than their other market transactions. Most people rely upon employment as their principal source of income. Pay serves as the major mechanism for the distribution of wealth in a market society. Work has to produce enough income to support an employee and his or her dependants, not only on a daily basis, but also for a lifetime. Beyond determining their material standard of living, work also provides people with a principal source of meaning in their lives. A job usually occupies a large proportion of the day. Through their work people seek personal fulfilment, and through participation in a workplace they obtain entry into a social community. Work can be exhausting, boring, and dangerous, but without it many people become socially excluded and lose any sense of personal worth.

To 'get a life', most people need work; yet work threatens to shackle them to an economic system that tends to treat workers like commodities, as merely another factor in the means of production. Observers of the Industrial Revolution revealed how the market system appeared to entail the consequential degradation of human beings, a logic of 'commodification'.

The manufacture of matches dates from 1833, from the discovery of the method of applying phosphorus to the match itself . . . The manufacture of matches, on account of its unhealthiness and unpleasantness, has such a bad reputation that only the most miserable part of the working class, half-starved widows and so forth, deliver up their children to it, their 'ragged half-starved, untaught children'. Of the witnesses examined by Commissioner White (1863), 270 were under 18, fifty under 10, ten only 8, and five only 6 years old. With a working day ranging from 12 to 14 or 15 hours, night-labour, irregular meal-times, and meals mostly taken in the workrooms themselves, pestilent with phosphorus, Dante would have found the worst horrors in his Inferno surpassed in this industry.[1]

The intensive division of labour, which Adam Smith so admired for its productive efficiency in the manufacture of pins,[2] at the same time seemed to lead inexorably to such instances of human degradation and exploitation among the matchmakers. Yet out of this industrial inferno sprang wealth, better living standards for most people, and new towns and communities full of civic pride. Even when the coal mines of Britain eventually shut at the end of the twentieth century, echoes of former material achievements and the social solidarity of industrialization could be heard as the miners' brass bands played on. Workers are compelled by economic necessity to comply with a system of production that tends to

---

[1] Karl Marx, *Capital*, vol. 1 (Harmondsworth: Penguin, 1976), p. 356, quoting in part from Children's Employment Commission, First Report, 1863 p. liv.
[2] A. Smith, *An Inquiry into the Nature and Causes of The Wealth of Nations* (1776, Harmondsworth: Penguin, 1970 edn), ch. 1.

treat them like commodities, yet within that system they seek and often find recognition for their dignity and humanity.

Employment law addresses the paradox encapsulated in the slogan 'labour is not a commodity'. It regulates employment relations for two principal purposes: to ensure that they function successfully as market transactions, and, at the same time, to protect workers against the economic logic of the commodification of labour. Its aim is not principally or exclusively to protect workers like the matchmakers against poor conditions and exploitation. Rather the problem addressed by employment law is the more complex one of both promoting the production of wealth through the division of labour while also channelling the relations of production to prevent the excesses of the logic of the market system from destroying human dignity and causing social injustice. It has to facilitate the intensive division of labour of the factory or office, yet curb the tendencies of the market system to treat workers as merely articles of commerce, without respect for their humanity.

Any resolution will be complex and contested. Karl Marx believed that no completely satisfactory resolution was possible without a total revolution in the economic and social system. He may have been right. But employment law at the beginning of the twenty-first century represents two hundred years of the evolution of pragmatic attempts to balance the logic of the market system with the liberal aspiration to ensure that individuals are treated with respect and justly, and that they have the opportunity to construct meaningful lives. There is no fixed settlement or solution. Experimentation and adaptation to new demands both from the market and from political aspirations compel continuous alterations in the content of employment law. Because this branch of the law regulates the key mechanisms for the production and distribution of wealth, and exercises a major influence on how our lives can become meaningful and fulfilled, the subject will always provoke controversy.

Employment law has evolved as a distinct subject of legal scholarship. It is also investigated under several other labels: labour law, industrial law, and social law. Different names for the subject betray contrasts in emphasis and scope. The primary focus of the subject, however, always concerns the contractual relation of employment, which is the legal expression of the economic and social relationship through which work is performed. This introductory chapter explains why the contract of employment requires distinctive support and regulation by the legal system, in order to enable it to function efficiently as a market transaction and a key mechanism in the division of labour. We then consider how the political aspirations to protect workers against the potentially degrading consequences of the market system have further shaped the evolution and structure of employment law.

I. THE CONTRACT OF EMPLOYMENT

Like other contracts, the contract of employment is a consensual relation between two parties involving an exchange: in this instance, work in return for pay. The standard rules for the formation of legally binding contracts apply to contracts of employment. Breach of the contract gives the injured party a right to claim a legal remedy such as compensatory damages. To this extent, a legal system regards the employment relation as like other contracts for market transactions. But we need to concentrate here on those features of the contract of employment that render the general law of contract unsuitable for handling disputes that may arise in connection with employment relations. Otto Kahn-Freund, one of the most influential writers about labour law, famously observed about this contractual relation:

> In its inception it is an act of submission, in its operation it is a condition of subordination, however much the submission and the subordination may be concealed by that indispensable figment of the legal mind known as the 'contract of employment'. The main object of labour law has always been, and we venture to say will always be, to be a countervailing force to counteract the inequality of bargaining power which is inherent and must be inherent in the employment relationship.[3]

We need to unpack this observation about the contract of employment. What is meant by these concepts of 'submission', 'subordination', and 'inequality of bargaining power'?

TAKE IT OR LEAVE IT

No doubt most employers are wealthier than workers. An employer normally represents a collective aggregation of capital, a corporation comprising shareholders and investors, whereas the individual employee bargains alone. As a combination of capital, an employer can try to use its market strength to impose terms on the job applicant as single trader. Employers come to the bargaining table armed with superior resources such as legal advice and experience. Such inequalities of bargaining

---

[3] P. Davies and M. Freedland, *Kahn-Freund's Labour and the Law*, 3rd edn (London: Stevens, 1983), p. 18.

power are of course endemic to a market society. These conditions apply to most purchases of goods by consumers from supermarkets and department stores. Is there some feature of the labour market that makes the employment relation different and may explain its separate legal treatment?

Adam Smith argued that a distinctive source of inequality of bargaining power in the labour market arose from the fact that workers typically require a job immediately to provide an income, whereas employers can refrain from hiring labour until the price is right with only the risk of a reduction of profits.[4] Although this insight explains one potential source of inequality of bargaining power, it is plainly not invariably applicable to employment relations. An employer may have an urgent requirement of productive capacity and have to take any workers available. A worker may have savings that reduce the urgency of finding a job, or may possess scarce skills such as those of an international soccer star, which eliminate the risk of unemployment. Furthermore, except in periods of high unemployment, employers rarely occupy a monopoly position, so workers usually enjoy the option of taking a job elsewhere. The case for saying that the employment relation is somehow unique or distinctive on account of systemic inequality of bargaining power therefore seems too much of a generalization.

Nevertheless, though not unique to the employment relation, an employer's superior bargaining position usually permits it to offer jobs on a 'take it or leave it basis'. Apart from some occasional haggling about the level of wages, the remaining terms of employment are likely to be set by the employer's standard-form contract. No doubt the employer takes the opportunity to fix the terms to its general economic advantage. Employment lawyers will help to draft some swingeing terms—for a fee. A job applicant searching for the best employment opportunity is unlikely to have the time to examine the competing standard forms on offer, even if the terms are available for inspection and intelligible to the layman. A job applicant is likely to be equally concerned about other matters, such as the working environment, the general standards of conduct of the employer, the character of staff with whom he or she will be working, the opportunities for promotion and job enrichment, and the training opportunities. Information about these aspects of the job is hard to obtain. Companies like to puff up their merits as equal opportunity employers, investors in people, and organizations that offer excellent

---

[4] Smith, above n. 2, p. 169.

prospects for career enhancement. Most people therefore accept the first apparently satisfactory job offer, rather than decline it in the hope that something better will turn up. And the widows and orphans in the match factory, with no skills to offer, took any work they could find. This bargaining process can be fairly described as 'submission'.

For consumers buying goods and services, legal regulation addresses the similar problems of take it or leave it standard-form contracts in two principal ways. The law promotes transparency in markets, so that consumers can more easily obtain reliable information on the qualities of products and make accurate price comparisons. Consumer protection laws also impose mandatory terms in transactions regarding the safety and reliability of products, in order to protect consumers from their worst mistakes. Employment law has evolved similar legal measures. Arguably regulation is needed more urgently in the context of employment, because the risks of economic and psychic disappointment arising from taking an unsuitable job are usually greater than disappointment arising from a mistaken purchase; and, owing to the need to secure an income, a job applicant may have little time to search for and reflect upon the available job opportunities. In promoting transparency and ensuring minimum standards of safety and fairness, employment law, like consumer law, aims to correct a risk of market failure arising from the combination of standard-form contracts and paucity of information. The rationale for this legal intervention is ultimately that, if employees had possessed this information at the time of the formation of the contract, they would have bargained for terms and conditions that corresponded to these minimum standards.

A LONG-TERM CONTRACT

For a simple job of short duration, such as hiring a person to remove the leaves from my garden, an elementary contract suffices. The performance of a particular task (removal of the leaves) is exchanged for a fixed sum of money, agreed in advance, and payable on completion of the job. Some casual work can be handled adequately by a simple contract of this type. But most jobs, and certainly nearly all the more desirable jobs, are intended to last for a period of time, perhaps many years. Employment relations, like other long-term contracts, pose particular difficulties that require differential treatment by the law.

The frequent hope and expectation of both employer and employee is that the employment relation will continue for a considerable period of time. Once contracts become long term, however, disputes may arise from either party trying to cheat. For example, an employer may instruct the worker to perform new, more arduous tasks, or the employer may try to reduce wages or fringe benefits unilaterally. Equally, workers may decide to avoid some unpleasant work, or to sneak off early. These deviations from the expected performance may constitute breach of contract, and so, in principle, the parties could take legal action. In practice, neither employer nor employee wants to terminate the relation and start litigation over relatively trivial matters in connection with the long-term contractual relation. The benefits to both parties of preserving the long-term employment relation usually outweigh the disadvantages of minor disappointments and disagreements. Some other way of resolving disputes about the details of performance needs to be created in order to avoid litigation over allegations of breach of contract that might destroy the employment relation entirely. The gardener who is not paid for sweeping up the leaves can sue for his money and refuse to work for me again. But in a long-term employment relation, neither party usually wishes to end the arrangement.

As in other long-term contracts, the management and resolution of conflict is a persistent and fundamental problem in contracts of employment. Part of the solution lies in the development of more complex rules and processes for managing and specifying what is expected explicitly and implicitly in each employment relation. These methods need to be supported by alternative dispute resolution techniques, such as grievance procedures that permit discussion and compromise to be reached. Employment law has a significant role to play both in the construction of processes for governing the relationship and in helping to create alternative dispute resolution procedures. Unlike most contractual relationships, for which the law assumes that its task is to provide a neutral court for the vindication of contractual rights, successful functioning of the employment relation requires the law to help the parties to find mechanisms and procedures to resolve disputes outside of the normal legal process. To assist this long-term economic relation to function efficiently, employment law needs to insulate the employment relationship against excessive posturing about legal rights and obligations, against what is sometimes called the 'juridification' of industrial relations.[5]

---

[5] G. Teubner (ed.), *Juridification of Social Spheres* (Berlin: Walter de Gruyter, 1987); Lord Wedderburn, R. Lewis, J. Clark (eds), *Labour Law and Industrial Relations* (Oxford: Clarendon Press, 1983).

INCOMPLETENESS AND AUTHORITY

An employer is rarely certain at the time of the formation of a long-term contract of employment about the precise nature, quantity, and timing of the requirements of the business for work of a particular kind. This contrasts with a commodity transaction, and the uncertainty compels the employer to insist that the contract should remain incomplete in its specifications of the work to be performed. In this way the employer retains a discretion to direct labour to its most productive location at any given time. In this respect, the contract is incomplete by design. This problem of incompleteness is not simply the normal one in contracts that the parties will not foresee every eventuality; nor is it incompleteness owing to the cost of writing a detailed contract. Here the contract is deliberately left indeterminate: the employer bargains for the right to direct the worker to perform a range of tasks according to the employer's requirements. For example, a worker may be hired as a street-cleaner, but managers determine on a day-to-day basis which streets should be cleaned, which tools should be available to the worker, and which tasks should be awarded priority. The contract is incomplete by design, because for efficient production the employer needs the flexibility to alter and adapt the details of work required at frequent, though unpredictable, times.

The paradigm of an employment contract thus contains an authority structure at its heart. In return for the payment of wages, the employer bargains for the right to direct the workforce to perform in the most productive way. An employee consents to obey these instructions, and so enters into a relation of subordination. This authority structure may be articulated through formal rules of the organization or day-to-day instructions from supervisors and managers. Since compliance with this authority structure is essential for the efficient operation of a contract that is incomplete by design, a disobedient employee must be sanctioned. The most visible sign of this authority structure is therefore the use of discipline by the employer, such as deductions from pay and dismissal from employment. But discipline is not the only way in which to secure compliance with authority structures.

Employers also use incentives to secure co-operation with the system of production. Co-operation requires work effort, the use of skill and judgement, and the exercise of responsibility. To encourage co-operation, employers use payment mechanisms such as bonus payments, promotion to higher-paid positions, and career ladders. Supervisors monitor performance, both for the purpose of allocating these rewards and to detect occasions meriting discipline. The employer creates a governance structure comprising managerial direction, hierarchies of authority, internal rules of the organization that allocate power and responsibilities, monitoring devices, techniques for the policing and disciplining of behaviour. This structure appears as an authoritarian regime that subordinates the employee.

Faced with this complex system of discretionary power laced with disciplinary sanctions and contingent incentives, employees will inevitably be concerned that the authority structure should operate fairly. There is plainly a danger that a manager may exercise the power to direct labour oppressively, to discipline workers unfairly, to bully and harass minority groups, to insist upon performance of work under dangerous conditions, and to distribute rewards inequitably. It is this authority structure that provides a focus point for the tension between employment as a mere market transaction and the need to respect the humanity and dignity of workers. Employees therefore press for institutional arrangements that monitor and control an employer's exercise of discretion. The ordinary law of contract cannot provide employees with much help, because its general approach is to enforce the contract as agreed between the parties. If the contract of employment provides the employer with a broad discretion to direct work and to monitor performance, ordinary contract principles would by and large enforce this contractual framework. Employment law therefore tends to introduce mandatory rules and procedures that aim to control any potential abuse of managerial authority. Of course, it is often bitterly contested where the law should draw the boundary between, on the one hand, exercises of managerial authority that count as an abuse of power, and on the other, harsh, but necessary and fair decisions in the interests of the business.

Some may insist that notwithstanding the persuasive argument that authority structures are based on the need for efficient production, any personal subordination constructed by the contract of employment is in itself objectionable, because it denies respect and dignity to the worker. Even if the need for some degree of control and co-ordination by management is conceded, the law can be called upon to support mandatory requirements of democracy at work with a view to sharing the power of direction with the workforce itself, thereby lessening the degree of subordination. Opposition to personal subordination also leads to support for the legal protection of civil liberties at work. An analogy can be drawn between the dangers presented by the discretionary power of the state and the discretionary power of employers. Employees need certain guarantees that managerial powers can never be used to override basic liberties and rights. These arguments have certainly influenced the evolution of employment law, but it has never accepted the view that employment relationships should be governed by legal requirements that precisely imitate the democratic institutions and the protection of civil liberties that public law applies to relations between citizen and state. Instead, employment law has developed a distinctive interpretation of the application of these liberal values to the workplace.

TIME AND COMMUNITY

A final reason for treating the employment relation as a special case that cannot be handled by the ordinary law of contract concerns the place of employment in the life cycle of workers. Performance of a contract of employment, unlike other contracts, usually occupies a substantial pro- portion of our lives. Whilst working we cannot deal with other essential needs such as eating, resting, and sleeping. Long hours of work also foreclose the possibility of pursuing other essential or valuable activities such as education, play, cultural experiences, and raising a family. The contract of employment has to treat workers differently from commodities, because they need time away from production to feed, rest, and reproduce. The employment relation has to grapple with the problem of balancing the employee's need to work, in order to acquire sufficient income to live and to support dependants, with these other essential needs.

The problem of achieving a balance between work and other aspects of the life cycle is surely one of the most complex facing society today. How can we build co-operative, participatory communities, in which people respect each other's interests, if individuals are compelled to spend nearly all their waking hours in the workplace? How can we best reconcile our desire to educate children to their maximum potential with the need to ensure that they have an adequate income? Should we place mandatory limits on working hours in order to enable people to enjoy play and cultural experiences outside work? How can we protect parents who want to raise a family from the adverse consequences for their employment prospects and levels of income that are likely to result from their restricted availability for work? How can we ensure that the elderly, who perhaps have become too infirm to support themselves through work, can obtain a satisfactory standard of living? Answers to these questions no doubt often turn to welfare provision by the state, but a full answer often requires selective measures of regulation of the employment relation.

The law governing the contract of employment has to prevent the complete commodification of labour, in order to leave the necessary time for workers to sustain themselves and build supportive communities.

DISTRIBUTIVE JUSTICE

The above analysis of a standard type of employment relation explains why the ordinary law of contract proves inadequate as a source of regulation for the employment relation. These features of the contract of employment relation also help us to articulate the reasons why labour is not a commodity, because they explain why the rules for ordinary commodity transactions cannot apply without modification to the employment relation. We have also elaborated upon Kahn-Freund's pithy summary of the distinctive qualities of employment relations. The contract of employment is usually in its inception an act of submission to a take it or leave it, standard-form contract with a shortage of information about further crucial aspects of the workplace. For long-term contracts of employment, the parties are bound together by economic interest, but also their relationship is plagued by the possibility of cheating or opportunism, which threatens to undermine its efficient functioning without adequate informal dispute resolution methods being available. The contract usually creates an authority structure as a consequence of the need to keep the worker's performance obligations indeterminate. Subordination of the employee flows from this authority structure, though again the law may temper this hierarchy by providing safeguards against abuse of power or by promoting techniques for sharing the power of direction. Finally, because labour is not a commodity, the contract of employment has to respect the worker's need to achieve a balance between work and life, to prevent working time from engulfing every other human and social activity. Employment law has evolved to cope with this unique combination of four features that represent the hallmark of a standard contract of employment: submission, opportunism, subordination, and the pressing encroachment of working time on life itself.

As well as elaborating on Kahn-Freund's remark, however, this analysis of the contract of employment suggests that employment law has to evolve special regulation of the employment relation so that it can function in ways that sustain in the long term an economically productive and wealth-enhancing system of production. Employment law is often not so much a 'countervailing force' as a necessary ingredient in constructing and protecting efficient relations of production. Unless an employer can satisfy all its needs for labour from the likes of the desperate widows and orphans in the matchmaking factory, the employer will have to negotiate with workers who are not prepared simply to submit to any terms and conditions, who will match opportunism by the employer with working practices of 'going slow' or 'making out', who will resist any perceived abuse of power, and demand fixed limits to their commitment to work. The complex division of labour of a market society depends on a precarious reconciliation of these competing interests in order for the relations of production to function efficiently. Employment law is needed to stabilize and protect the explicit and implicit expectations of the parties to these long-term economic relations.

But how to achieve that aim of supporting the division of labour becomes inextricably entwined in broader questions of distributive justice. Employment is a major institution for the distribution of wealth and, more indirectly, power in modern societies. The issue of how the employment relation should be regulated to enable it to function satisfactorily at all becomes dominated by wider considerations of how to influence the distributive effects of the market, which in turn broaden into fundamental questions of social justice and the legitimacy of the state.

2. THE SHIFTING OBJECTIVES OF EMPLOYMENT LAW

Employment law, poised on the front line of the deepest controversies of a market society, has been tossed in the winds of ideological controversy and of transformations in the economy. Looking back over the two centuries of industrialization in western countries, it is possible to discern two broad strategies for stabilizing and regulating employment relations that have profoundly influenced the evolution of the law. An understanding of these strategies, if only in outline, assists us in discerning the central choices that have been made in the evolution of employment law. But the weaknesses of these strategies, both politically and economically, also help us to appreciate that at the beginning of the twenty-first century we may be witnessing in Europe the evolution of a new consensus on how best to regulate the employment relation.

FREEDOM OF CONTRACT

Notwithstanding the special characteristics of the employment relationship described above, a liberal paradigm remains sceptical of the need for, and the merits of, any special system of regulation or employment law. By locating employment as a contractual relationship, private law ensures that workers are protected from compulsory labour and serfdom. The principle of freedom of contract removes the possibility of workers being treated exactly like commodities, because by giving them the power to choose, the principle ensures the elementary respect for the dignity, autonomy, and equality of citizens. So too the principle ensures a measure of justice and fairness by permitting everyone to seek work without discrimination and obstructions to competition. Furthermore, freedom of contract permits the parties to regulate their own relationship in order to deal with the special difficulties presented by the unique combination of characteristics of the employment relationship. The parties are likely to have the best information about where their interests lie, and therefore they should be permitted to forge a compromise between their competing interests without interference by a paternalistic state. Provided that these conditions of freedom of contract are secured by the legal system, employment relations are likely to be efficient in the sense of maximizing the total wealth of the parties, whilst at the same time workers will be protected against being treated as merely a factor in production.

This powerful liberal theory questions especially whether special regulation of the employment relationship in fact achieves any of its intended objectives. By meddling with freedom of contract, legal regulation risks the creation of inefficiencies or rigidities, which in turn may produce three kinds of undesirable outcome. First, friction in the labour market prevents equilibrium levels of employment. For example, if the law fixes a minimum wage, there is a danger that some workers will be priced out of employment altogether. A second possible consequence of rigidities is inflation caused by pressures for wage demands unsupported by commensurate increases in productivity. A third effect of rigidities is said to be a redistribution of wealth in favour of certain groups who benefit from regulation at the expense of those who are rendered unemployed or who lack the power to obtain equivalent benefits. Legal regulation that imposes mandatory terms on the parties or insulates one party from market forces may have all three of these adverse effects.

A further objection to any kind of social regulation, including employment law, raises fears about the loss of competitiveness in international markets. Most regulation imposes on employers an additional cost of production, either by increasing the cost of labour or by imposing additional administrative expense in complying with regulatory requirements. By raising the costs of units of production, the regulation may either reduce sales in international competitive markets or reduce profits, with a consequential damage to investment. These economic considerations predict that states can obtain a competitive advantage in the global economy by minimizing social regulation. These incentives for a 'race to the bottom' in employment law standards can only be countered by transnational or universal labour standards accepted by all trading nations.

In our subsequent examination of employment law and its effects on the labour market, we will discover that the predictions of these simple economic models do not always hold true in practice. Nevertheless, this liberal paradigm for employment law predominated in the nineteenth century, when it corresponded to the laissez-faire spirit of the age, and was embodied in the doctrines of private law. From time to time, it is true, the Victorian legislator was shocked into action by reliable accounts of terrible conditions in factories and mines.

J. Murray, 12 years of age, says: 'I turn jigger and run moulds. I come at 6. Sometimes I come at 4. I worked all night last night, till 6 o'clock this morning. I have not been in bed since the night before last. There were eight or nine other boys working last night. All but one have come this morning. I get 3 shillings and sixpence. I do not get any more for working at night. I worked two nights last week.'[6]

Such reports led to the strengthening of the 'Ten Hours Act' of 1847, which had patently failed to limit the hours of work of women and children in factories. Although such legislative prohibitions against the worst conditions in factories tended to prove more symbolic than effective, these minimum standards were strenuously resisted by employers both on the ground that the state had no right to intervene in private contractual relations, and on the ground that the regulation handicapped employers in competitive markets, so that it would lead eventually to business closure and unemployment. Nevertheless, we do find in the nineteenth century considerable regulation of employment that was regarded as more or less consistent with the liberal paradigm. Regulation could be presented as a paternalist intervention on behalf of groups such as children and women who could not bargain for themselves. Alternatively, regulation could be justified as tackling fraudulent practices in the labour market, such as the device of paying workers not in cash but by credit at the employer's shop, an abuse together with others that were prohibited by the Truck Acts.

---

[6] Marx, *Capital*, above n. 1, p. 354, drawing on the report of the Children's Employment Commission, First Report, Appendix, 1863.

This liberal paradigm has once again become highly influential. It lies at the root of calls for deregulation and flexibility in the labour markets.[7] These concerns are also central to contemporary European employment policy. For most of the twentieth century, however, a rival set of principles tended to steer the evolution of employment law in most industrialized countries.

INDUSTRIAL PLURALISM

The starting point of an alternative paradigm, which we can call industrial pluralism,[8] concerns the distributive effects of the liberal framework. A market society produces considerable inequalities in wealth. The rewards for work depend ultimately neither on the market value of the product, nor on the profits of the business, which are retained by the employer, but on the forces of supply and demand for labour. Employees can improve their income only by increasing their bargaining position in the labour market, either by acquiring scarce skills or by restricting the supply of labour. Since the inception of industrialization, employees have attempted to control the supply of labour by combining together to bargain for better wages, and using the threat of a withdrawal of labour to improve their bargaining position. Such a course of strike action is fraught with difficulties. The employer may simply hire an alternative workforce from the unemployed. The solidarity of the workforce tends to crumble when confronted with the urgent need to earn a wage to feed the family. Any agreement to pay higher wages may simply be torn up later when the employer has secured a stronger bargaining position. Nevertheless, collective action resulting in a collective agreement is often the most effective way for workers to improve their pay.

Governments do not quietly observe these bargaining strategies from the sidelines. On the contrary, the structure, operation, and effects of the labour market are always a matter of keen public interest. Since wages determine the level of welfare of most citizens, governments have to respond to demands for social justice. Moreover the total wealth of a society depends heavily upon efficient and uninterrupted productive activities. Governments fear widespread industrial conflict owing to its

---

[7] Described in P. Davies and M. Freedland, *Labour Legislation and Public Policy* (Oxford: Clarendon Press, 1993), ch. 10.

[8] A. Fox, *Beyond Contract: Work, Power and Trust Relations* (London: Faber, 1974), ch. 6; H. A. Clegg, 'Pluralism in Industrial Relations' (1975) 13 *British Journal of Industrial Relations* 309; K. Stone, 'The Post-War Paradigm in American Labor Law' (1981) 90 Yale LJ 1509.

potential damage to the economy by reducing production and discouraging investment. For all these reasons, the state has never stood by
and tolerated any kind of bargaining strategy adopted by workers and
employers. Instead, governments often use all the power at their disposal
to control bargaining in the labour market, not only through the law, but
also through police and military power.

In Britain in the nineteenth century, at the inception of industrialization, the formation of a combination or trade union was regarded by the
law as a criminal conspiracy, and action designed to assert collective
power such as stopping work to reinforce demands was a criminal offence.
Pickets outside the factory gates to deter other workers from taking their
jobs were regarded as unlawful assemblies and rioters. Even after 1825
when the Combination Acts had been repealed, and workers were permitted to form trade unions, industrial action taken to reinforce demands for
better wages or reduced hours remained a criminal offence until 1875.
The magistrates, who were often the owners of the factories as well, were
not embarrassed to use their powers of imprisonment and transportation
to break strikes.[9] Yet the state ultimately lacked the resources to enforce
this oppressive regime. Nor did it seem prudent to do so. From the
inception of the mechanized factory system workplace conflict threatened
to escalate into much broader class conflict.

A fear of class conflict leading to revolution initially reinforced
employers' demands for coercive measures against workers' organizations
and their activities, but eventually it created the necessary condition for
forging a political compromise designed to avoid the threat permanently.
In the United Kingdom and the rest of Western Europe the compromise
established by the early decades of the twentieth century permitted the
formation of collective organizations for the limited purpose of bargaining over terms of employment and conditions in the workplace. The
Trade Disputes Act of 1906 secured in England the removal of the
remaining legal obstacles to the formation of effective institutions of
collective bargaining between employers and unions of workers. Industrial collective action was permitted by the law, but closely controlled and
insulated to prevent it from escalating into a broader political conflict
about the control of state power.[10] After much legal controversy, unions
were permitted to engage in political activities, but only to the extent of

---

[9] Lord Wedderburn, *The Worker and the Law*, 3rd edn (London: Sweet & Maxwell, 1986)
pp. 512–21.
[10] A. Fox, *History and Heritage: The Social Origins of the British Industrial Relations
System* (London: Allen & Unwin, 1985).

providing funding for parliamentary democratic parties under restrictive conditions.[11] In France and Germany the principal institutional arrangements were only settled after the war in 1919.[12] In all cases, however, as Dahrendorf has observed: 'Industrial conflict has been severed from the antagonisms that divide political society; it is carried out in relative isolation.'[13]

In most legal systems in Europe this political compromise led to a fresh code of labour law that specified the rights of workers to form collective organizations such as trade unions, to enter into binding collective bargaining arrangements with an employer or groups of employers, and to use strikes and other forms of industrial action in order to support their bargaining position. In the United States, as well, the National Labor Relations Act of 1935 proclaimed:

Employees shall have the right to self-organization, to form, join, or assist labor organizations, to bargain collectively through representatives of their own choosing, and to engage in other concerted activities for the purpose of collective bargaining or other mutual aid or protection.[14]

This legal framework was justified in part on the ground that it served to produce a fairer distribution of wealth, and in part on the more pragmatic ground that it avoided the escalation of industrial conflict into political revolution. The model of industrial relations that it constructed involved the recognition of an inevitable conflict of interest between employers and employees, together with an acceptance of the legitimacy of the claims of both groups. The promotion of collective bargaining acknowledged the legitimacy of sharing power within an organization between these groups, so that the trade union, as the representative of the workers, deserved a say in how the enterprise was run and in the distribution of rewards. This power sharing in industrial enterprises was described as 'pluralist', for it rejected the view that employers should have the exclusive power to manage the business in their own interests. The collective agreement served as a 'peace treaty', which contained vital 'procedural agreements' that established routine methods for negotiation or arbitration of disputes.[15]

---

[11] Originally Trade Union Act 1913, now Trade Union and Labour Relations (Consolidation) Act 1992, ss. 71–96.

[12] A. Jacobs, 'Collective Self-Regulation', in B. Hepple (ed.), *The Making of Labour Law in Europe* (London: Mansell, 1986).

[13] R. Dahrendorf, *Class and Class Conflict in Industrial Society* (London: Routledge & Kegan Paul, 1959), p. 277.

[14] 29 USC, s. 157.

[15] Davies and Freedland, above n. 3, pp. 154, 162.

From the perspective of industrial pluralism, it becomes public policy
to promote collective bargaining and collective procedures as a necessary
institution for the reduction of social conflict. In the UK, governments
awarded priority to this policy, with varying degrees of enthusiasm,
from 1919 to 1979. The policy dominated the reasoning of the two most
influential official reports on industrial relations in the twentieth century: the Whitely Committee that in 1917 proposed Joint Industrial
Councils for every industrial sector and the extension of 'Trade Boards'
as a way of establishing collective bargaining in the 'sweated trades' (i.e.
low-paid, non-union, workers);[16] and the Donovan Commission which
recommended in 1968 that systematic, orderly, plant-level collective
bargaining was the best solution to the widely perceived problem that
Britain was 'strike-prone'.[17] Perhaps the clearest legislative statement of
this policy occurred in 1975. A new independent body, the Advisory,
Conciliation and Arbitration Service (ACAS), was 'charged with the
general duty of promoting the improvement of industrial relations, and
in particular of encouraging the extension of collective bargaining and
the development and, where necessary, reform of collective bargaining
machinery'.[18]

With the assistance of such laws and other techniques for the promotion of collective bargaining, for much of the twentieth century unions in
industrialized societies were able to acquire sufficient organizational solidarity to fix the rates of pay for the majority of the workforce. The
working conditions of large factories and businesses were conducive to
union organization, for the workers were gathered together in the same
place, they shared a common interest in pay and conditions because their
contracts were homogenous, and they could halt production on a con-
veyor belt merely by withdrawing their labour. The extent to which
unions were able to use collective organization to influence other aspects
of the management of the business remained much more contentious, and
either as a result of legal restriction or the weakness of worker solidarity,
the system of collective bargaining in industrialized countries rarely
extended beyond some key terms of the employment relation such as
wages, hours, and the allocation of work.

---

[16] Interim Report on Joint Standing Industrial Councils, Cd. 8606 (1917).

[17] Report of the Royal Commission on Trade Unions and Employers' Associations,
Cmnd. 3623 (1968).

[18] Employment Protection Act 1975, s. 1(2).

3. AN EMERGING EUROPEAN MODEL

The history of employment law in Britain and most of the industrialized world can be told as an unceasing struggle between these two paradigms. The liberal framework emphasizes the importance of efficient and competitive businesses, which need to be supported by legal regulation that maximizes freedom of contract in the labour market and forbids obstructions to competition. In contrast, the industrial pluralist framework emphasizes for reasons of fairness and respect for the dignity of workers the importance of institutional arrangements that achieve joint regulation of the workplace or industrial sector. Employment law is necessary under either paradigm, for not only do the distinctive problems of the contract of employment described earlier have to be managed, but also the law has to prevent attacks on the preferred paradigm. Under the freedom of contract model the principal aim of employment law concerns the protection of a competitive labour market from interference and market failures; under the industrial pluralist model, the law enacts a series of 'social rights' that guarantee the essential features of the industrial relations system of collective bargaining.

This history remains important to an understanding of contemporary employment law, with its embedded series of historic compromises and pragmatic solutions. But we also need to appreciate contemporary currents in political thought and social policy in Europe that tend to impose a different agenda for employment law. In the European Community three key themes seem to be driving employment law in new directions at the beginning of the twenty-first century: social inclusion, competitiveness, and citizenship. These themes are all present in the basic Treaty provision on the objectives of European employment law:

The Community and the Member States, having in mind *fundamental social rights* . . . shall have as their objectives the promotion of employment, improved living and working conditions, so as to make possible their harmonisation while the improvement is being maintained, proper social protection, dialogue between management and labour, the development of human resources with a view to lasting high employment and the combating of *exclusion*.

To this end the Community and the Member States shall implement measures which take account of the diverse forms of national practices, in particular in the field of contractual relations, and the need to maintain the *competitiveness* of the Community economy.[19]

---

[19] Treaty Establishing the European Community, Art. 136, italics added.

SOCIAL INCLUSION

Once work is allocated by a labour market, three significant consequences follow. First, an employer has the power to allocate jobs to particular individuals and to reject others for any reason whatsoever. Second, exclusion from work entails for workers and their dependants denial of the means of support. Markets lack any sense of social responsibility. Third, exclusion from work deprives individuals of the opportunity to participate fully in the intangible advantages of their community. These non-material benefits derived from work can include opportunities to make friendships, to achieve social status within a community, and to engage in meaningful activities including participation in the community. In modern politics we describe these implications of a market society as the problem of social exclusion. Those who cannot obtain work suffer from social exclusion. They are denied the best way to obtain an income to provide the material goods necessary for subsistence or better. They have to rely instead on such welfare support as those in work agree to provide from taxation. But even with sufficient welfare benefits, the unemployed are denied the opportunity provided by work to participate in the intangible advantages of their community and to gain social status and a sense of fulfilment. Without work, the slender threads of community that bind citizens of a market society together become sundered, leading sometimes to a breakdown in order or in social cohesion.

To avoid or reduce these potential sources of breakdown in the social system, employment law functions with other aspects of government policies to reduce or minimize social exclusion. Although the most important elements in the strategy of combating social exclusion concern taxation, welfare payments, education, and macro-economic policies aimed at promoting full employment, employment law plays a vital subsidiary role. In order to combat persistent patterns of social exclusion, the law regulates employers' hiring decisions and dismissals. How intensive these controls should be is deeply contested, but most industrialized countries now have laws outlawing various forms of discrimination in hiring and provide controls over employers' decisions to terminate the employment of a worker. It is unlawful, for instance, in modern times for an employer to make hiring decisions on the ground of sex, race, or membership of a trade union. Modern employment laws also control to a lesser extent the employer's power to terminate employment relations without just cause. Regulation can also address other causes of social exclusion by, for example, requiring employers to train their workforce in new skills or to offer terms of employment that offer hours of work that are compatible with the employee's obligations towards dependants. Although these different laws about discrimination, dismissal, family-friendly measures, and improvements to the employability of workers can be justified in a number of ways, one of their central goals is to assist in tackling the underlying problem of social exclusion in a market society. Employment law thus tries to achieve much more than to protect a liberal freedom to work. In addition, the law controls directly and indirectly the size of the labour market, it imposes duties on employers not to create barriers to employment opportunities for certain groups, and it imposes duties on citizens to look for work. The achievement of these ambitious tasks requires intensive and wide-ranging regulations, which together comprise an institutional structure for fair employment opportunities.

COMPETITIVENESS

A second theme that profoundly influences contemporary employment law arises from the ambitious attempts of governments to improve the competitiveness of businesses and national economies. In order to survive in an increasingly globalized economic system, businesses have to obtain a competitive edge against rivals, often located in other countries, where rates of pay may be lower, natural resources more plentiful, or the work-force more highly skilled. To some extent the ambition of improving the competitiveness of businesses has led governments to deregulate or reduce employment laws, in order to reduce the costs to business and to increase their flexibility in acquiring labour power efficiently. As well as often being politically unpopular, however, deregulation achieves little to improve the long-term competitiveness of businesses. What is required rather is systems of management that attract investment, because they offer efficient production, innovative products, and a highly skilled, co-operative workforce that uses its knowledge to improve productive efficiency, to ensure quality, and to assist in making innovations. Employment law can be used to provide an institutional framework for the workplace that provides support for such competitive enterprises to flourish.

How best to achieve this goal has become a central problem for employment law. It is clear that improvements in competitiveness require considerable flexibility and co-operation from the workforce, who may be unwilling to oblige without receiving in return reliable assurances of fair treatment, employment security, and some commensurate flexibility on the part of employers. Moreover, legal rights are unlikely to provide sufficient reassurance given the practical difficulties faced by individuals of enforcing them and the need to avoid constant disruptive disputes in the course of production. Better mechanisms may be found in institutions that enable the workforce to participate in the management of the business and to have a say in decisions that require flexibility and co-operation. Such 'partnership' institutions which give workers a 'voice' in the governance of the business organization may involve traditional forms of collective bargaining, but are more likely to extend to novel institutions such as consultation committees and 'works councils', which enable employers and representatives of employees to agree strategies and safeguards in the pursuit of a more competitive business.

CITIZENSHIP

A third theme that pervades contemporary discussions of employment is signalled by the term citizenship. This idea is not confined to the traditional liberal account of the entitlements of a citizen to participate in a democratic system of government and to have civil liberties protected against abuse of state power. The modern notion of citizenship embraces a broader range of social issues, such as education, culture, and employment. It suggests that citizens have fundamental social rights as well—to have access to education, health care, cultural activities, and jobs. But these rights are not conceived as welfare entitlements. Rather social rights also depend on the citizen respecting his or her responsibilities as well. In the case of employment, for instance, a worker's social right is respected by the government providing assistance in the form of education, training, and services to help in job search, but the worker also has obligations to take up these opportunities and genuinely seek employment. The notion of citizenship thus expresses both an attachment to traditional civil liberties and also a recognition of the need for states to provide social rights or enabling conditions for individual well-being. At the same time, it implies a weakening of the unreserved commitment of the Welfare State to provide for everyone through general taxation, for citizenship only confers opportunities for well-being, and does not guarantee them to those who act in ways that are regarded as irresponsible.

Within this theme of citizenship we can detect a growing insistence not only that traditional civil liberties should be protected against the state but also that the state owes its citizens a duty to secure those liberties in other contexts such as the workplace. For example, in the past it was accepted that the right to privacy would be infringed by a government's monitoring of telephone calls, but today the question is whether employees should be protected by the state against their employers' monitoring of personal telephone calls and email messages. Similarly, in the past the right to freedom of speech was thought to have no application to the workplace, but now we ask whether some freedom of speech, such as occasions when a 'whistleblower' reveals crime and corruption to the police, should be protected against the employer's disciplinary powers. In short, the former sharp contrast between the public sphere of rights and the private sphere of market relations where civil liberties had no application is increasingly questioned. It is no longer accepted that workers leave their rights of citizenship at the doors to the workplace. The question is rather how far civil liberties should be protected against an employer's exercise of market power.

In addition, the modern notion of citizenship suggests that the range of rights should be extended to include social rights, including some basic rights for workers. Some of these social rights, such as the freedom to join an independent trade union and to take part in industrial action were intrinsic to the industrial pluralist strategy, and have been asserted for a long time by the ILO and in international Conventions. But modern statements of social rights include a wider range of issues, such as health and safety in the workplace, fair treatment, and fair pay. In the Charter of Fundamental Rights of the European Union 2000, for instance, the rights include a right to access to vocational training, the freedom to choose an occupation, a right to be protected against discrimination, a right to information and consultation within an undertaking, a right to fair and just working conditions, and protection against unjustified dismissal. Although this Charter is not directly legally enforceable, it articulates through its combination of traditional civil liberties and an expanded range of social rights, a modern vision of citizenship for the European Union, which has profound implications for employment law.

A CONCEPT OF EMPLOYMENT LAW

Employment law lacks a conventional structure for its exposition. Indeed, the boundaries of the subject are unclear, and its basic principles, so long contested between liberals and industrial pluralists, remain controversial. Nor can employment law draw on traditional classifications of the law for its structure, for the contextual focus on the employment relation forces the exposition of the law to traverse nearly every category of public and private law, from the ordinary private law of contract to the complexities of European constitutional, human rights, and competition law. In the end, the scope and content of the subject depends on a concept of the point of legal regulation of the employment relation.

The framework of this book takes three contemporary themes—social inclusion, competitiveness, and citizenship—as the basis for its organization. The division of the book into three parts, each focused on a particular theme, carries with it the danger that these policy objectives may be misunderstood as addressing separate problems, whereas in practice of course all three themes influence governments and other participants in the legal process as they address every particular issue in employment law. Nevertheless, the division into themes enables us to grasp more fully the character of these policy goals, and their special weight in particular contexts, and their detailed legal implications, and it facilitates a careful analysis of the dilemmas that these novel objectives present for employment law. This concept of employment law suggests that at the beginning of the twenty-first century these three themes provide the core of a distinctive European response to the puzzles presented by the cry that labour is not a commodity.

2

Regulating the Workplace

Two years after the passing of the National Minimum Wage Act 1998 in the UK, the Trades Union Congress (TUC), an organization to which most British unions are affiliated, estimated that about 170,000 workers were not receiving the minimum wage to which they were entitled. That is a lot of people, and clearly the TUC believed that they had produced damning evidence of the failure of the law. But from a historical perspective on employment law, far from being a failure, this result amounted to an incredible success story. Compare this result, for instance, to the repeated history of the ineffectiveness of employment legislation such as the 'Ten Hours' laws that we noted in the previous chapter were completely evaded. Despite that legislation, which restricted the hours of work of children in factories and at nights, J. Murray, aged 12, worked twenty-four hours without a break. Before examining how employment law articulates the policy objectives described in the previous chapter, it is important to consider the difficulties that confront the implementation of any regulation of employment relations.

The central problem is how to achieve full compliance. Intimately connected to that issue of compliance is the need to develop regulatory systems that are sensitive to the diversity of contractual arrangements and workplaces in which work is performed. Examination of these problems alerts us to the possibility that mandatory legal regulation that grants rights and imposes obligations may not always prove effective or sufficiently sensitive to the context. Alternative methods of regulation, such as the promotion of self-regulation without imposing precise standards, may in fact secure the policy goals more satisfactorily. Employment law has been the source of some of the most innovative regulatory techniques and continues to provide a site for radical experimentation.

I. COMPLIANCE, REFLEXIVITY, AND PROCEDURAL REGULATION

Even for generally law-abiding citizens, the incentives for disobedience to labour standards are often too pressing to be ignored. Consider the case of an employer that pays its workers less than a statutory minimum wage. The employer is naturally reluctant to increase costs to comply with the law, and may worry that its competitors who ignore the law will be able to undercut its prices for products and services. Assuming, probably unrealistically, that employees are aware of their statutory rights, they may nevertheless be unwilling to raise the issue of breach of regulation with their employer for fear of retaliatory action such as dismissal. In any case, the employer is likely to respond to their claim by saying that if the employees do not want the low-paid job, they can leave, because others will be happy to take their places. Economic interest and sometimes necessity induce systematic disobedience to labour standards. In effect, both employers and employees are frequently prepared to connive at the subversion of employment laws.

This problem of securing compliance with labour standards can be alleviated by making the regulation more sensitive to the differences between industrial sectors, types of working arrangement, and the qualities of the worker. In the case of a statutory minimum wage, for instance, it is possible to create exceptions, to vary the minimum wage according to industrial sectors, or to set different rates according to the qualities of the worker such as setting a lower rate for young people. These variations create complexity, however, which tends to reduce levels of compliance, because employers and workers become unsure what detailed rules apply to their relationship.[1] Nor is there a logical stopping point in devising measures that increase regulatory complexity, for each business and each employment relation has its idiosyncratic features that may call for adjustment of the labour standard. Without such refinement, a general standard may either be ignored or misapplied, or prove counterproductive in that it might cause loss of jobs or add unnecessarily to the costs of the business. General standards that apply to all employment relationships create the risk of inefficiency in the sense that they may impose costs upon employers which either are unnecessary to the achievement of the goal of the regulation or far exceed any benefits produced by the regulation. In sum, to avoid inefficiency and ineffectiveness,

---

[1] C. S. Diver, 'The Optimal Precision of Administrative Rules' (1983) 93 Yale LJ 65.

legal regulation of employment must be 'reflexive', in that it must respond and be sensitive to the variety of contexts to which it applies.[2]

In the pursuit of its policy objectives, employment law has to confront this dual problem of securing high levels of compliance with standards whilst at the same time being reflexive. In theory, adequate policing of standards can solve the problem of compliance. The early British legislation on dangerous conditions in factories appointed inspectors, whose job was to enforce observance of the regulations. Inspectors increase levels of compliance, because connivance by employees becomes less significant, and employers may fear the increased risk of the costs of fines and other sanctions flowing from higher detection rates. Yet it would require a huge army of inspectors, who could credibly threaten stiff penalties, in order to secure full compliance. The costs of such a system have always seemed prohibitive to governments. Although most industrialized countries have inspectors to enforce various labour standards, they never have the resources to ensure full compliance. In the United Kingdom today, for instance, there are about 700 safety inspectors, who need to visit around half a million establishments, which results often in four- or five-year gaps between inspections.[3]

An alternative method for securing better compliance is to increase the incentives for individual employees to enforce labour standards. Individual employees can be granted the right to pursue a claim against their employer for substantial compensation for breach of legal regulations through a simple legal procedure. This model applies in Britain, for instance, to claims for equal pay for women, for incorrect deductions from pay, and for unfair dismissal. Though avoiding the costs of the army of inspectors, this model does create costs for governments in running the legal process that decides individual claims. Employees may still prove reluctant to enforce their rights, however, even if the law provides protection against retaliatory action by the employer, for they may judge that the measure of probable compensation is outweighed by the risks to their continued employment, promotion prospects, and their employability in the labour market. It is possible to alter this assessment by such techniques as awards of punitive compensation, simple and inexpensive procedures, and by placing the burden of proof on the employer. But ultimately employees will always be reluctant to enter into litigious

[2] R. Rogowski and T. Wilthagen (eds), *Reflexive Labour Law* (Deventer: Kluwer, 1994); I. Ayres, and J. Braithwaite, *Responsive Regulation: Transcending the Deregulation Debate* (Oxford: Oxford University Press, 1992).

[3] R. Baldwin, *Rules and Government* (Oxford: Oxford University Press, 1995), p. 144.

conflict with their employer, with the consequence that employers will not be induced to comply with legal regulation in full.

These weaknesses from the point of view of compliance of both a public law model represented by inspectors and a private law model of individual employment law rights to compensation have compelled employment law to seek innovative solutions. The most distinctive technique involves procedural regulation that requires or induces self-regulation by employers and workers through negotiation. Under this technique, the law specifies the processes that have to be followed and the institutional framework through which negotiations should be conducted, but refrains from setting detailed substantive standards. Collective bargaining between employers and trade unions provides an example of such procedural regulation, where the law specifies the processes and the conditions under which collective bargaining should occur, but does not determine the outcomes of bargaining in terms of the standards set by the agreement. But many other procedural and institutional mechanisms can be used for similar purposes. For example, in the UK, the EC, and many other countries, legislation requires the establishment of a health and safety committee in each workplace, which consists of representatives of management and the workforce, and which has the tasks of identifying risks to health and safety and agreeing measures to reduce or eliminate risks.[4]

This style of procedural regulation has advantages with respect to both reflexivity and compliance. Collective self-regulation permits the parties to agree standards that are practicable and efficient for each workplace, and which can be modified easily in the light of experience. These procedures harness the information available to the workforce about regulatory issues such as safety problems and their expertise in how they might be solved efficiently.[5] Once the self-regulation has been established, it is likely to achieve high levels of compliance, both because it has been agreed by all sides, and because the parties to the agreement, and in particular trade union officials, are likely to monitor compliance closely. Advocates of procedural regulation argue further that these procedural institutions such as collective bargaining are indispensable for the

---

[4] EC Directive 89/391 Art. 11; Health and Safety at Work Act, etc. 1974, s. 2(3),(6); Safety Representative and Safety Committee Regulations 1977 SI 1977/500; Health and Safety (Consultation with Employees) Regulations 1996 SI 1996/1513.

[5] L. S. Bacow, *Bargaining for Job Safety and Health* (Cambridge Mass.: MIT Press, 1980); J. Rees, *Reforming the Workplace: A Study of Self-Regulation in Occupational Safety* (Philadelphia: University of Pennsylvania Press, 1988).

effective enforcement of other regulatory techniques. The early protective legislation became more effective when the inspectors were
supplemented by trade union officials who could rely on collective
organizational strength to insist on compliance by the employer.[6]

The danger exists, of course, that the collectively agreed standards will
be pitched very low, so that they do not accord with the aspirations of the
legislator. To guard against the worst outcomes, the legislator can fix
minimum requirements that must be observed by self-regulation. But
anything more than minimum standards would detract from the potential
advantages of procedural regulation. These advantages of high levels of
compliance and reflexivity depend ultimately on the goals of the regulation not being regarded by employers as simply imposing another cost on
the business, but rather as becoming one of the goals of the business
organisation. By following its own procedures, as modified by legal
requirements for particular procedures such as health and safety committees, the business organization reaches decisions that approximate to the
goals of employment law.[7]

Through its historical reliance upon procedural regulation, and in particular the promotion of collective bargaining as an instrument of self-
regulation, employment law has evolved a distinctive character. The
study of collective self-regulation becomes central to the legal enquiry,
because of its superior combination of effectiveness and reflexivity compared to other regulatory techniques.[8] Nevertheless, it is important to
recognize the inherent limitations of procedural regulation and collective
bargaining as a regulatory technique for implementing the goals of
employment law. The scope of issues covered by collective bargaining,
the standards achieved, and the extent to which the union can secure
compliance with the negotiated agreement depend ultimately upon the
strength of the union's bargaining position on a particular issue. High
levels of unemployment, weak organization, and reluctance of workers to
press their claims through strike action tend to weaken the union's bargaining position and diminish the impact of self-regulation through collective bargaining. A second weakness of collective bargaining is that a
union usually operates within a democratic framework, so that its policies

---

[6] P. Davies and M. Freedland, *Kahn-Freund's Labour and the Law*, 3rd edn (London:
Stevens, 1983), p. 19.
[7] G. Teubner, *Law as an Autopoietic System* (Oxford: Blackwell, 1993), ch. 5.
[8] K. Klare, 'Countervailing Workers' Power as a Regulatory Strategy', in H. Collins,
P. Davies, and R. Rideout, *Legal Regulation of the Employment Relation* (London: Kluwer
Law International, 2000), p. 63.

must conform to the wishes of the majority of its members. This form of government creates the risk that the interests of minorities or groups who do not take an active part in union affairs will not receive adequate attention. The union may pay lip-service to their interests, but with an eye on the wishes of the majority not exercise its industrial muscle to prosecute vigorously the claims of a particular section of the workforce, such as women.[9] A third weakness is the difficulty encountered by the law in compelling employers to comply with procedural regulation such as that requiring recognition of trade unions for the purposes of collective bargaining. In particular, it is hard for the law to detect employers who go through the motions of the procedure without in fact taking the bargaining process seriously. Finally, and perhaps most important of all, there are some interests of workers that we may want to regard as inalienable rights, such as the right not to be discriminated against on grounds of race or sex. To subject such rights to trade-offs and qualifications during the process of collective self-regulation may be regarded as a denial of the fundamental importance of such rights to workers as citizens.[10]

Despite these potential weaknesses and criticisms of collective bargaining as a regulatory instrument, the reasons for its adoption described earlier remain compelling in many contexts. Or at least some supplementary element of procedural regulation may often be the preferred mechanism for achieving legislative goals rather than the straightforward imposition of mandatory general standards backed by criminal penalties or civil claims for compensation. Of course, employment law can use many other regulatory techniques beyond these simple alternatives.[11] Recent experiments include tax breaks as an incentive for employers to adopt systems of remuneration that include employee share ownership schemes; Codes of Practice and other types of 'soft law', which, though not legally binding, provide more determinate guidance on how to comply with general standards; subsidies to employers to encourage employment of particular categories of worker such as the young and inexperienced; and an exploration of all the varieties of alternative dispute resolution. In each experiment, employment law is grappling with

[9] J. Conaghan, 'Feminism and Labour Law: Contesting the Terrain', in A. Morris and T. O'Donnel, *Feminist Perspectives on Employment Law* (London: Cavendish, 1999), pp. 13, 23.

[10] H. Collins, 'Against Abstentionism in Labour Law', in J. Eekelaar and J. Bell (eds), *Oxford Essays in Jurisprudence Third Series* (Oxford: Clarendon Press, 1987), p. 79.

[11] A. Ogus, 'New Techniques for Social Regulation: Decentralisation and Diversity', in Collins, Davies, and Rideout, above n. 8, p. 83.

the problem of securing better compliance whilst being sensitive to the needs of particular businesses and groups of workers.

2. REGULATING CONTRACTS

Most employment law operates by interfering directly or indirectly with the fundamental legal institution at the heart of the employment relation: the contract of employment. In the previous chapter we noted the distinctive combination of features that are characteristic of this contract. Legal regulation has to grapple with the special characteristics of this contractual mechanism for the division of labour. Because the contract of employment is regarded in law as a species of contractual relationship, it falls under the umbrella of the general presumption of private law systems in favour of freedom of contract. The starting point of the legal analysis is invariably that the parties should be free to reach whatever agreement they choose. Employment law interferes with that freedom by imposing mandatory standards, or by introducing procedures that lead to variations in the agreement. Three significant effects of this contractual framework for regulation of employment need to be highlighted at this stage.

RULE–BOOKS

As for any other contractual relationship, the standard legal analysis places considerable emphasis on the express terms of the agreement as the mechanism that establishes the respective legal rights and obligations of the parties. Given that the employer is likely to impose a standard-form contract to fix these express terms, this legal analysis immediately tends to favour the power of the employer to dictate the express terms of the agreement. Yet the most significant effect of the contractual framework consists paradoxically in the power of the employer to refrain from introducing express terms of the contract. By adopting a contract that is incomplete by design whilst bargaining for the power to direct the workforce, the employer can obtain a broad power to secure all its interests under the contract whilst granting sparse contractual rights to employees. The visible embodiments of this technique of control and subordination are the 'works rules' or 'staff handbooks'.

The employer promulgates rules and procedures to which employees are required to conform under the express or implied terms of the contract of employment. The employer can change these internal rules of the organization at will by issuing fresh instructions, because the employer usually avoids making any of this code a part of the express terms of the contract. For example, the employer may establish a disciplinary procedure, which may foster on the part of employees an expectation of fair treatment. Yet if the employer ignores this procedure, this deviation does not establish a breach of contract, provided that the procedure laid down in the handbook has not been incorporated into the express terms of the contract. Although courts sometimes determine on the basis of the apparent intention of the parties that some element of the handbook such as a disciplinary procedure or a health benefit has been expressly incorporated as a term of the contract of employment, or perhaps represents a separate collateral contract, it is more likely that the court will regard the rule-book as merely a set of standing instructions issued under the general authority of management to direct the workforce. It follows that any expectations that an employee may have acquired from reliance upon the rules cannot usually be protected directly as a contractual right. Nor can the employee rely upon the rules as the exhaustive description of contractual duties, for they cannot limit the more general contractual duty to comply with the reasonable instructions of management within the flexibility demanded by the express terms of the contract.[12]

IMPLIED TERMS

In addition to what is encompassed by the express terms of the contract, the legal obligations engendered by the employment relation are defined by implied terms or, in civil law countries, by general principles of private law. Implied terms are justified in the common law on the ground that they represent the implicit understandings and expectations of the parties to the contract. In reality, they tend to betray judicial perceptions of what obligations should be undertaken by the parties. In the nineteenth century, the judges drew upon the former legal tradition of status obligations to insert authority relations into contracts. The economic relation between employer and worker was described in the same terminology, a contract between master and servant, and into this contract the courts implied legal obligations that preserved an authority relation.[13] The key ingredients were the implied obligations of obedience and fidelity. A worker is under an implied obligation to obey all lawful instructions of the employer. A worker is also under an implied obligation to serve his

---

[12] See Chapter 5.
[13] A. Fox, *Beyond Contract: Work, Power and Trust Relations* (London: Faber, 1974), Chapter 4.

master faithfully. A worker must do what he is told, and even in the absence of express instructions, should not act in ways that are detrimental to the employer's business. Breach of these implied terms amounts to a breach of contract, for which the common law developed by judges permitted the employer to use the self-help remedy of summary or immediate dismissal.

Implied terms (or the equivalent supplementary general principles of private law) remain the most powerful instrument available to the courts to regulate contracts for work. Judicial perceptions of the implicit expectations of the parties have slowly evolved, which has resulted in the development of further implied terms or supplementary rules. Three key developments should be highlighted. First, courts have accepted that employers owe an obligation with respect to the safety of the workforce. In the common law, this implied obligation parallels the tortious or delictual duty to take reasonable care of the personal safety of others. Second, courts have regulated through implied terms or supplementary rules how an employer should exercise the authority to give orders and to organize production. Although the judges preserve the authority relation, through implied terms they can place outer limits on its exercise to deter arbitrary or outrageous managerial behaviour. Legal systems express these outer limits in different ways, such as an obligation not to act in bad faith or an obligation not to abuse legal rights. In the UK, the principal implied term that serves this function is the duty not to act in a way that is calculated to destroy mutual trust and confidence between the parties.[14] For example, an employer who constantly harasses and bullies a particular worker, or who is unfairly critical and personally abusive, would be in breach of this implied term. The third area in which the courts have evolved important default rules concerns the employer's power to dismiss or terminate the employment relation. Regulation of this power is crucial, for the implicit threat of dismissal provides the employer with the most powerful sanction to reinforce management instructions and to deter unwanted conduct on the part of employees. Most legal systems in western industrialized countries have developed supplementary rules to the effect that the power of dismissal should not be exercised in bad faith or be abused. The common law is exceptional in this respect, because the courts have usually imposed merely a procedural requirement that an employer should give reasonable notice of dismissal, and have rejected the

[14] *Mahmoud v. Bank of Credit and Commerce International SA* [1998] AC 20, HL; see Chapter 5.

idea of an implicit obligation to refrain from bad faith terminations of the contract.[15]

Although implied terms share with civil law systems of general principles of private law this technique of inserting general obligations into contracts of employment, there is one crucial difference. General principles may be supplementary or mandatory. But implied terms are regarded as default rules, which can always be excluded by the express terms of the contract. Except by statutory provision, implied terms are never mandatory rules that can override the express terms of the contract. Nevertheless, the courts can construe express terms narrowly in order to avoid any conflict with a default rule. For example, in *Johnstone v. Bloomsbury Health Authority*,[16] the contract of a junior hospital doctor required him to work a standard 40-hour week, but also granted the employer the right to require a further 48 hours of overtime. The employee claimed that excessive hours of work would foreseeably damage his health, and therefore instructions to work all the overtime amounted to a breach by the employer of the implied term to take reasonable care not to injure the employee's health. Although the court accepted that the implied term had been broken, it found great difficulty in explaining how in exercising an express power under the contract to direct the employee to perform overtime work the employer could be in breach of an implied term. Browne-Wilkinson VC produced an elegant solution. He conceded that if the contract imposed an absolute obligation to work a further 48 hours' overtime, there could be no breach of the implied term. In this case, however, the employer had a discretion to order overtime up to 48 hours' and that discretion was impliedly qualified by the employer's ordinary duty not to injure the employee by instructing the junior doctor to work long hours when that would foreseeably damage his health.

Implied terms also perform the function of inserting customs and conventions of the workplace into the legal construction of the employment relationship. Customs of the workplace may become implied terms if they are 'reasonable, certain, and notorious'. An employer may consolidate many of these conventions in the discretionary rule-book, but the custom may have independent legal effect as an implied term, if it has been observed consistently in practice. Many concessions won by employees, such as restrictive working practices and breaks, may be observed as a matter of custom rather than express contractual entitlement, but they may have legal effect as customary implied terms. Once

---

[15] See Chapter 8.   [16] [1992] QB 333, CA.

determined to constitute customary implied terms, conventions of the workplace place restrictions on the employer's implied discretionary powers under the contract of employment.

SCOPE OF EMPLOYMENT REGULATION

One last implication of the contractual framework of the legal analysis of workplace relations needs to be highlighted at the outset. Freedom of contract permits the employer to acquire labour through an enormous variety of contractual relations. An employer may hire one worker on a contract that pays the worker by the hour or week for performing services according to the instructions of the managers, and hire another worker to perform tasks in return for payment for each piece of work completed. Although these workers may in fact be performing exactly the same range of tasks, the contractual framework differs, which produces significant consequences for the parties. For example, if the need for work diminishes, under the arrangement by which the worker is paid for her time, wages fall due even if no work was available, whereas if the worker is paid by the piece, no wages are payable if no task was completed. Contracts for the performance of work can allocate all the associated risks in a bewildering variety of ways. No doubt the employer usually selects the form of contract that seems likely to produce the most efficient result from the employer's perspective. Given this harmony between considerations of freedom of contract and efficiency, predictably the law is extremely reluctant to constrain that choice.

The variety of patterns of working relation presents two kinds of problem for any attempted legal regulation. In the first place, as a central instance of the need for reflexivity in employment law, general legal regulation has to cope with the diversity of contractual arrangements. A minimum wage law that specifies a minimum payment for an hour's work, for instance, can apply straightforwardly to an employee paid by the hour for work, but how might it apply to piecework, commissions on sales, salaried workers who receive a fixed wage regardless of hours worked, or the tips given to waiters in restaurants by customers in addition to any wages from the owner of the restaurant? Similarly, a mandatory law of unfair dismissal applies easily to contracts for indefinite employment, but how can it analyse the position of the failure to renew a fixed-term contract, a change in a professional person selected to provide a service, or a refusal to offer any more work to casual workers? Given that all that has happened in these examples from the point of view of the ordinary law of contract is a refusal to offer work, has there been a dismissal at all? These are practical problems provoked by the diversity of contractual arrangements that compel complexity in regulation.

The second problem concerns the scope of employment regulation. In order to determine the application of any statutory or analogous regulation of contracts for the performance of work, the regulation has to determine the types of contracts to which it applies. For example, legislation that mandates a minimum wage has to identify the types of contracts that concern wages as opposed to fees or other species of payment for services; and legislation that grants workers a right not to be unfairly dismissed has similarly to determine its field of application. Given the enormous variety and subtle differences between contracts for the performance of work, the scope of regulation or what is sometimes called the 'personal scope of labour law' is frequently hard to determine. The difficulty lies both in deciding what kinds of contracts should be covered in view of the policy objectives of the regulation, and then in implementing that decision through clear legal rules that determine the scope of the regulation. Consider, for instance, the 'putting out' system used for homeworkers engaged in making products such as clothing and soft toys. The principal business supplies materials to a person working at home, who makes the goods with the help of friends and family, and receives payment by the piece when the goods are collected. Should employment laws apply to this relationship? Should we apply the minimum wage law, and if so, how might this be achieved given that the principal business pays a lump sum for the work, and is unaware of and indifferent to the number of workers and the amount of time taken? If the principal business stops giving work to the homeworker, should we apply the law of unfair dismissal? If there is a suspicion of discrimination against the homeworker, should we apply the protection of anti-discrimination laws to this relationship? We may not be able to produce a single answer to these questions, so that the scope of employment laws may differ according to the question posed. Under UK law, for instance, the homeworker may be protected against discrimination and low wages, but perhaps not against unfair termination of the putting-out arrangement.[17]

The practical importance of these two problems dramatically increased (or more accurately resurfaced) in the last quarter of the twentieth century. The full-time contract of employment of indefinite duration, which

[17] Though an unfair dismissal claim was permitted in *Nethermere (St. Neots) Ltd v. Gardiner* [1984] ICR 612, CA.

became dominant in the first half of the twentieth century,[18] now applies to only about half of the workforce in Britain. There has been a growth in temporary work, casual work, agency work, employment under fixed-term contracts or for a particular task, and about a quarter of the national labour force work part-time for less than 30 hours per week. In addition, payment systems are much more likely to be linked in a variety of ways to performance and profits.[19] At the extreme end of these new configurations of contractual relations, employees become self-employed, selling their services to perform a defined task for a fixed price. For example, dairies in the UK used to sell milk to customers at their doorsteps by employing milkmen driving a fleet of vans (milk-floats). But now the milkmen have to purchase a franchise to sell the milk to a particular area, and rent or purchase the floats. They purchase the milk from the dairy, and their income depends upon the mark-up on the resale to the customer. From the perspective of the dairy this new arrangement provides milkmen with an incentive to increase the quantity of sales in a highly competitive market and reduces the costs of monitoring performance by the milkmen. The milkmen rather than the dairy also bear the risk of customers failing to pay bills and the cost of credit. The hierarchy of the former institutional arrangements is replaced by a contractual link that shifts many of the risks of the business on to the milkmen.[20] Despite these risks, self-employment has many attractions to workers, for it reduces the intensity of supervision and discipline, and it has the potential to produce a greater income. From the legal point of view, what is significant is not that the transfer from employment to self-employed franchisee was a perfect substitute from the perspective of the employer, and possibly a more efficient arrangement, but rather that the milkmen, by becoming self-employed, divested themselves of most of their employment law rights. The workers perform the same tasks, delivering milk and collecting payment, but the new franchise arrangement not only shifts various risks on to the workers, such as declining product demand, non-payment by customers, and inability to work through sickness, but also probably removes the workers from the scope of nearly all employment laws.

---

[18] S. Deakin, 'Legal Origins of Wage Labour: The Evolution of the Contract of Employment from Industrialisation to the Welfare State', in L. Clarke, P. de Gijsel, and J. Janssen (eds), *The Dynamics of Wage Relations in the New Europe* (Dordrecht: Kluwer, 2000).

[19] N. Millward, A. Bryson, and J. Forth, *All Change at Work?* (London: Routledge, 2000), chs 2 and 6.

[20] J. O. Davidson, 'What do Franchisors Do? Control and Commercialisation in Milk Distribution' (1984) 8 *Work, Employment & Society* 23.

This effect is produced because employment law starts from the presumption that it never applies to contracts between two businesses. Although sensible in theory, this boundary becomes contestable when the business supplying the services is a single self-employed worker. Especially if this worker is effectively economically dependent on the other business, as in the case of the milkmen, the self-employed contractor may be subject to similar features in its contractual relationship to those that provide the hall-mark of employment. The contract may be a standard form, which confers authority and discretion upon the larger business, and which as a long-term arrangement may require informal methods for resolving disputes, and present identical problems to the self-employed contractor regarding the balance between life and working time. Nevertheless, employment regulation normally excludes from its scope contracts between businesses. As a result, for instance, the milkmen who became franchisees almost certainly lost nearly all their legal rights under employment law, such as mandatory standards about minimum wages and maximum hours, protection against unfair dismissal, and access to alternative dispute mechanisms. This effect raises the suspicion that employers may choose between different forms of contract for acquiring labour, if they are efficient substitutes, on the basis of which contractual arrangement avoids the legal incidents of employment law.

One of the least satisfactory aspects of many employment law systems is the way in which the allocation of the risk of economic insecurity on to the worker also tends to exclude the worker from protection of employment law rights. A casual worker, who is only contacted when there is a job to be performed, may not accrue the period of service necessary to claim employment law rights, and may even be regarded as an independent contractor rather than an employee. For example in *O'Kelly v. Trusthouse Forte*,[21] waiters were hired for banquets at a hotel, often working several nights a week, but with no commitment on either side to provide regular work or service. When the waiters tried to secure union representation, the employer removed them from the list of people to whom work would be offered. But the waiters had no legal claim against the employer for this anti-union discrimination. Protection of the right to union membership or freedom of association is limited in Britain to employees. The waiters were held to be independent contractors rather than employees, because they bore the risk of the absence of work, so their claim for anti-union discrimination failed.

[21] [1984] QB 90, CA.

Short of compelling employers to use a limited range of contracts for the purpose of acquiring work from others, employment regulation has to define the scope of application of each law to particular kinds of contracts. A rough pattern emerges in which health and safety regulation applies to anyone in the workplace, discrimination laws apply to anyone seeking to offer personal services, and other rights arising in the course of work, such as rights to a minimum wage or protection from dismissal, apply to contracts of employment and sometimes to contracts which are similar, because they provide for the performance of work by an individual.[22] But this broad pattern in employment regulation is not followed consistently, and in any case tends to break down in borderline cases, where it can produce unsatisfactory results. Consider, for instance, the case where a woman failed to obtain a contract to distribute newspapers in a locality from the publishers of the newspaper. Her claim for sex discrimination failed at the first hurdle by falling outside the scope of the regulation, because the dominant purpose of a distributorship was not for the applicant to provide services personally, but rather for her to manage others in the performance of the task.[23] The effect of the decision was that her suspicion that the newspaper proprietor would not offer distributorships to women was never investigated, because the distributorship was regarded as a business-to-business contract, and therefore not covered by discrimination laws at all. The acceptance of the risks associated with a distributorship rather than simply being a manager of the newspaper's delivery service entailed not only exclusion from legal rights arising in the course of employment but also denial of the more fundamental rights of citizenship and social inclusion provided by anti-discrimination laws.

The typical position of temporary workers issued with work by agencies brings together these themes of the contractual framework through which employment law has to operate. About 2 per cent of the workforce in the UK find their jobs through agencies. In the standard-form contracts issued by these agencies, the terms usually specify that the workers are self-employed businesses and not employed by either the agency or its clients, yet the terms also specify that the temporary workers must also satisfy the requirements of obedience and loyalty to the agency and its clients as if they were employees of both. The apparent effect of this

---

[22] A. Supiot, *Beyond Employment* (Oxford: Oxford University Press, 2001), chs 1 and 2; P. Davies and M. Freedland, 'Employees, workers, and the autonomy of labour law', in Collins, Davies, and Rideout, above n. 8, p. 267.
[23] *Mirror Group Newspapers v. Gunning* [1986] ICR 145, CA.

contractual arrangement is that most employment law rights do not apply
to temporary workers: no minimum wage, no maximum hours, no protection against dismissal, and probably exclusion from many social welfare
benefits. Not only do these temporary agency workers have no promise of
any work at all, but also, even when they receive an assignment, the
contract tries to exclude as much of employment protection legislation as
possible, whilst ensuring that the worker owes strict duties of obedience
and fidelity like an employee. This calculated avoidance of regulation is so
transparent that courts may be able to ignore the form of the contract as
one between businesses and insist that in substance it amounts at least in
some respects to the type of contract to which employment law applies.[24]

Alternatively, employment regulation may itself deem certain kinds of
relationship, such as the temporary agency worker, to fall within its scope,
despite its contractual form. The resulting problem of regulatory complexity, where each right is conferred on certain types of contracts for the
performance of work, reaches its apogee in measures that effectively
grant the government the power to confer employment law rights on any
group of workers if they turn out not to be covered and the government
thinks that they ought to receive protection.[25] In effect the scope of
employment law becomes determined on a case-by-case, discretionary,
political evaluation of the merits of conferring a particular legal right on a
particular group of workers. Freedom of contract in the creation of contracts for the performance of work undermines any coherence and transparency in the legal test for determining the proper scope of employment
law.

3. THE CASE FOR MANDATORY REGULATION

We have noted that procedural regulation may be superior in some
instances in its effectiveness and reflexivity as a regulatory technique for
employment relations, but there remains a case for mandatory legislation
of substantive standards. In the case of low pay, for instance, though
workers may obtain more significant gains from collective bargaining,
most governments of industrialized societies have enacted a minimum
wage to set a floor below which no worker should fall, no matter how
weak their bargaining power. Yet the use of mandatory regulation, even
in this minimum standard-setting role, has been subject to sustained

---

[24] *McMeechan v. Secretary of State for Employment* [1997] ICR 549, CA.
[25] Employment Relations Act 1999, s. 21.

criticism from an economic perspective. The central argument is that mandatory regulation not only is generally ineffective, but also tends to back-fire, in the sense that the regulation ends up harming those whom the regulation was designed to help. In the case of a minimum wage law, for instance, though it is conceded that some workers may benefit, it is predicted that those who are paid the least will be disadvantaged, because employers will respond to the potential increased labour costs by dismissing these workers. Instead of receiving higher pay, some economists predict that the low paid will suffer even greater poverty arising from the predicament of unemployment. This argument against mandatory regulation is generalized, so that it applies to any regulation that imposes costs on employers, which, it is usually assumed, includes all employment law.

The deregulatory strategy implied by this economic analysis of mandatory labour standards has certainly had a profound influence on governments' approaches to employment law. In the UK, for instance, before any laws are introduced, they are subject to a regulatory impact assessment, which tries to measure the net costs to employers and their likely negative consequences for employees. Yet it has also been demonstrated on many occasions that the economic model that is used to support deregulation is far too simple to explain and predict the real effects of mandatory employment laws. A minimum wage law may in fact produce a net increase in levels of employment, because the higher wages attract unemployed workers back into the labour market to fill vacancies.[26] Similarly, a law of unfair dismissal may have no unemployment effects but merely induce employers to adopt more cautious hiring procedures. Empirical studies demonstrate at the least that the simple economic predictions of the impact of mandatory regulation are not invariably correct, and that employment laws may sometimes achieve most of their intended distributive effects without undesirable side-effects.

More significantly, a case can often be made for predicting that mandatory employment laws in fact serve to reduce labour costs or in the long run improve the competitiveness of businesses. The reduction of costs may be achieved by legal rules providing savings on such matters as transaction costs, that is the costs of making contracts, by providing a standard package of terms. Similarly, legally constituted institutions may provide a less costly and disruptive technique for the resolution of disputes. Improvements to competitiveness may be indirectly achieved by regulation. In order to comply with mandatory labour standards, an

---

[26] Below p. 81.

employer may need to invest in capital equipment and train the workforce more thoroughly, which in the long run may improve productive efficiency, in the sense of reducing unit costs while improving quality, features of businesses which are so often the keys to survival and profitability in competitive markets.[27] It can also be argued that mandatory rules that provide reliable safeguards for employees against the abuse of managerial power or other risks may serve to encourage co-operation by the workforce, leading in turn to greater productive efficiency.[28] For example, if employers are required by law to disclose information in advance about changes to the organization, to provide necessary training on the introduction of new technology, and to pay generous compensation to workers who lose their jobs for business reasons, these mandatory requirements may make the workforce more willing to accept changes and even to suggest changes that improve the competitiveness of the business. It is true that employers can do all these things on their own initiative, and many do so in order to obtain the benefits to competitiveness. The case for mandatory regulation relies on the extra reassurance provided to the workforce by legal safeguards, and the weakening of the employer's concern that rival businesses may undercut prices, at least in the short term, by not incurring similar expenses.

Earlier it was noted that the 'one size fits all' quality of mandatory regulation of labour standards creates difficulties when it is applied to all industrial sectors involving very different kinds of working relationship. These disadvantages of mandatory regulation can be avoided by permitting contractual adjustment of the standard. Employees may agree to relinquish or modify their rights under the legislation in return for some alternative benefit that they value more highly. The obvious danger here is that the employer will merely use the standard-form contract of employment to eliminate these rights without further discussion and without any compensatory benefits. This practice has occurred, for instance, in connection with the EC Directive on working time that permits employees to agree to a longer working week than 48 hours. Although employment law usually responds to this danger by invalidating

---

[27] W. Sengenberger, 'Labour Standards: An Institutional Framework for Restructuring and Development', in W. Sengenberger and D. Campbell (eds), *Creating Economic Opportunities: The Role of Labour Standards in Industrial Restructuring* (Geneva: International Institute for Labour Studies, 1994), p. 3; S. Deakin and F. Wilkinson, 'Labour Law and Economic Theory: A Reappraisal', in Collins, Davies, Rideout, above n. 8, 29.

[28] H. Collins, 'Regulating the Employment Relation for Competitiveness' (2001) 30 *Industrial Law Journal* 15.

contractual agreements that purport to exclude statutory rights, there is an alternative of permitting collective self-regulation to negotiate modifications of rights. Such a process carries with it much less risk that the employer's superior bargaining power will be used to eviscerate employment standards, and it enables the collective negotiation to adapt the regulation to the particular circumstances of the business and the needs of employees. Mandatory regulation combined with the possibility of particular and partial derogations from the rules produced by collective procedural methods may ultimately strike the most satisfactory balance between reflexivity and compliance.

4. GLOBALIZATION AND LEVELS OF REGULATION

The combination of instantaneous global communications, rapid transport, and electronic transfers of vast sums of capital by tapping a few keys on a computer terminal have produced the phenomenon of globalization. The economic health of a region or state depends much more than hitherto on economic conditions around the world. Multi-national enterprises, often with resources as large as those of a small country, provide business with an institutional framework through which to direct their operations around the world and enable them to switch investment and production easily and at their discretion. The phenomenon of globalization has increasingly threatened national-level employment law and labour market regulation. Governments fear that protective labour laws will induce businesses to invest in other jurisdictions with lower labour standards and labour costs. There is a danger that countries will enter a 'race to the bottom', that is compete for investment with each other by offering the lowest employment law standards. Western industrialized countries observe how some Asian countries with no significant employment laws seem to attract a disproportionate level of capital investment, and draw the lesson that deregulation is necessary in the interests of the national economy.

This threat posed by regulatory competition to employment law and labour standards can be exaggerated, because it does not affect all business sectors equally. You cannot sell hamburgers in a high street restaurant in the UK using cheap, unregulated labour in India. But modern communications technology enables employers to export a remarkable range of jobs, including growth areas in the service sector such as call centres. When considering new employment laws, governments are keenly aware of the potential risks posed by high labour standards to capital investment and levels of employment. One possible response is to create transnational employment rules for an economic bloc such as the European Community.[29] Within an economic bloc, uniform rules exclude regulatory competition and remove the danger of capital flight for this reason from one Member State to another.

In its inception, however, the European Community rejected this aim of uniform minimum labour standards, partly because the founders believed the risk of a race to the bottom was slight, and partly because it was expected that national diversity would help to spread the benefits of a single market to all parts of Europe.[30] In the course of half a century, however, the European Community has increasingly intervened through Directives that have an impact on the movement of capital by the enactment of employment law standards. For example, there are general rules requiring workers to be informed and consulted prior to plant closures, mass dismissals, and sales of the business. The scope of EC employment laws has expanded to respond to other perceived problems of 'social dumping', that is the use of cheap, unregulated labour from one Member State to take work from relatively well-paid and protected employees in another. It is only recently, however, that the Member States have granted the EC the competence to legislate in employment law more generally, such as health and safety issues, working conditions, and anti-discrimination. Nevertheless, many of the key issues of employment law such as pay, collective bargaining, industrial action, and individual dismissals from employment remain within the sovereignty of Member States, and therefore exposed to the problem of regulatory competition in Europe.[31] The reason for restricting the competence of the EC in these respects is not that these issues are irrelevant to the thematic priorities of social inclusion, competitiveness, and citizenship. Rather these topics concern the sensitive political compromises forged in each Member State, to which EC needs to adopt a reflexive stance by respecting the autonomy of national systems of industrial relations.

It should be appreciated that securing the agreement of all or a

---

[29] S. Deakin and F. Wilkinson, 'Rights vs Efficiency? The Economic Case for Transnational Labour Standards' (1994) 23 *Industrial Law Journal* 289.

[30] S. Deakin, 'Labour Law as Market Regulation: the Economic Foundations of European Social Policy', in P. Davies *et al.* (eds), *European Community Labour Law: Principles and Perspectives* (Oxford: Oxford University Press, 1996), p. 63.

[31] Treaty Establishing the European Community, Art. 137 defines the principal competences of the EC with respect to employment law.

majority of Member States to a particular legislative proposal often poses considerable difficulties. Governments may emphasize different policy objectives and have opposing views on how shared objectives such as competitiveness might be best achieved. To reduce the intensity of these disagreements, the Community has introduced the 'Open Method of Co-ordination' for employment policy and social exclusion. Member States are encouraged through routine reporting and dialogue to review their own and others' policies and achievements with respect to competitiveness and social inclusion with a view to establishing standards of best practice, benchmarks, and targets.[32] Perhaps league tables will follow. Although this dialogue does not lead directly to the enactment of employment laws at Community level, it enables Member States to evolve a consensus about priorities and the best methods for promoting those policies, which in turn may facilitate agreement on common labour standards.

Sometimes an even greater obstacle to agreement and harmonization arises from the differences between the employment law traditions in each country. Although EC Directives are usually expressed in terms of abstract principles rather than detailed rules, each legal system has to find a way of accommodating new initiatives within its existing legal framework. There are many examples where an abstract principle that makes sense in one country is hard to fit into the rules and institutions of another. For instance, several EC Directives require employers to inform and consult representatives of the workforce about particular issues. This principle makes sense in countries that already require employers to create a Works Council comprised of representatives of the workforce for the purpose of informing and consulting employees. But in the UK, in the absence of a recognized trade union, there may be no representatives or institutions for consultation, so this principle of information and consultation is hard to accommodate in an effective manner for all workplaces.

In order to overcome the obstacles to securing agreement between Member States, the EC has developed in the sophisticated regulatory traditions of labour law a new method for enacting social regulation. The Treaty enables representatives of employers and trade union leaders to negotiate labour standards through what is called a 'Social Dialogue'.[33] If the parties reach agreement through this form of transnational collective

---

[32] Treaty Establishing the European Community, Art. 125–30; S. Ball, 'The European Employment Strategy: The Will but not the Way?' (2001) 30 ILJ 353.
[33] Treaty Establishing the European Community, Art. 139.

self-regulation, the Community can then enact the agreed standards as a binding Directive. Although it is not always possible to reach a consensus through the Social Dialogue, this procedure has already produced Directives on parental leave, part-time work, and fixed-term work. As an example of innovative regulatory techniques in employment law, the procedural approach represented by the Social Dialogue reveals how a reflexive strategy can work at supra-national level to achieve practicable labour standards supported by the legitimacy gained through the participation and agreement of the interest groups.[34]

These techniques for controlling regulatory competition within economic blocs cannot be used at a fully international level in the absence of suitable institutions of governance. Through its agency the ILO, the United Nations promulgates labour standards in the form of international Conventions. States have the option of subscribing to these standards, and if they ratify them, the ILO monitors conformity by issuing reports about violations of standards. But the Conventions do not create legal rights for workers that can be relied upon in legal proceedings. And governments can ignore critical reports, or simply 'denounce' or withdraw from a particular Convention. The UK has ratified about 80 Conventions, that is less than half of those promulgated by the ILO. British law probably does not even conform to some of the Conventions which have been ratified, such as the Convention on freedom of association with respect to trade union membership and activities.

It must be doubted, however, whether it is feasible to create universal labour standards, given the different stages of economic development around the world and the diversity of cultural and political traditions. Consider the vexing example of child labour, which the ILO has sought to eradicate. In many developing countries that depend heavily on small-scale agriculture, the whole family work in the fields to achieve subsistence-level farming. Elimination of child labour in such circumstances might impose severe economic hardship and seems impracticable and subversive of the culture of such communities. In contrast, prohibitions on child labour, at least during school hours and at nights, seems possible and desirable in western industrialized countries, and indeed this principle has been enacted at EC level.[35]

Agreement on general mandatory standards at international level

---

[34] A. Lo Faro, *Regulating Social Europe* (Oxford: Hart, 2000); C. Barnard, 'The Social Partners and the Governance Agenda' (2002) *European LJ* 80.
[35] EC Directive 94/23 on the protection of young people at work.

seems both impossible and probably in many instances undesirable because it does not satisfy a requirement of reflexivity. Nevertheless, it is possible to respond in many other ways to our genuine concern for the plight of workers in foreign developing countries,[36] even if this concern is combined with the fear of knock-on effects of regulatory competition. Economic blocs or even the World Trade Organisation itself can try to ensure the extra-territorial effects of the labour standards of their members. Another possibility is product labelling, so that goods produced according to fair labour standards can be marked as such, thereby permitting consumers to use their purchasing power to favour employers that conform to those standards.[37] Yet a further possibility is to try to induce multinational enterprises that have their head offices in western countries to conform to minimum standards wherever their production is located in the world.[38] Such measures may help to discourage the worst forms of exploitation, but it is hard to solve the problem of the effective policing of conformity to these standards in order to detect cheating, especially in the absence of local trade union organizations.

This brief examination of the problems presented by globalization and different levels of regulation merely repeats in a different context the central problem considered in this chapter. Simply passing a law, or agreeing to a grand international declaration, is unlikely to have much impact on the practical operation of employment relations. The labour standard may be flouted, avoided by contractual techniques, or simply dismissed as irrelevant to the particular relations of production. Despite international, EC, and national prohibitions, some children work at night in factories in Britain even today, because employers, always mindful of the bottom line in the business accounts, tend to adopt a strategy of efficient breach of regulation. Achieving high levels of compliance with employment law requires regulatory techniques that use a reflexive strategy, ones which try to accommodate the economic interests of both employer and employee through processes of negotiation. Mandatory laws that set transparent minimum standards, such as a national minimum wage, can achieve a fair level of compliance. Mandatory law can further provide institutional frameworks for peaceful negotiations leading

---

[36] K. Stone, 'Labour and the Global Economy: Four Approaches to Transnational Labor Regulation' (1995) 16 *Michigan Journal of International Law* 987.

[37] R. B. Freeman, 'A hard-headed look at labour standards', in W. Sengenberger and D. Campbell (eds), *International Labour Standards and Economic Interdependence* (Geneva: International Institute for Labour Studies, ILO, 1994), p. 79.

[38] B. Hepple, 'New Approaches to International Regulation' (1997) 26 ILJ 353.

to collective self-regulation, which is likely to achieve higher levels of compliance and reflexive standards. Beyond this basic framework, however, to achieve high levels of compliance, employment law has to experiment with a wide range of strategies that nudge and induce, rather than command, businesses and governments acting as employers to incorporate the objectives of employment law within the procedures and objectives of those organizations.

Part II

Social Inclusion

3

Opportunity and Discrimination

In 1966, the English Court of Appeal considered a claim by a woman that the Jockey Club had effectively barred her from becoming a licensed horse trainer. Instead, the licence had to be held by her male employee, the 'head lad'. Lord Denning MR held that the claimant could obtain an interim injunction against the bar on the ground that the Jockey Club, by operating an unwritten exclusionary rule against women, had acted arbitrarily, capriciously, and contrary to public policy in restraint of trade.[1] He added, 'It is not as if the training of horses could be regarded as an unsuitable occupation for a woman, like that of a jockey or speedway-rider. It is an occupation . . . which women can do as well as men; and there would seem to be no reason why they should be excluded from it'.

From the perspective of legal doctrine, this decision was a radical step. The Jockey Club's rejection of the application for a licence could be regarded as just a refusal to enter a contract with the claimant—merely an exercise of the fundamental right of freedom of contract. To override that civil liberty, Lord Denning appealed to a person's 'right to work', a right for which he could cite no clear legal authority. He relied on ancient precedent, from the time of Chief Justice Coke in the early seventeenth century, when the notion of the freedom to pursue an occupation was used to break the power of the guilds of skilled craftsmen in the *Ipswich Taylor's* case.[2] There was no more obvious legal claim available to a woman against discrimination in the labour market—no general law against sex discrimination in employment in the UK. The first elementary prohibition on race discrimination had only been enacted the year before in a pale imitation of the American Civil Rights Act 1964. It was still a time in which sex stereotypes permeated legal discourse, as Lord Denning unconsciously revealed by insisting that he was only intervening because being a horse trainer, unlike the jobs of racing horses or motorcycles, was a suitable occupation for a woman.

In little more than a quarter of a century, however, Europe has

---

[1] *Nagle v. Feilden* [1966] 2 QB 633, CA.   [2] (1614) 11 Co Rep 53.

developed a comprehensive framework of anti-discrimination laws. The revised Treaty of the European Community, in its opening statement of principles in Articles 12 and 13, empowers the Council of Ministers to legislate for the purpose of combating discrimination based on nationality, sex, racial or ethnic origin, religion or belief, disability, age, or sexual orientation. The purpose of anti-discrimination laws in the context of employment is to ensure that no one is prevented from obtaining a job or is subject to some other detriment in the terms of employment solely because the worker has one of these characteristics. Employers can still choose the best person for the job and pay people different wages, and in that sense they can discriminate between applicants and employees on the basis of such criteria as competence, qualifications, and experience. With few exceptions, what anti-discrimination laws prohibit is an employer's use of rules or practices that deliberately disadvantage or unintentionally have the effect of unjustifiably disadvantaging people in the labour market owing to their possession of one of the listed characteristics. Today there would be no legal difficulty in a woman bringing a legal claim against her discriminatory exclusion from almost any kind of job, whether it be horse-trainer, jockey, racing driver, or even 'head lad'.

The justifications for this detailed regulation of employers' hiring and employment practices combine elements of all three of the guiding themes of modern employment law. Anti-discrimination laws evidently reflect a constitutional principle of government that requires equal treatment under the law for all citizens. But in developing the idea of citizenship in the workplace, this constitutional principle is both extended and qualified.[3] The requirement of equal treatment in discrimination laws applies not only to government but also to private employers' decisions in the labour market. Yet its province is confined to discrimination on the grounds of the particular listed characteristics. These characteristics have been chosen because of a history of disadvantage for these groups in the labour market or segments of the labour market. Discrimination laws also serve the economic goal of competitiveness. The exclusion of people from work or particular occupations on grounds of their characteristics regardless of their actual abilities to perform the work can only damage the productivity and profits of businesses in the long run, for it deprives employers of some of the best workers with relevant knowledge and skills.

These justifications for anti-discrimination laws explain why unequal

---

[3] J. Gardner, 'Liberals and Unlawful Discrimination' (1989) 9 *Oxford Journal of Legal Studies* 1.

treatment is wrong in principle and inefficient in practice, but the third theme of social inclusion explains why employment law needs to insist that employers should positively embrace diversity in the workplace. Anti-discrimination laws help to establish social cohesion. In a country containing ethnic diversity and many different sources of political and cultural identity, we have to respect these differences and yet not permit them to become a source of social division and alienation from civil society. A key ingredient in creating social cohesion is to ensure that no person is excluded from jobs or the better jobs merely because of their membership of a group. Discrimination laws pursue the goal of social inclusion, because they require employers to dismantle unnecessary barriers to employment for all groups in a multicultural and diverse society and to promote opportunities for all groups. With access to employment comes the opportunity to participate more fully in society and to become integrated.[4]

Passing a law against discrimination in employment does not, of course, ensure social inclusion for the protected group. Patterns and practices of discrimination are rooted deeply in the institutions and conventions of society. No doubt we all carry with us a host of cultural prejudices against and in favour of particular groups. Discrimination laws cannot change these cultural prejudices overnight, but they can force employers to examine the need for rules, procedures, and practices that have the effect of disproportionately excluding or disadvantaging particular groups. An employer might legitimately use as a criterion for decision the requirement that employees should be reliable in their attendance at the workplace. If, however, this criterion is combined with an assumption by the employer that certain groups such as some racial minorities or married women are unreliable, the criterion of reliability will in practice entail different treatment by reference to group membership. The law requires the employer to examine each job applicant on his or her merits with respect to any criterion such as reliability, and not to use a further proxy in making a decision that invokes stereotypes about members of a particular group. Similarly, the law may question whether the possession of a particular qualification is strictly necessary for successful performance of a job. In some cases it will be necessary, as in the case of a medical qualification to work as a doctor. In other cases, however, the qualification

---

[4] I. M. Young, *Justice and the Politics of Difference* (Princeton: Princeton University Press, 1990); H. Collins, 'Discrimination, Equality, and Social Inclusion' (2003) 66 *Modern LR* 16.

such as an English language GCSE may not be necessary in the sense that some other qualification that establishes competence in the English language would serve equally well, and an insistence upon the requirement of a GCSE might in practice disproportionately exclude racial, ethnic, and national minorities. Discrimination laws try to compel employers to examine the need for such rules, and, if they are unnecessary, to force employers to dismantle such obstacles to employment opportunities for some groups.

Legal regulation of discrimination has evolved in a piecemeal fashion. As each protected group has been added to the scheme, discrete legislation has been enacted. For example, in the United Kingdom the Sex Discrimination Act 1975 concerns discrimination against women, men, married persons, and in a subsequent amendment those who have undergone gender reassignment; and the Race Relations Act 1976 includes discrimination on grounds of colour, race, nationality, or ethnicity. There are further statutes and regulations addressing discrimination against other protected groups, and the legal position in Britain is further complicated by the need to conform to the extensive and detailed EC Treaty provisions and Directives. Although the structure of these laws is not always identical, three central questions always have to be considered. First, how is unlawful discrimination in relation to employment on one of the prohibited grounds established? Second, on what grounds, if any, may an employer attempt to justify the discrimination? Third, what remedies are available for the eradication of discrimination?

I. PROVING DISCRIMINATION

In the past, as we saw in the horse-trainer case, discrimination could often be established by reference to the express rules and statements of the employer. Certain jobs were reserved for men, gays were excluded from the military forces, and job advertisements stated upper age limits. The effect of anti-discrimination laws in the labour market has been that nearly all of this explicit discrimination on prohibited grounds has now been eliminated. Yet more subtle forms of deliberate, covert, or unconscious discrimination persist. Often the major problem that claimants face is one of proof. In order to bring a successful claim against discrimination before a tribunal, an applicant has to prove the case for the existence of deliberate or unintended discrimination.

One way to prove discrimination is to demonstrate that the employer's rule necessarily involves different and adverse treatment for one of the protected groups. For example, if an employer refuses to hire pregnant workers, a pregnant woman who is refused a job can establish discrimination because she can establish that 'but for' her sex, she would have been treated differently and not to her disadvantage. The rule does not directly refer to sex as a criterion, but since only women can become pregnant, the rule necessarily involves different treatment for men and women. Under this method of proof, for instance, at a time when state pensions became payable for women at aged 60 and men at 65, an employer's rule of compulsory retirement at state pensionable age was sex discrimination.[5]

The limits of this method of proof of discrimination were reached in *Grant v. South-West Trains Ltd.*[6] The employer offered employees the benefit of concessions for travel for partners of employees, who were defined as spouses or a person of the opposite sex with whom there had been a relationship for at least two years. A female employee claimed sex discrimination on the ground that her lesbian partner did not qualify for the concession. Sexual orientation discrimination was not prohibited at that time, so the more obvious basis for the claim was unavailable. The case for saying that the rule involved sex discrimination was that, if the employee had been a man and her partner the same person, her partner would have received the travel benefit. But the European Court of Justice (ECJ) rejected the claim, arguing that the rule applied equally to male and female workers who were living with a person of the same sex, so there was no sex discrimination. The Court was no doubt reluctant to introduce sexual orientation as a prohibited ground for discrimination without a clear legislative mandate, and the employer clearly did not intend to discriminate on the ground of sex. Yet there remains the logical problem that under the rule, if the sex of the employee had been different, her partner would have received the benefit. Perhaps the solution lies in the point that not merely her sex mattered, but also her sexual orientation: changes in both were necessary for the benefit to have been conferred. This method of proof of discrimination requires only one change, that of sex, to be critical to an alteration of the effect of the employer's rule.

In the absence of an explicit rule or requirement imposed by an employer that is tainted by discrimination, an applicant may attempt to prove discrimination through circumstantial evidence. It may be possible to demonstrate, for instance, that despite the fact that many members of

---

[5] *Marshall v. Southampton and South West Hampshire Area Health Authority* C–152/84 [1986] ECR 723, [1986] QB 401, ECJ.
[6] C–249/96 [1998] ECR I-3739, [1998] ICR 449, ECJ.

racial minorities had applied for jobs with a particular employer, none or very few had been successful. A court or tribunal may be willing to draw from such statistical evidence the inference of a discernible pattern in the disproportionate failure of the minority group to obtain jobs. If so, the employer will be required to provide a satisfactory explanation of this pattern in order to rebut this inference of unequal treatment. *King v. The Great Britain-China Centre*[7] illustrates how such a claim of covert or unconscious discrimination may be established. A job applicant claimed racial discrimination by the employer when she was not short-listed for a job. The first step towards proving the case is for the applicant to use a statutory procedure to send a questionnaire to the employer asking for an explanation of the decision and any further statistical information that may be required. If the employer gives an evasive or equivocal reply, a tribunal may infer discrimination from that fact alone. The questionnaire may also produce relevant statistical evidence. In this case it was established that 5 of the 30 candidates for the job were ethnic Chinese, but none was put on the short-list of 8 for interview. Furthermore, no ethnic Chinese had ever been employed at the Centre. The applicant could also demonstrate that her formal qualifications fulfilled the requirements of the job specification. From this evidence the tribunal could infer discrimination unless the employer could put forward an adequate and satisfactory explanation of the decision that involved no breach of the principle of equal treatment. In the absence of such a convincing explanation, the applicant's claim should be successful, as happened in this case. This method of drawing inferences about discrimination is necessary because, as Neill LJ observed in this case: 'Few employers will be prepared to admit such discrimination even to themselves. In some cases the discrimination will not be ill-intentioned but merely based on an assumption "he or she would not have fitted in" '.

Yet this method of inferring discrimination from circumstantial evidence must overcome many obstacles. Employers may not collect relevant statistical evidence such as the ethnicity of job applicants. Employers may produce rationalizations for their decision that appear unimpeachable, such as the claim that other applicants were better qualified. To undermine that assertion, the applicant requires detailed information about the qualifications of other job candidates, which again may not be available, in order to demonstrate that the subsequent rationalization was not the true

---

[7] [1992] ICR 516, CA.

ground of the decision. Outside the public sector of employment,[8] there is no legal obligation to record such statistics, and nor have the tribunals been willing to compel employers to incur the expense of constructing relevant statistics retrospectively. But equal opportunities monitoring is recommended in Codes of Practice, and failure to follow these Codes is a factor that tribunals take into account when assessing whether to draw the inference of discrimination. An employer that does not follow an explicit equal opportunities policy will find it harder to rebut the inference that covert or unconscious discrimination lay buried at the root of the decision.

There remains a third method for proving discrimination, which is known in Europe as 'indirect discrimination' and in the United States as 'disparate impact'. Here the challenge is made to a rule or practice that on its face respects the principle of equal treatment, but the effect of which is disproportionately to exclude a protected group. For instance, a height and weight requirement for prison guards might be applied equally to job applicants, but its effect is likely to exclude women disproportionately compared to men. A criterion of previous experience in the same line of work applied equally to all candidates for a job is likely to have the effect of disproportionately excluding groups who have previously been excluded from that trade or profession. A requirement of a particular British qualification will similarly have the effect of disproportionately excluding migrant foreign nationals. The law of indirect discrimination examines how equal treatment may have the effect, whether or not intended or foreseen, of continuing patterns of exclusion.

The difficulty presented by the notion of indirect discrimination is that any rule or practice that is neutral on its face could put one or more groups at a small particular disadvantage. As we shall shortly see, employers can put forward a defence of justification in order to rebut a complaint of indirect discrimination. But the law also tries to establish a threshold for indirect discrimination, so that minor or incidental discriminatory effects of neutral rules cannot provide the basis for proof of discrimination. The question posed by the ECJ is whether a 'considerably smaller proportion' of the disfavoured group than the privileged group is able to satisfy the criterion or requirement. In some cases, common knowledge may suffice to persuade a court, as in the case where a height requirement of 6 ft excludes women disproportionately compared

---

[8] The Race Relations (Amendment) Act 2000, s. 2(1), amending the Race Relations Act 1976, ss. 71, 71A–71E.

to men. But where an employer denies the disparate impact of a rule and questions commonly held views about social patterns, courts cannot easily avoid an investigation of statistical evidence. These statistics are relevant both to establishing the disproportionate adverse effect on a particular group and to demonstrating that the threshold of significance has been met.

The legal test does not specify which statistics are relevant or any precise measure of statistical significance. In a typical case of a hiring condition or requirement, the relevant statistics concern two ratios or proportions. The first ratio is formed by the proportion of the disfavoured group to the privileged group in the labour market that can satisfy all the hiring conditions. The second ratio examines the proportions between the two groups in the labour market if the disputed hiring condition is omitted. For example, if the disputed condition concerns a full-time work requirement that may exclude women disproportionately, the first ratio consists of the proportion of women to men who can satisfy all the requirements for the job, and the second ratio consists of the proportion of women to men that satisfy all the requirements apart from the disputed full-time work requirement. It is the difference between those two ratios or proportions that establishes the indirectly discriminatory effect of the hiring condition. Where the claimant asserts that the employer's practices within the workplace have an indirectly discriminatory effect, such as making it harder for employees in the disfavoured group to gain promotion or retain their jobs in the event of compulsory redundancies, a similar statistical comparison should apply, except that the pool of workers is likely to be confined to employees.

The correctness of these statistical comparisons is not always accepted. On one side, it is disputed, especially in the United States, whether it is fair to establish indirect discrimination in hiring rules without confining the comparison to job applicants rather than suitably qualified people in the labour market. This view emphasizes that the purpose of the law is equal treatment, and that the employer should not be regarded as having treated people unequally on the basis of uniform criteria unless those people had in fact applied for jobs. This argument is vulnerable to the objection that people will not usually apply for jobs if they believe there is no prospect of success. On the other side, the correctness of the statistical comparisons may be challenged because they do not always tackle patterns of disadvantage. For instance, in the case of selection for dismissal for economic reasons or redundancy on the basis of length of service, it is possible that in the context of a particular workplace this seniority rule has no disproportionate adverse impact on women, as will be the case in an all-female workforce. Yet in the labour force as a whole, it is clear that women on average have shorter periods of service with a particular employer, because they often take breaks from paid employment following childbirth. For those advocates of anti-discrimination laws who hope that the law can make a significant contribution to the achievement of equality of outcomes in the labour market, it is essential to root out any practices that might cause disproportionate disadvantage, even if in a particular case the disproportion cannot be demonstrated. Disputes about the relevant pool of workers for statistical comparison thus expose disagreements about whether the anti-discrimination legislation requires merely equal treatment in the labour market or whether it aspires to a greater ambition to achieve a more equal distribution of better jobs.[9] From the perspective of social inclusion, what is important is that as many unnecessary barriers to job opportunities as possible should be dismantled. Although equal or proportionate distribution of jobs or better jobs is not an aim of the law, evidence of inequalities in outcomes may signal the presence of such barriers to employment opportunity.

Even where the relevant statistics are agreed and available, a court still has to interpret them in order to determine the threshold requirement whether a 'considerably smaller' proportion of the disfavoured group can comply with the apparently neutral rule or practice. This problem of interpretation was explored in a challenge to the consistency of UK employment law with EC sex discrimination law. In 1985, the UK imposed a qualifying period of two years of continuous employment with a particular employer before employees became entitled to the protection of the law of unfair dismissal. It was argued that this qualifying period discriminated against women in practice, because women often take breaks from paid employment to meet family responsibilities, with the effect that a considerably smaller proportion of women than men could satisfy the requirement of having held a particular job continuously for two years. A reference was made to the ECJ to determine the correct approach to the interpretation of statistics. The ECJ indicated that the appropriate method was to examine the proportion of the male workforce that satisfied the requirement compared to men who did not, carry out the same investigation for women, and then compare the proportions. In 1991, about 74.5 per cent of men were qualified, compared to 67.4 per cent of women. The ECJ hinted that the statistics did not appear to

[9] C. Barnard and B. Hepple, 'Substantive Equality' (2000) 59 *Cambridge LJ* 562.

establish sufficient disparate impact. On the return of the case to the English courts for a final determination on the facts, however, a majority of the House of Lords upheld the women's claim on this point.[10] The majority made the disparity appear greater by taking a percentage of the percentage figures above. It could be asserted that there was a 9 per cent difference in qualifying rates between men and women. The difference could also be expressed as a proportion, so that for every 10 men who qualified, only 9 women did so. This difference was sufficient to satisfy the threshold requirement that a considerably smaller proportion of women could satisfy the neutral rule.

In view of the complexity of these statistical exercises, the courts have tended recently to accept that the disparate impact of a rule has been established on the basis of relatively slender evidence. In a case where London Underground altered the shifts of train drivers, the 2,000 male drivers all accepted the new shifts, but one of the 21 female drivers decided that she had to give up her job owing to her family responsibilities. The Court of Appeal refused to interfere with the decision of the tribunal that the threshold had been met.[11] The tribunal was entitled to view the statistics in the light of the common knowledge that single parents who experienced difficulty in balancing the requirements of work and childcare are predominantly women. Such decisions may reduce but not eliminate the obstacle presented by the threshold requirement for establishing indirect discrimination. Nevertheless, many claims of indirect discrimination now turn more crucially on the issue of whether the employer can justify the neutral rule.

2. JUSTIFYING DISCRIMINATION

Once discrimination has been established by one of the methods described above, an employer may seek to justify the decision or rule. The law carefully circumscribes the grounds for justifying discrimination. The underlying principle is a test of proportionality. Breaches of the equal treatment principle can be permitted, but only if the measure serves an important purpose, is rationally related to the achievement of that purpose, and no alternative measure that avoids discrimination is available. The precise legal formulation of this principle varies according

---

[10] *R v. Secretary of State for Employment, ex p Seymour Smith* [1995] ICR 889, Div Ct, CA, C–167/97 [1999] ICR 447, ECJ, [2000] ICR 244, HL..
[11] *London Underground Ltd v. Edwards (No. 2)* [1998] IRLR 364, CA.

to the method by which discrimination has been proved. An employer may justify a rule that explicitly or implicitly discriminates either on the ground that the characteristic is a genuine and proportionate occupational qualification or that the employer is implementing a permitted and proportionate form of positive discrimination. Where the indirect discriminatory effect of a neutral rule or practice has been established by statistical evidence, an employer can justify it by showing that the rule or practice is required by the business of the employer and satisfies a test of proportionality.

DISCRIMINATORY OCCUPATIONAL QUALIFICATIONS

We should be sceptical about claims that a particular group cannot perform certain jobs. Such claims often depend implicitly on stereotypes that denigrate the group as a whole. When such propositions are tested in practice, such as the claim that women cannot race horses or motorcycles, almost invariably they prove false. Under EC law such discriminatory occupational qualifications, even though genuinely believed to be necessary for a legitimate purpose, can be tested by reference to the principle of proportionality. Discrimination against foreign nationals is permitted in the civil service of national governments. Assuming this exception is justified on the ground of their doubtful loyalty, the principle of proportionality asks whether the exclusion should apply to the whole civil service or merely to those jobs where issues of national security may arise. Similarly, to ban women from front-line military forces assumes that women as a group without exception cannot be good fighters or will disrupt combat operations. The ECJ has permitted the UK government to maintain its ban on women in military jobs that involved front-line fighting, accepting that national governments have a margin of discretion when they adopt measures that they consider necessary in order to guarantee national security.[12] However, the German complete ban on women in armed military service was held to be a disproportionate exclusion, because it was unnecessary to achieve the aim of national security.[13]

Employers sometimes defend discriminatory occupational qualifications on the ground that their customers have that preference. This argument may sometimes be acceptable where a person of the wrong sex or race could not convincingly perform the job, as in the case of actors

---

[12] C–273/97 *Sirdar v. The Army Board and Secretary of State for Defence* [1999] ECR I-7403, [2000] IRLR 47, ECJ.
[13] C–285/98 *Kreil v. Germany* [2000] ECR I-0069, ECJ.

and actresses needed to play a particular part. But to accept this argument more broadly would permit employers to rely upon the prejudices of customers. If an employer advertises for an attractive female receptionist, believing that customers want to be greeted by such a person, the effect of permitting such an exception would be to reinforce harmful stereotypes which discrimination law aims to eliminate. The legal test in the UK is whether the employee provides individuals with personal services promoting their welfare and those services can most effectively be provided by a member of the particular group.[14] The width of this exception has been tested in relation to local authorities' attempts to respond to multicultural communities by restricting jobs to particular ethnic minorities corresponding to those receiving the service. A nursery school that advertised for an 'Afro–Caribbean worker', who understood Afro–Caribbean culture and the importance of anti-racist and anti-sexist child-care fell within this exception, but only because the tribunal accepted that the service of reading and speaking with children in their dialect could be provided more effectively by someone of the same ethnic origin.[15] An employer cannot discriminate on the basis of race or ethnic origins in order to facilitate a sensitivity to cultural differences in general; each job must be assessed to consider whether the service in question can be more effectively provided by a member of a particular racial or ethnic group.[16]

Sex discrimination legislation also permits discrimination to protect privacy and decency. Again we should be sceptical about the need for such an exception. There are almost always ways in which an employer can make provision to protect privacy and decency at small cost, without the need to exclude one sex from the job entirely. In any case, it should be left to the choice of the job applicant whether or not the risk of infringements of privacy and decency are objectionable. A woman may leap at the chance to become an astronaut, even if the job does involve living and sleeping in a confined space with men for weeks at a time.

POSITIVE DISCRIMINATION

Because discrimination laws prohibit employers from using criteria that exclude groups by reference to their identity, these laws also prohibit measures intended to favour disadvantaged groups. Thus an employer who tries to give preference to women and racial minorities in recruit-

---

[14] Sex Discrimination Act 1975, s. 7(2)(e); Race Relations Act 1976, s. 5(2)(d).
[15] *Tottenham Green Under Fives' Centre v. Marshall (No. 2)* [1991] ICR 320, EAT.
[16] *Lambeth London Borough Council v. CRE* [1990] ICR 768, CA.

ment incurs the risk that its hiring rule will be challenged as unlawful discrimination by a white man. This restriction on measures of positive discrimination reveals a tension between, on the one hand, respect for the constitutional principle of equal treatment, and on the other hand, the social policy goal of anti-discrimination legislation to promote a more inclusive society. How to resolve this tension presents one of the hardest issues in discrimination law. Claims that a particular instance of discrimination is merely benign need to be scrutinized carefully, because any departure from strict equality of opportunity looks suspiciously unfair to those who are disadvantaged. American courts correctly say in this context that any rule that invokes group identity on its face is a 'suspect classification', which must be subject to 'strict scrutiny'.

One kind of positive discrimination is to permit or require an employer to accommodate differences between groups. In the case of women, for instance, employers are legally required to provide benefits in relation to pregnancy that have no equivalent for men. Similarly, employers are under a legal duty to make reasonable adjustments of terms and working conditions in order to enable disabled workers to obtain jobs. Equal treatment in such cases, even assuming we could find some intelligible way to implement the requirement to treat like cases alike in such contexts, would plainly reinforce rather than relieve the disadvantage of women and disabled workers in the labour market. For this reason, discrimination laws derogate from equal treatment in order to require special treatment that respects the difference between groups in the cases of pregnancy and disability.

A more controversial question is whether employers should be permitted or required to adopt hiring rules or practices that seek to reverse the effects of past discrimination.[17] If an employer has in the past excluded women or racial minorities, so that they occupy a disproportionately small number of jobs or of better jobs compared to their qualifications and their availability in the labour market, should the employer be permitted or required to introduce quotas or targets for recruitment with a view to eliminating the effects of past discrimination? The problem with such affirmative action measures is that members of the disadvantaged group, typically white men, can immediately claim that they are being denied equality of opportunity by the system of targets or quotas.

European law permits Member States to derogate from the equal treatment principle under a test of proportionality. Specific measures to

---

[17] R. Dworkin, *A Matter of Principle* (Oxford: Oxford University Press, 1986), Pt V.

prevent or compensate for disadvantages in obtaining employment are permitted provided that they are necessary and proportionate to that objective.[18] Does this exception permit an employer to use targets or quotas for recruitment? The ECJ has used the principle of proportionality to rule out affirmative action measures except 'tie-breakers'. If two candidates are equally well qualified for a job, in order to compensate for past discriminatory practices the employer may favour the group such as women or a racial minority, which is disproportionately under-represented in the workforce or in a particular job classification. For instance, the Court approved a German civil service rule that awarded preference to women over men in promotion to positions where women accounted for less than half of the incumbents provided that the woman was equally competent and suitable for the post and that there were no reasons specific to the male candidate that tilted the balance in his favour.[19] In contrast, the Court disapproved a Swedish positive action rule in favour of women in jobs where they were underrepresented and had sufficient qualifications, where men could only obtain the job if the difference in qualifications was so great that the preference for women 'would give rise to a breach of the requirement of objectivity in the making of appointments'.[20] The Court permits 'tie-breaker' hiring and promotion rules, if they do not on their face necessarily derogate from the principle of equal treatment based on individual merit, because it is recognized that gender stereotypes tend in practice to lead to the disproportionate selection of men, even when women have scored equally under the relevant job-related criteria for selection. But more aggressive measures of affirmative action that permit advantage to be given to a particular group are likely to be regarded as contrary to the principle of proportionality.

American law has permitted stronger measures of affirmative action, though only targets rather than fixed quotas are allowed. Where direct discrimination in the past has been proven, a court may order a remedy under which the employer must pursue targets for the recruitment of the underrepresented group in order to redress the balance. An employer may also adopt an affirmative action plan for recruitment, in order to improve the representation of a particular group towards the level it would have achieved if past discrimination had not occurred. But in

---

[18] Treaty Establishing the EC, Art. 141(4); Directive 2000/43, Art. 5; Directive 2000/78, Art. 7.

[19] C–409/95 *Marschall v. Land Nordrhein-Westfalen* [1997] ECR I-6363, ECJ.

[20] C–407/98 *Abrahamsson & Anderson v. Fogelqvist* [2000] ECR I-5530, ECJ.

neither case will the courts permit fixed quotas for recruitment as opposed to equal opportunity procedures designed to achieve targets.[21]

The law in the UK does not ostensibly permit positive discrimination. Governments seem reluctant to breach the principle of equal treatment contained in the law of direct discrimination. The nearest that UK law comes to affirmative action occurs in Northern Ireland, where an Equality Commission can order an employer to adopt measures that will seek to redress the past denial of equal opportunities to members of a particular religious faith, though these measures do not include strict quotas. The crucial test case for the need for positive action in England may be the police service, where racial minorities are severely underrepresented. Although the government is prepared to set targets for recruitment of minorities in the public sector, the persistent failure of public authorities to meet these targets or anything close to them raises the question of the need for a more vigorous form of positive discrimination. The case is strengthened in the case of the police, where it is surely important that the service should have the confidence of the local people, and this confidence must depend in part upon the service appearing representative of that community. Apart from some sections of the public sector where special considerations of representative diversity may require more exacting requirements of positive action, however, the aim of social inclusion does not require strict quotas or the like. The objective is to remove barriers to employment opportunities, not to impose a pattern of distribution of jobs among different groups.

PROPORTIONALITY OF INDIRECT DISCRIMINATION

Where proof of indirect discrimination is established by the disparate impact of a neutral rule on a particular group, an employer may try to justify the rule or practice. First, the employer must demonstrate that the requirement serves 'a real need on the part of the undertaking'.[22] Such a need might include a requirement that employees should have a particular qualification or have experience of a particular kind of work, in order to perform the job competently. Second, the employer must demonstrate that the business need could not be satisfied by a different requirement that did not have the effect of indirect discrimination. For example, the employer might fail to satisfy this second element that the requirement be

---

[21] *Regents of University of California v. Bakke*, 438 US 265, 98 S Ct 2733 (1978); *Adarand Constructors, Inc v. Pena* 115 S Ct 2097 (1995).

[22] Case C-170/84 *Bilka-Kaufhaus GmbH v. Weber von Hartz* [1986] ECR 1607, ECJ.

'necessary' in a case where an employer insists upon a particular qualification when other equivalent qualifications would be satisfactory and avoid
disparate impact. This dual-pronged test of justification is known in the
USA as the 'business necessity' test, and in Europe as the requirement of
'proportionality'.

The employer's defence of justification is the legal moment when two
driving policy ambitions of employment law clash head-on. Social inclusion demands the elimination of artificial and unnecessary barriers to
work in order to help disadvantaged groups to be integrated. But the
policy of encouraging the competitiveness of business insists that nothing
should be done to prevent employers from making efficient decisions,
including the recruitment of the best workers. The task of reconciling
these policy objectives is given to the courts in their interpretations of the
defence of justification and their applications of the defence to particular
circumstances. The impact of the law depends greatly on how much
evidence the courts are prepared to demand from employers of the need
for the requirement and the unavailability of appropriate alternatives that
would avoid indirect discriminatory effects.

One way in which employers may justify a criterion for employment
that has indirect discriminatory effects is to assert that possession of this
requirement such as a formal qualification is necessary for an employee to
be able to perform the job competently and efficiently. A court must
question this assertion in order to determine whether or not the requirement or qualification is indeed related to competent and efficient performance of the job. Formal educational qualifications may not always be
job related in the sense that workers without those qualifications or poss-
essing alternative qualifications may be able to perform the job equally
well. Similarly, size and strength requirements may be necessary for some
jobs, but because they are likely to exclude women disproportionately, it
is necessary for a court to examine whether the job's requirements actually demand those qualities. Courts can sometimes be criticized for not
being as rigorous in their scrutiny of formal requirements for jobs. In one
case, a university restricted an appointment in its student careers' service
to graduates between the ages of 27 and 35. On the assumption that this
requirement indirectly discriminated against women, the university put
forward a justification for the requirement that it was desirable that career
advisers be not too far removed in age from students. Age was being used
here as a proxy for the ability to communicate effectively with young
people. The court permitted this justification without demanding from
the employer evidence that age was a reliable guide to the ability to

engage with students.[23] My experience suggests that such evidence would not have been forthcoming: for effective communication with students, it is not age that matters, but attitude.

Another way in which an employer may justify a requirement that has a disparate impact is to insist that it serves other business interests such as administrative efficiency, a harmonious and more productive working environment, or the retention of a skilled workforce. Such arguments may not suffice as justifications under the American test that the requirement must be 'job related for the position in question and consistent with business necessity'.[24] The EC test of proportionality, however, acknowledges the possibility of such broader justifications, even though they carry with them the danger of either reinserting unfavourable stereotypes or simply endorsing employers' practices based upon tradition and convenience. For example, a school operated a compulsory retirement age of 60 for all staff except maintenance workers and gardeners for whom the age set was 65. Nearly all the teaching and clerical staff were women, whereas the maintenance workers and gardeners were all men. Although the age limit for employment was held to be indirectly discriminatory against women, the employer succeeded in justifying the rule on the ground that a later retirement age was necessary because of the difficulty of recruiting and retaining maintenance workers and gardeners.[25] The court does not seem to have paid attention to the second prong of the proportionality test, which asks whether some other rule, such as a retirement age of 65 for all staff, could have avoided the disparate impact, while adequately meeting the employer's retention needs without imposing a significant cost on the employer. It is in this respect that UK courts have not always followed strictly the EC principle of proportionality when applying national legislation. It is often stated that justification 'requires an objective balance between the discriminatory effect of the condition and the reasonable needs of the party who applies the condition'.[26] What this formulation omits is an investigation of whether the needs of the employer could be met by some other condition or by making some exceptions.

It is important to notice that the European test of proportionality has the potential to permit employers to seek to justify rules that have an indirect discriminatory effect on the ground that they serve to combat

[23] *University of Manchester v. Jones* [1993] ICR 474, CA.
[24] Civil Rights Act 1991, s. 105.
[25] *Bullock v. Alice Ottley School* [1993] ICR 138, CA.
[26] Balcolme LJ, *Hampson v. Department of Education and Science* [1989] ICR 179, CA.

social exclusion. For example, in a case concerning an employer's child-care facility reserved exclusively for women employees, the ECJ concluded that the employer's measure failed a test of proportionality, because it excluded male employees who take care of children by themselves.[27] The employer's rule should have been aimed more precisely at the problem of social exclusion faced by single parents. If the facility had been available to any single parent, regardless of sex, its indirectly discriminatory effect of favouring women employees, who no doubt constitute the vast majority of single parents, would have been justifiable under the test of proportionality as pursuing the legitimate aim of social inclusion.

The EC test of proportionality also accepts another kind of justification defence for Member States whose laws are challenged on the ground that they are inconsistent with EC principles of discrimination law. In the example considered earlier of the challenge to the legal requirement that employees should have two years of continuous service before becoming qualified to claim unfair dismissal, the UK government, having lost on the point that the requirement was not indirectly discriminatory, eventually won on the basis of a justification defence. The government claimed that the aim of the law was to reduce levels of unemployment by reducing the deterrent effect on employers of hiring more staff caused by the risk that they might have to pay compensation for unfair dismissal when terminating employment. The evidence for this 'unemployment effect' of the law of unfair dismissal was extremely thin. In a survey a few employers had said that employment protection laws in general might inhibit their recruitment policies. Nevertheless, the House of Lords upheld the justification, because the rule reflected a legitimate aim of social policy (the reduction of unemployment), and the government could reasonably consider that the means chosen were suitable for attaining that aim. This loose scrutiny of the justification for legislation with indirect discriminatory effects can be explained as a sensible reluctance on the part of the courts to question the validity of a democratically elected government's policies. But it should be remembered that in those areas within the competence of the EC, national governments have given up sovereignty by the undertaking to act in accordance with the Treaty and Directives. Member States have a margin of appreciation in how they achieve compliance with EC principles, but there must always come a point when a

---

[27] C–476/99 *Lommers v. Minster Van Landbow, Natuurbeheer en Visserij* [2002] IRLR 430, ECJ.

national interpretation of a principle amounts to a denial of that principle. National courts as well as the ECJ are under a duty to draw that line.

ACCOMMODATING DISABILITY

At first sight the law governing disability discrimination differs in its structure from the remainder of anti-discrimination laws. Disabled persons are defined as those with a physical or mental impairment which has a substantial and long-term adverse effect on the ability to carry out normal day-to-day activities.[28] Equal treatment of disabled persons is important, because it seems likely that prejudice accounts for the greatly disproportionate number of disabled persons who are unable to obtain work. Yet equal treatment in many cases would still result in exclusion. The physically disabled may not be able to perform some kinds of manual work, or may not be able to enter and move about the workplace. A blind person may not be able to work with an ordinary computer or carry out clerical tasks. The requirements of employers in such cases, such as manual dexterity, ability to move easily, and to read a computer screen, are plainly related to the performance of the job and appear to be necessary. Such requirements applied equally would have an indirect discriminatory effect against disabled persons, but an employer would usually be able to satisfy the normal tests of justification applied in discrimination law. In order to tackle social exclusion, therefore, disability discrimination law adopts a different standard.

UK law imposes upon employers a duty to make reasonable adjustment of requirements and working conditions that place disabled persons under a substantial disadvantage compared to others in competing for jobs.[29] Fulfilment of this duty might require the employer to make the premises more accessible, to reallocate some duties to other workers, to acquire special equipment, to offer suitable alternative work, and to introduce particular safety measures. The duty only requires the employer to take reasonable steps, so that measures which are impracticable, unsafe, extremely expensive, or disruptive to efficient production would not be required. Even if an employer fails to take reasonable steps to accommodate the needs of disabled persons, the employer may still justify this omission for a substantial and material reason. In particular, the employer may demonstrate that even if reasonable steps had been

---

[28] Disability Discrimination Act 1997, s. 1.
[29] Disability Discrimination Act 1997, s. 6.

taken, the decision to exclude the disabled person would still have been justified because, for instance, the applicant would still not have been in a position to perform the job at the necessary level of competence and efficiency. In the comparable American terminology, the employer may treat a disabled person differently if after reasonable accommodations were made, the applicant still could not perform the essential functions of the job. Once again, therefore, the courts are charged with balancing the policy of social inclusion against the policy of encouraging the efficiency and competitiveness of business.

Although disability discrimination law differs in respect of its formulation of the justification defence from the remainder of anti-discrimination laws, the difference is not as great as first appears. The duty to make reasonable adjustments for disabilities finds a parallel in the examination of the necessity of an employer's rule in justifications for indirect sex and race discrimination. In the case mentioned earlier concerning the introduction of a new shift system by London Underground,[30] the female single parent established indirect discrimination because the tribunal accepted that the new hours of work were disproportionately detrimental to women. The employers demonstrated that the new shift system served a business need, but their justification defence failed eventually because they were unable to demonstrate that they could not accommodate the applicant's needs by creating an exception to the shift system for single parents. Indeed, the employer had originally proposed such an exception, but later withdrew it following discussions with the union. This decision demonstrates how a careful investigation of alternatives to the rule adopted by the employer can reveal that the rule does not satisfy the test of proportionality. The requirement that the employer should have considered alternatives to a rule with a foreseeable indirect discriminatory impact before implementing it, in effect amounts to a duty to make reasonable accommodation for disadvantaged groups in the rules and terms of employment.

It can be argued that the approach taken in disability discrimination to impose on employers a duty to make reasonable adjustments should be applied to all socially excluded groups. We should respect and make allowances for the different needs of disadvantaged groups. For instance, because only women can become pregnant, we should respect that difference by according women rights to different treatment. Similarly, disabled workers may require special help to enable them to perform their

---

[30] *London Underground Ltd v. Edwards* [1997] IRLR 157, EAT.

jobs, and we should acknowledge their special needs by requiring employers to treat them differently. An analogous principle will be applied to older workers when age discrimination laws are enacted. The aim of social inclusion requires this element of different or unequal treatment in order to overcome barriers to worthwhile employment opportunities.

3. ERADICATING DISCRIMINATION

We must doubt the effectiveness of these elaborate laws against discrimination in employment. The legislation relies upon individual civil claims for compensation for losses caused by breach of an individual's rights as the principal enforcement mechanism, a strategy which we have noted is generally extremely weak. A person who is denied a job or who suffers a detriment in employment on prohibited grounds of discrimination can bring a claim before a tribunal for compensation, for a declaration that discrimination has occurred, and for a recommendation that the employer should act to reduce or obviate the adverse effect on the complainant. Unusually in a British employment law context, the measure of compensation has no upper limit, and compensation can be awarded for injury to feelings as well as economic loss. Compensation can be awarded for both direct and indirect discrimination, though in the latter case a tribunal is only permitted to award compensation when it is 'just and equitable'. An enforcement strategy that relies upon employees bringing claims against their employer for what are usually modest amounts of compensation is predictably going to have only a marginal impact on the behaviour of employers. Given that problems of discrimination are deep-rooted and often unconscious or the product of unquestioned convention, it is evident that an effective enforcement strategy leading to high levels of compliance requires other methods.

Responding to this need for more effective enforcement, in Britain for each of the separate discrimination laws an independent public agency is charged with the tasks of promoting the aims of the legislation. These Commissions can issue Codes of Practice to employers, make recommendations to the government concerning necessary reforms, and conduct research into discrimination problems. The Commissions can also advise and support individual employees who wish to bring an individual claim against an employer. In a path-breaking constitutional decision, the Equal Opportunities Commission, which addresses sex discrimination, succeeded in obtaining 'standing' in a public law claim in order to mount a pre-emptive challenge under EC law to the validity of rules in the national law of unfair dismissal that differentiated between full-time and part-time employees.[31] A more controversial power of the Commissions consists in carrying out a formal investigation of a particular employer. Such a power might be used to consider all the rules and practices of an employer with a view to assessing whether or not they reveal covert discrimination or produce unjustifiable indirect discrimination. But such a sweeping power of investigation of private employers has been resisted in the legislation and the courts. In effect a Commission can only conduct an effective investigation if it has a belief that unlawful discriminatory acts have occurred and it gives the alleged discriminators a prior opportunity to make representations to rebut the allegation.[32] These requirements turn a formal investigation into an accusatory procedure with time-consuming and expensive safeguards for individuals and employers, which in practice render the procedure impracticable.

The problem here, as elsewhere in labour law, is to devise a procedure that induces employers to adopt best practice without at the same time using threats of punishment that will drive employers to resist an open investigation and evaluation of their existing practice. Northern Ireland provides the closest approximation to such a model, for the legislation imposes monitoring of the composition of the workforce with respect to religious belief on all employers, and the Equality Commission can initiate an investigation for the purpose of considering what action for promoting equality of opportunity ought to be taken.[33] Having identified any necessary action, the Commission must use its best endeavours to obtain a voluntary undertaking from the employer to take such action as is, in all the circumstances, reasonable and appropriate. This mechanism provides a route around the accusatory model that may end in a punitive legal sanction for breach of a non-discrimination order.

Although enforcement by an independent agency may improve the effectiveness of anti-discrimination laws, this method does not attempt to introduce the technique of participatory self-regulation that we have already noted to be a distinctive and generally more effective method of regulation in the workplace. The case for a more participatory process of determining employment practices is particularly strong in the case of

[31] *EOC v. Secretary of State for Employment* [1995] I AC 1, HL.
[32] Race Relations Act 1976, ss. 49, 50; *R v. Commission for Racial Equality ex p Prestige Group plc* [1984] ICR 472, HL.
[33] The Fair Employment and Treatment (Northern Ireland) Order 1998, SI 1998/3162 (N.I. 21).

discrimination, because such a process is likely in itself to promote respect for diversity and inclusiveness, and at the same time to facilitate minority groups in asserting and defining their particular needs.[34] For instance, once given a chance to influence working conditions, women are likely to articulate demands that will assist them to manage work and the care of dependent children in ways that may not have occurred to the employer. Despite these potential benefits of participatory self-regulation, legislation has not yet endorsed this approach by requiring, for example, the creation of equal opportunity committees in workplaces. Reforms of this kind,[35] perhaps linked more generally to mechanisms for auditing the extent to which companies respect their obligations of citizenship, might achieve considerably more impact than the current regulatory scheme, which, one suspects, suppresses without eradicating unlawful discrimination.

[34] S. Fredman, 'Equality: A New Generation?' (2001) 30 *Industrial LJ* 145, 164.
[35] B. Hepple, M. Coussey, and T. Choudhury, *Equality: A New Framework* (Oxford: Hart, 2000).

4

Work and Life

The red flag, that potent symbol of class struggle, was perhaps first raised in Britain by the Luddites. This name was given to secret organizations of skilled weavers, who, at the beginning of the nineteenth century, reacted violently to a combination of the government's abandonment of Tudor paternalist social legislation and of the arrival of cotton mills, whose power-looms threatened their jobs and way of life.

On 20 April a major affray took place at Middleton, where Daniel Burton's power-loom mill was attacked by several thousands. The mill was assailed with volley upon volley of stones, and its defenders replied with musket-fire, killing three and wounding some more. On the next morning the threatening crowds assembled in ever greater strength, and were joined at mid-day by—*a body of men, consisting of from one to two hundred, some of them armed with muskets with fixed bayonets, and other with colliers' picks, [who] marched into the village in procession, and joined the rioters. At the head of this armed banditti a Man of Straw was carried, representing the renowned General Ludd whose standard-bearer waved a sort of red flag . . .*

The mill proving impregnable, the rioters burned the mill-owner's house. They were then met by the military, at whose hands at least seven were killed and many more wounded.[1]

The sound of muskets aimed at the Luddites outside Daniel Burton's power-loom mill in 1812 announced the advent of a new social division of labour.[2] Industrialized production methods needed the introduction of factories to obtain the advantages of mechanization. For the first time, the economic system required a sharp division in space and time between paid work and other activities. In the preceding agricultural and craft systems of production, no rigid division could be drawn between work and activities at home. All members of the household including women and children would contribute their labour to the production of crops and

---

[1] E. P. Thompson, *The Making of the English Working Class* (Harmondsworth: Penguin, 1968), pp. 620–1, quoting from the *Leeds Mercury*, report from Middleton, 25 April 1812.
[2] N. J. Smelser, *Social Change in the Industrial Revolution* (Chicago: University of Chicago Press, 1959).

artefacts, as well as performing household chores. The rhythm of work was largely determined by the seasons and the division of labour within the household. The patriarchy of the family served as the co-ordinating mechanism for work within the household, and social status in the village provided an authority structure for the co-ordination of agricultural production. The invention of the factory created a new architectural space for paid work, a new division of working time in the day, and a precise authority structure of owners, managers, and foremen, unrelated to previous attributions of status in the community. The Luddites' foaming anger at the satanic mills was provoked in part by their loss of autonomy in determining the rhythm and place of work, and in part by their resistance to the new authority structures of the mill owners.

Standing in front of the mill gates, the Luddites were confronted with the new geography of industrialization. There was a physical separation of the workplace and the home. This new frontier of space also entailed a separation of time. The day was divided between time at work and time outside work. Unlike work in the household, working time was no longer interspersed with other activities such as domestic chores, socializing, and resting. Nor was there any flexibility about working time in the factory.[3] If a workman was late, the gates were shut, and the worker was excluded from work and income. The owner of the business determined the amount of working time: the hours were those offered as the terms of employment. In the artificial light of the factory, the working day extended into the night as well, leaving scant time for anything else, and seriously damaging the health of the workers. No longer could the skilled craftsman determine the pace of work, for production had to be co-ordinated within the division of labour and be performed with standardized intensity. The owners of factories prohibited social interactions at work; people caught chatting or away from their workstation were summarily dismissed.

This separation of the workplace in space and time also implied a new division of labour in the household. Those who were in the workplace could not perform domestic work such as shopping, cleaning, washing, and child-rearing. What evolved from this constraint was a strikingly powerful sexual division of labour in industrialized societies. Men went to a workplace to earn a wage; women stayed at home to perform domestic work, supplemented in many instances by casual, part-time work.

---

[3] E. P. Thompson, 'Time, Work-Discipline, and Industrial Capitalism' (1967) 38 *Past and Present* 56.

Although this pattern was never uniform, it acquired almost moral force: a woman's place was in the home, and a woman's job was to run the household and to care for the children. As late as the 1950s in Britain, in some business sectors women were expected to resign their jobs on marriage and confine themselves to domestic work. This was unpaid work, and therefore no value was attached to it by a market society, which in turn contributed to the ideology that women were unequal, second-class citizens.

Although we now take for granted the consequences of separation of the workplace that the Luddites bitterly contested, the social problem of establishing a balance between work and life remains as alive today as ever. We seek a satisfactory division of time between, on the one hand, paid work in the workplace, and on the other domestic unpaid work and leisure activities. In a contemporary context, the problem arises particularly acutely for families with dependent children where these days both partners usually take paid work. How can the parents juggle paid work with childcare? Moreover, the older problem that employers dictate the hours and pace of work remains applicable to all workers, who for mostly economic reasons feel bound to accept jobs involving long hours at an intensive pace. As well as coping with the need to fulfil domestic chores and responsibilities, workers increasingly also want time off from paid work to enjoy leisure and community activities. How can a person perform a good job that is well remunerated and also find time to fulfil caring responsibilities, share the household chores fairly, as well as have time for leisure and community activities? The attempt to find practical answers to these questions has been, and will continue to be, one of the central tasks for employment law.

A simple economic model can assist our analysis of how employment law tackles this problem. Paid work in the workplace provides an employee with a stream of income. By increasing the time spent in the workplace, an employee can usually obtain greater rewards, either through extra payments for overtime or through promotion for hard work. But the increase in income must be set against the lack of time to perform unpaid domestic work and to enjoy leisure activities. Each employee has to make a trade-off between paid work and unpaid activities. In making this decision, a crucial variable is the amount of additional income obtained from longer working hours. If a job is well paid, the additional income can be spent on buying services or employing others to perform domestic work. For example, a well-paid parent can afford to pay for childcare and to purchase prepared meals. If work is badly paid, however, a worker may decide that it is more efficient to work few hours, if at all, and to spend time on domestic work, though as a consequence the family may be forced to live in relative poverty. This model assumes that work opportunities will be available for any number of hours that the worker chooses. This assumption usually proves false, however, for employers offer jobs in standard packages, often requiring at least forty hours a week, and they not infrequently expect longer working hours. This barrier to flexible hours of work can effectively exclude workers from any jobs, or more commonly from the better paid jobs. Workers who find that, owing to poor pay and inflexible hours, they have to forgo employment opportunities for the sake of domestic responsibilities and other obligations, often become socially excluded.

Although very simple, this economic model points towards certain measures that employment law can apply with a view to enabling people to achieve a more satisfactory balance between paid work and the rest of their lives, and to avoid social exclusion. Low wages are a prime target: if good rates of pay are available, workers can take jobs, improve their standard of living, and achieve a better balance between work and domestic responsibilities. Hours of work, in terms of both the length of the working week and the flexibility of employment opportunities, are also a key target for legislation to address the work/life balance. As well as regulating in this way the terms of employment, governments can obviously assist workers to achieve a better balance through public provision of services such as care for children and elderly dependants. The generosity of the social security and welfare system is also an important factor in determining whether it is worthwhile for many people to take paid work and the level of poverty if they cannot find a suitable job. We concentrate here on regulation of the terms of employment, but will note incidentally some of the key social welfare provisions that have an impact on how people achieve a satisfactory balance between paid work and the rest of their lives.

I. A LIVING WAGE

Most industrialized countries tackle the problem of low pay with a mandatory minimum wage law. These laws fix a minimum rate per hour for adult workers, though they usually permit some excluded categories of workers and set lower rates for some groups such as young people. As well as setting a national minimum wage, the state can enhance the rewards from paid work both by increasing income through the welfare system and by supplying free or affordable public services. The welfare system can provide 'in work benefits' or 'earned income tax credits' (negative income tax), which provide additional income on the basis of means testing to those receiving low pay whilst maintaining dependants. The kinds of publicly funded services that enable people to take paid work include childcare, through both nurseries and a free education system, and training in skills that enable workers to apply for job opportunities. All these measures combine together to produce a living wage in the sense that the income produced from work is sufficient to enable people to combine paid work in a satisfactory balance with the other dimensions of their lives. In addition, a national minimum wage may have positive effects on competitiveness. Some employers may be forced to organize their production more efficiently, in order to be able to pay higher wages.

In Britain, the National Minimum Wage Act 1998 arrived astonishingly late, given the early industrialization of the country and the fact that many other industrialized countries enacted such laws in the first half of the twentieth century. The minimum wage is fixed by a minister on the advice of a Low Pay Commission. The Commission consists of a body of experts, who are under a duty to consult representatives of employers and workers, and are placed under a duty to consider when making recommendations their effect on the economy of the UK and on competitiveness. The same rate applies universally regardless of region or sector, with the exception of workers under the age of 26 for whom a lower rate may be set. The reasons for the comparative delay in enacting a national minimum wage are instructive for an understanding of the options and complexities of employment regulation. Four perennial objections to the enactment of a national minimum wage can be detected. We shall consider these objections and the responses to them.

EMPLOYMENT EFFECTS

First, a neo-classical economic model suggests strongly that, if the price of labour is increased by a minimum wage law, its effect will be to increase unemployment by reducing the demand for labour from employers. A national minimum wage certainly runs the risk of back-firing in the sense that it may cause the unemployment of those it is designed to help. To some extent the setting of lower rates for groups such as young workers can reduce this unemployment effect. But a more powerful answer to this objection reverts to the simply economic model of why people opt for paid work.

A national minimum wage increases the attraction of paid work, especially if it is linked to in-work welfare benefits. Thus, although a national minimum wage may reduce demand for labour, at the same time it is likely to increase supply, so that job vacancies become filled. Provided the minimum wage rate is fixed at the optimum level, the net effect may be neutral or even positive on the unemployment statistics. For instance, a study of the effects on employment in fast food restaurants of an increase in the New Jersey minimum wage in 1992 demonstrated an expansion in the amount of employment.[4] The study was controlled by a comparison with eastern Pennsylvania, where similar general economic conditions pertained, but where there was no increase in the minimum wage and no increase in levels of employment. In New Jersey, the study also found that employment growth was higher at restaurants that were forced to increase their wages than at restaurants that already paid the new minimum wage. Similarly, in the Low Pay Commission's assessment of the impact of Britain's national minimum wage, their conclusion was that more than a million workers benefited from an increase in income, adding about 0.5 per cent to the national wage bill, with no measurable impact on overall levels of employment, and with positive employment effects in many low-paying sectors.[5]

These economic analyses and reports demonstrate both that there is some elasticity in the price of labour, in the sense that employers can be required to pay higher rates without immediately depressing the demand for labour, and that the supply side is also affected by motivating people to take paid work and fill vacancies. The lesson to draw is that the objection that a minimum wage law will necessarily back-fire is unfounded, provided that the statutory rate is fixed at the optimum level.

INDUSTRIAL PLURALISM

A second objection to a national minimum wage law is that it may impede the development of collective bargaining. If workers are assured of a minimum rate, they may lack the motivation to join trade unions and to use the threat of industrial action to increase levels of pay through collective bargaining agreements. In other words, a national minimum wage poses an indirect threat to the industrial pluralist strategy of promoting collective bargaining to regulate every workplace. The force of this

---

[4] D. Card and A. B. Krueger, *Myth and Measurement: The New Economics of the Minimum Wage* (Princeton: Princeton University Press, 1995).
[5] Low Pay Commission, Second Report, *The National Minimum Wage: The Story So Far*, February 2000 (www.lowpay.gov.uk), ch. 8.

objection explains to a considerable extent the late enactment of a national minimum wage law in Britain.

In the UK, from 1909 a scheme operated to address the problem of low wages in the 'sweated trades'. The scheme involved the creation of what became known as Wages Councils.[6] These councils comprised representatives of employers and employees in a particular industry, together with independent members who mediated a compromise minimum wage rate. The Councils were originally authorized to set (with the approval of the relevant minister) a minimum hourly wage and terms about paid leave, but their power to fix terms was extended in 1975 to include all the basic terms and conditions of employment in an industrial sector. The minimum wage orders were enforced by inspectors, who had the responsibility to bring prosecutions against employers who failed to comply. By the 1950s there were more than 60 Wages Councils fixing basic rates of pay for millions of workers. The main attraction of Wages Councils as a regulatory technique for fixing a minimum wage was that they fitted into an industrial pluralist scheme. The Councils were regarded as a proxy and a start-up mechanism for collective bargaining in those industrial sectors where union organization was difficult, as in catering and retailing, owing to the dispersal of workers among small employers. Thus a Wages Council could only be established for workers on low wages if 'no adequate machinery' existed for collective determination of pay.[7] The hope was that collective bargaining would in time replace Wages Councils. This expectation fitted into the general strategy of industrial pluralism that better and more comprehensive regulation of labour market conditions could be achieved by industrial-sector or company-level agreements between employers and unions. Furthermore, collective bargaining and its proxy of Wages Councils could also be extremely sensitive to potential unemployment effects by setting different rates for each trade and region according to its particular labour market conditions. By the 1960s, however, trade unions began to suspect that Wages Councils, far from being a route towards the creation of collective bargaining in all industrial sectors, actually impeded the development of collective bargaining. This concern led to legislative changes that permitted the abolition of Wages Councils, even where no effective collective bargaining

---

[6] Trade Boards Act 1909; Wages Councils Act 1945; Wages Councils Act 1979; P. Davies and M. Freedland, *Labour Law: Text and Materials*, 2nd edn (London: Weidenfeld & Nicolson, 1984), p. 144.

[7] Wages Councils Act 1979, s. 1(2).

machinery existed.[8] Although many Wages Councils were removed under these procedures, leaving only 26 at the time of the final abolition of the institution in 1993,[9] the absence of a Council did not result in the development of effective collective bargaining.[10]

Although Wages Councils were abolished on the basis of government policies that endorsed the neo-classical economic objections to any regulation of minimum rates of pay, their history was entwined with the more general fate of the industrial pluralist strategy. It became apparent that the expectation that Wages Councils would become redundant once they had kick-started collective bargaining was never realistic for many industrial sectors. Effective union organization was substantially blocked in many sectors of the secondary labour market, where small, widely dispersed, employers used temporary, casual, or part-time workers, with a high labour turnover. As union membership and strength declined in the economy as a whole after 1980, the prospects for collective bargaining in these labour markets became even bleaker. Furthermore, during the 1980s employers and government policy turned against multi-employer or industrial-sector collective bargaining, believing that it caused rigidities in the labour market that had unemployment and inflationary effects. Nor were Wages Councils in fact delivering minimum rates of pay that had a significant impact on low wages. They were often criticized for establishing unnecessarily low minima, which were in fact below the rates that most workers in those industries were already earning. The vision born at the beginning of the twentieth century that, by promoting collective bargaining through institutional mechanisms, a government could both eliminate the problem of low pay and usher in a comprehensive industrial pluralist solution to the conflicts engendered by a market order, turned out to be a chimera. Structural impediments to the development of union organization in some industrial sectors prevent collective bargaining from becoming a universal solution to problems in regulating the labour market. At the very least, the vision of industrial pluralism has to be qualified by an acceptance of the need for comprehensive minimum labour standards, including a national minimum wage, to protect the interests of the weakest groups of workers.

---

[8] Wages Councils Act 1979, ss. 5 and 6.

[9] There remained the Council established under the Agricultural Wages Act 1948.

[10] C. Craig, J. Rubery, R. Tarling, and F. Wilkinson, *Labour Market Structure, Industrial Organisation and Low Pay* (Cambridge: Cambridge University Press, 1982).

COMPLIANCE

A third perennial objection to a national minimum wage law is that it is
likely to prove ineffective in practice. Individual workers who receive
less than the required minimum may not raise the issue with employers, because they fear retaliatory action such as dismissal. In other
words, the problem of collusive disobedience to legal regulation proves
a major obstacle to the effectiveness of any minimum wage rules. This
problem of compliance is compounded by ignorance of the legal
minimum, a problem that was accentuated under the Wages Councils
system that fixed different minimum rates for each industrial sector.
Although a well-publicized single national rate largely overcomes this
obstacle, the difficulties surrounding employee enforcement of the
standard remain.

The traditional solution to this compliance problem has been for governments to create an inspectorate, which can examine the wages records
of an employer, either on its own initiative or following a tip-off from a
worker, and prosecute an employer that fails to pay the minimum wage.
The National Minimum Wage Act 1998, together with detailed regulations,[11] places a duty upon employers to keep records of wages and to
issue employees with a statement of wages for the purpose of assisting the
worker to ascertain whether the wages comply with the national minimum wage. In order to remedy violations of the national minimum wage,
an inspector can issue an 'enforcement notice' on an employer requiring
payment of arrears and future payments in accordance with the national
minimum wage. The employer can appeal against an erroneous enforcement notice to an employment tribunal. If the employer fails to comply
with a valid enforcement notice, the inspector may bring an action for
arrears of wages on behalf of the worker. In addition, the inspector can
enforce a financial penalty against the employer, which is calculated at the
rate of twice the hourly rate of the minimum wage for each day that the
employer has failed to comply with the enforcement notice. An employer
who refuses or wilfully neglects to pay the minimum wage is also guilty of
a criminal offence punishable by a fine. Of course, the effectiveness of this
policing mechanism depends heavily on the resources of the inspectorate
combined with the accuracy and completeness of an employer's records.
In 1980 it was estimated that about 35 per cent of employers failed to

---

[11] National Minimum Wage Regulations 1999, SI 1999/584; B. Simpson, 'Implementing
the National Minimum Wage—The 1999 Regulations (1999) 28 *Industrial* LJ 171.

comply with Wages Council orders.[12] This proportion has certainly dropped to a few percentage points with the introduction of a single, well-publicized, national minimum wage, policed now by the formidable resources of the Inland Revenue tax inspectors. Individual employees can also bring a claim for arrears of wages, and they have statutory protection against retaliatory action in the form of dismissal or other detriment.

COMPLEXITY

A final objection to a national minimum wage is that the legal regime has to be extraordinarily complex, in order to regulate all the different types of remuneration systems found in employment relations. How, for instance, can a minimum rate per hour be applied to workers remunerated on the basis of piecework, or by commissions on sales, or from tips in restaurants? Some remuneration consists of benefits in kind, such as board and lodging, transport, and goods, so the regulation must decide whether and to what extent such benefits should be included in the hourly rate. Indeed, employers might seek to avoid the impact of the regulation by introducing complex and contingent payment systems that could obstruct official scrutiny and might operate to the disadvantage of low-paid workers. This legal problem of attributing all benefits to a calculation of an hourly rate that can be compared to the statutory minimum is not insuperable, though it certainly leads to regulatory complexity, which in turn tends to obstruct enforcement.

In the detailed British regulations, provision is made for the variety of contingent payment systems. With respect to piecework, for instance, the technique is to ascertain the actual hours worked or a fair estimate of them over the payment period, and then to calculate the hourly rate. To prevent avoidance of the statutory minimum rate, the regulation applies to the broader category of 'workers', with special extensions for agency workers and homeworkers. In addition, the statute creates a presumption in civil proceedings that an individual qualifies for the minimum wage, which an employer has to rebut. For the purpose of calculating the time during which the worker is working, 'on-call' periods when the employee is required to be awake and available at or near a place of work count towards the hours. Thus a security guard who sleeps on the premises is only working during periods when he or she is required to be awake, but a fireman or a doctor who is at home and free to do more or less what he or

[12] Low Pay Unit/Equal Opportunities Commission, *Minimum Wages for Women* (London, 1980).

she likes, whilst always being available in the event of an emergency telephone call, is not working for this purpose. In a controversial exclusion in the legislation, when a worker is taking an authorized rest period, the time spent does not count towards hours of work unless otherwise provided in the contract. This exemption may make employers more willing to grant rest breaks, but if we are really concerned to help workers to establish a satisfactory work/life balance, surely they should be entitled to take the occasional paid tea-break?

These four objections to the enactment of a minimum wage law, though not without substance, do not appear in the final analysis to provide sufficient reason to refrain from using this regulatory lever to assist people to achieve a better work/life balance. On its own, however, a minimum wage law will not ensure that everyone can earn a sufficient amount from paid work to achieve a decent standard of living and to manage household responsibilities. A state's welfare system needs to provide additional income to those household units with non-working dependants that have to survive on a single, low-paid job. In recent years in Britain the technique for delivering these welfare benefits has switched from direct social security payments to a system of tax credits, so that the benefits are paid through the wage packet. From the government's perspective this method of delivery is cheaper administratively, it permits the consolidation of the various benefits into a single payment, and, of course, it targets the benefits only on those who are prepared to take a job. The policy is social inclusion, not the promotion of welfare dependency.

2. EQUAL PAY

About two-thirds of the beneficiaries of the National Minimum Wage Act 1998 in Britain were women. This disproportionate effect reveals how the problem of establishing a satisfactory balance between work and life is especially significant for women. In order to reconcile the demands of childcare and other domestic chores, women often feel constrained to accept lower-paid, part-time, or casual jobs that offer the necessary flexibility of hours. Furthermore, they may be discouraged from investing in the skills and training necessary to obtain better jobs, if they do not expect to be able to follow the career paths involving full-time, continuous employment, through which they can realize the financial benefits from such investments in human capital. One effect of these considerations is to crowd women into lower-paid jobs, which itself may cause a problem of over-supply that permits employers to reduce wages further.

These factors explain why women were the disproportionate beneficiaries of the minimum wage law. They also may explain why women's pay is on average less than 80 per cent of men's pay, and why over a life-time on average women may earn about £250,000 less than a man. These broad statistics conceal wide variations according to occupation, but whatever comparisons are made, a wage gap opens up between men and women.

Is this gender effect found in statistics about wages explicable entirely by reference to the factors described above, such as women's lower investment in marketable skills and preference for jobs with flexible or shorter hours, or is there also discrimination in the labour market, so that women receive lower rates of pay for the same work as men? Although blatant discrimination in pay is rare these days, some statistical evidence points to the persistence of unconscious discrimination in payment systems.[13] If a job is predominantly performed by women, it is often regarded as 'women's work', and it is assumed to be probably less valuable and deserving of lower rates of pay. To the extent that unconscious discrimination in pay persists, the attractions of paid work will be reduced for women, making it harder for them to achieve the desired work/life balance. Legal regulation may help to combat this form of discrimination, though it should be appreciated that latent institutional discrimination is an extremely difficult target to identify and control.

The equal pay principle, which is enshrined in Article 141 of the Treaty of the European Community, has applied in the UK since 1975.[14] The national legislation requires an employer to pay a woman the same as a man for similar work or work of equal value. This requirement applies to every and each separate benefit received by an employee under the contract.[15] A claimant has to find a person of the opposite sex employed by the same or an 'associated' employer, who performs similar work or work to which equal value is attributed, and who receives higher pay. The fact that the work appears to be much the same is not conclusive, however, since if the two workers have different qualifications, skills, and experience, a tribunal may conclude that the work being performed is not really the same or of equal value.

A problem that often faces a claimant is that occupational segregation prevents such comparisons from being drawn. Partly through the choices described above and no doubt partly as a result of sex discrimination,

---

[13] A. McColgan, *Just Wages for Women* (Oxford: Clarendon Press, 1997), ch. 6.
[14] Equal Pay Act 1971.
[15] *Hayward v. Cammell Laird Shipbuilders Ltd* [1998] 1 AC 894, HL.

women may find themselves in occupations almost exclusively performed by women. To overcome this barrier, a claimant can compare her work to that performed by another male employee doing a different job to which equal value is attributed. This valuation can be based either on an employer's job evaluation scheme, or, in the absence of such a scheme, on an expert determination called for by an employment tribunal. This procedure permits comparisons to be made across occupations, as in the case of *Enderby v. Frenchay Health Authority*,[16] where a female senior speech therapist drew a comparison with senior hospital pharmacists and clinical psychologists who were predominantly men. A prima facie case of sex discrimination is established once a tribunal determines that the jobs in the comparison are of equal value, though paid unequally, and performed predominantly by persons of the opposite sex.

An employer then has the burden of demonstrating that the difference in pay was not the result of sex discrimination but was due instead to an objective material factor. It is not enough for the employer to prove the absence of intentional or direct discrimination in pay rates. An employer usually relies on institutional structures, such as different collective bargaining arrangements or separate wage scales, to establish an objective cause of the difference. Even those apparently sex-blind structures will not suffice to establish a material factor defence to a claim for equal pay, if those payment systems have an indirect discriminatory effect and cannot satisfy a test of proportionality. For example, in *Enderby v. Frenchay Health Authority* the tribunal found that the difference in pay was due to different collective bargaining structures and different structures within the professions, and that internally these pay scales did not directly or indirectly discriminate. But the ECJ held that this finding was insufficient to establish a material factor defence for the employer. If the jobs were of equal value, and speech therapists were predominantly women whereas the other comparator professions were predominantly occupied by men, then the bargaining and professional structures created a form of indirect discrimination in pay, so the employer had to satisfy in addition a test of proportionality. For this purpose, the employer has to demonstrate that the different payment structures correspond to a real need on the part of the employer, are appropriate with a view to achieving the objectives pursued, and are necessary to that end. The most common way for employers to establish such a defence is to rely upon market forces, that is to demonstrate that the different rates of pay in the payment systems

---

[16] C–127/92 [1993] ECR I-5535, ECJ.

respond to factors concerned with the supply of persons with those professional skills. For example, in *Enderby* the employer might point to the need to pay a particular profession more in order to recruit and retain these employees. Even when the employer establishes this market forces defence, it may not be a complete defence, if the need to recruit and retain members of a particular professional group explains only part of the difference in pay.

The effect of decisions such as that in *Enderby* is to permit women to challenge differences in payment linked to occupational segregation, but only up to a point. An employer cannot simply rely on different institutional structures to justify payment differentials. When there is apparently indirect discrimination arising from the gendered nature of occupational groupings, the employer has to demonstrate that market forces explain and account for all the difference in pay. The problem with accepting that argument is, of course, that women may have selected particular occupations because those jobs offered a more satisfactory work/life balance, with a consequent 'crowding effect' in such professions. Market forces should therefore not be regarded as some objective, invisible hand, but the product of women's difficult decisions about how to manage a work/life balance. In *Ratcliffe v. North Yorkshire County Council*,[17] workers producing school meals brought a claim for equal pay after their wages had been reduced following a competitive tendering operation. This work is performed almost exclusively by women—hence the name 'dinner ladies'. They compared their pay to jobs performed predominantly by men, which were formerly paid the same under the employer's payment system. The claim was successful, because the tribunal concluded that the variation in pay was ultimately due to a perception that this was women's work and could therefore be paid less. But the claim nearly failed, because the Court of Appeal accepted that it was also true that a pay cut had been imposed to reflect labour market rates for this type of work, which were low owing to the market forces factor that women are attracted to and crowd into this kind of work as it matches their skills and fits in with family responsibilities. The House of Lords, however, restored the tribunal's decision. Despite such victories for women, it remains true that the material factor defence can operate to condone and reinforce the negative effects on income from paid work that women often experience as a result of feeling the need to draw the balance between paid work and other responsibilities in ways that exclude them

[17] [1995] ICR 833, HL.

from jobs and careers that offer the highest rewards. Furthermore, a legal claim depends upon an individual worker commencing litigation, not a step that most employees will be willing to take as long as they have a job. Although the Equal Opportunities Commission (EOC) advises women and sometimes assists with the often complex litigation (as in the *Enderby* case), there must be serious doubt whether this regulatory technique of permitting claims by individual employees is likely to have much impact on the problem of unequal pay for women. A more effective approach would consist of inducements to employers to carry out their own careful examination of payment systems, in order to identify instances of latent discrimination based upon unconscious stereotypes. The EOC has developed a technical model for employers to carry out internal pay reviews. What is required in addition is either an incentive for employers to carry out such reviews rigorously and honestly or perhaps a penalty if they do not. Although the equal pay laws may not be completely effective in tackling latent discrimination in payment systems, they have helped to make paid work more attractive for women, thus enabling them to make a more satisfactory choice about the balance between paid work and other responsibilities.

3. FLEXIBLE HOURS

A final key target for the law with respect to improving the work/life balance concerns hours of work. The highest-paid jobs are typically full-time jobs. In Britain, notorious for its 'long-hours culture', a full-time job typically involves about 44 hours per week including both paid and unpaid overtime, and about one in eight full-time employees works more than 48 hours each week. These long hours are typically accepted by workers on the grounds of either a financial need for overtime payments or a desire to earn promotion to a higher salary. Once one takes into account additional time spent commuting, it is apparent that full-time jobs do not permit much opportunity to carry out other responsibilities and to enjoy leisure time.

About a quarter of all jobs in Britain require less than full-time work. Employers have increasingly offered part-time work opportunities, partly because it enables them to increase the labour force at times of peak demand, and partly to meet labour shortages because such opportunities appeal to people, the vast majority being women, who seek to balance paid work with substantial domestic commitments. But part-time work opportunities are not a panacea for the problem of the work/life balance.

Most part-time jobs are paid at the lower end of the spectrum of wage rates, and the hours offered, as determined by an employer, are often few, so that these jobs rarely provide a living wage.

Until recently, UK law made little attempt to regulate hours of work apart from paternalist interventions in favour of children (and previously women). Except where considerations of public safety were involved, as in the case of truck drivers, employers were left free to design job packages for reasons of productive efficiency. The objections to legal regulation were much the same as those raised against a statutory minimum wage: control over hours might have unemployment or negative income effects, might interfere with the development of collective bargaining, might in any case be ineffective owing to collusion, and, finally, would pose what might turn out to amount to an unmanageable regulatory task. But new laws have been required by the European Community.[18] This legislation reflects the widespread practice in European countries of controlling maximum hours of work for such purposes as to protect the health of employees and to some extent to create jobs for the unemployed.

But the EC Directive is largely a paper tiger. It fixes an upper limit of 48 hours per week for work, a high limit compared to the ILO proposed norm of 40 hours.[19] The Directive excludes from its coverage both wide sectors of the labour market such as transport and many occupations that typically require work for longer hours such as doctors and senior managers. In addition, the legislation for the time being permits individual employees to agree to opt out of the upper limit, which an employer can achieve by simply inserting a suitable term in the contract of employment. The comparable US legislation also avoids fixing a mandatory upper limit on hours, but merely requires an employer to pay higher overtime rates.[20] There is plainly no political will to prevent the creation of full-time jobs with long hours; where a more rigid system has been attempted, as in France, it is not a popular measure with workers who thereby suffer a diminution of income.

In any case, the more pertinent problem for the work/life balance issue is not so much long hours of work, but that of enabling workers to obtain jobs with the right balance for them. The law grants almost unrestricted flexibility to employers to create jobs with patterns of time that suit their

---

[18] Directive 93/104/EC; Working Time Regulations 1998, SI 1998/1833.
[19] ILO Convention 116.
[20] Fair Labor Standards Act 1938, 29 USC s. 201; Germany uses both techniques of upper limit and pay supplement.

productive requirements, and job seekers have to accept the best offer available even if it does not meet their needs. In particular, as long as the higher-paid jobs are full time, workers are typically left with the invidious choice between low pay or an unbalanced and destructive work/life balance. What workers plainly need is access to good jobs that require lower hours of work, and the opportunity to vary hours of work as their personal circumstances change.

This need reveals a further dimension of the idea that labour is not a commodity: everyone goes through a life cycle—child, student, worker, parent, retirement—though with considerable variations, and paid work has to be accommodated within this constantly shifting life experience. Part-time work could be regarded, as it is said to be in Sweden, not as a dead end, but rather as partial leave during a lifetime employment biography with guarantees of a right to resume full-time work as personal circumstances change.[21] A full response to such needs would effectively transfer the power to determine the pattern of hours for jobs from employers to employees. Such a radical intervention in the managerial discretion to organize production has not been attempted. Nonetheless, legal regulation has been edging towards such a position.

The first step in this direction was to grant rights to women to paid maternity leave with the right to return to work afterwards.[22] This legislation ended the business practice of terminating employment in the event of pregnancy. The right has subsequently been extended to new fathers to take a short period of leave. These 'family-friendly' measures have been further supplemented to give both parents a legal right to short periods of time off work to care for young children and to deal with family emergencies.[23] There are many other rights to time off that also help people to balance the requirements of work with other personal needs and responsibilities, such as the right to paid time off for young people for study or training.[24] All these measures, though especially useful to parents in juggling the demands of work and home, do not really tackle the underlying problem that the employer in practice determines hours of work.

Women have enjoyed some success through litigation under sex

---

[21] G. Bosch, P. Dakins, and F. Michon, *Times are Changing: Working Time in 14 Industrialised Countries* (Geneva: ILO, International Institute for Labour Studies, 1994).

[22] Directive 92/85/EC; Employment Rights Act 1996, Pt VIII; Maternity and Parental Leave, Etc. Regulations 1999, SI 1999/3312.

[23] Directive 96/34/EC; Employment Rights Act 1996, s. 57A.

[24] Employment Rights Act 1996, s. 63A.

discrimination laws in persuading courts that an employer's insistence on full-time work is indirect discrimination. Here the argument is that women are disproportionately adversely affected by the requirement of full-time working owing to their childcare responsibilities. Once this point is accepted, the employer has to justify the requirement under the test of proportionality. Although the courts have sometimes accepted that the additional cost and possible loss of productivity that may be linked to part-time work and job-sharing can justify a requirement of full-time work,[25] such justifications have increasingly been subjected to greater scrutiny, in order to ask whether or not the employer might have been able to make a reasonable accommodation to the claimant's need for different hours of work.[26]

One last legal avenue with the potential for challenging an employer's determination of hours of work relies on the right to freedom of thought, conscience, and religion protected by the European Convention for the Protection of Human Rights.[27] This right includes a freedom to worship and practise religious observance, subject to various standard limitations such as proportionality and respect for the rights of others. Can a worker rely on this right to demand that an employer should offer flexible hours to permit religious observance? The prospects for such a claim look poor following the failure of a Muslim schoolteacher to win the right to take time off on Friday afternoons to attend prayers at the Mosque.[28] Even so, the Convention right to practise religious observance may offer some protection to workers who want to resist changes to their hours of work imposed by the employer. A refusal by an employee to accept such changes on the ground of religious belief might be protected indirectly by the availability of a claim for unfair dismissal if the employer insists upon the variation in hours. Furthermore, the anti-discrimination principle in employment embraced by the EC now includes indirect religious discrimination, so that employers' neutral rules that have an indirect disadvantageous impact on religious minorities will have to be justified under a test of proportionality.[29] In the light of the growing respect for multicultural diversity in Britain, a court seized today with a similar issue to that posed by the Muslim schoolteacher might expect an employer to

---

[25] *Clymo v. Wandsworth London Borough Council* [1989] ICR 250, EAT.

[26] *London Underground Ltd v. Edwards (No. 2)* [1997] IRLR 157, EAT, [1998] IRLR 364, CA; above p. 72.

[27] Article 9, incorporated into UK law by the Human Rights Act 1998; Chapter 10 below.

[28] *Ahmad v. UK* (1982) 4 EHHR 126, ECHR; below p. 213.

[29] EC Directive 2000/78.

make reasonable accommodations in the hours of work for employees with minority religious beliefs.

It seems unlikely, however, that all workers will be given a general right to choose their own hours of work and to vary them from time to time. Employers strongly object to the potential disruption and additional costs that such a right might cause. What seems to be emerging instead is the idea of a right to ask the employer to consider a variation in hours, together with an obligation on the employer to justify its refusal. The seeds of this idea can be found in an EC Directive on the fair treatment of part-time workers.[30] The main principle in the Directive is that part-time workers should be treated equally, though pro rata, with full-time employers, unless the difference can be justified on objective grounds.[31] But the Directive also requires that, as far as possible, employers should give consideration to requests by workers to transfer from full-time work to part-time work, and vice versa. This idea of a 'right to ask' has been taken up by UK legislation that gives parents of pre-school age children protection against retaliatory action by an employer if they ask for a variation in hours, and imposes an obligation on the employer to produce business or economic reasons for rejecting the request.[32] An employee can contest a negative result in an employment tribunal, though only on the limited grounds that the correct procedure has not been followed or that the employer has failed to explain why the business grounds for refusal apply. The tribunal is not empowered to review the commercial decision itself, but can require an employer to reconsider its refusal to permit variations in working time. This model, though currently limited to parents of young children and disabled children, has the potential to provide a blueprint for a mechanism that would enable all workers to enjoy a better chance to secure a satisfactory work/life balance, whilst at the same time recognizing that employers may have genuine business reasons for being unwilling to accommodate flexibility in hours of work.

4. THE ROLE OF GOVERNMENT

Legal regulation of the work/life balance has to be viewed against the background of rapidly changing social division of labour, shifts in the

---

[30] EC Directive 98/49.

[31] The Part-time Workers (Prevention of Less Favourable Treatment) Regulations 2000, SI 2000/1551.

[32] Employment Rights Act 1996, s. 80F (as amended by the Employment Act 2002, s. 47).

types of jobs available, and a reconsideration of the role of the state in supporting welfare and eliminating social exclusion.[33] The male bread-winner model of family units has ceased to represent the position of the majority of households in Britain, with the proliferation of single-parent units and dual-income households. The greater equality accorded to women in the political sphere is reflected in their demand for good jobs and in men's willingness to accept a fairer division of labour in the home. Most adults now wish to combine a well-paid job with more time for family and other responsibilities and more leisure time. The majority of jobs are no longer in industrial production in factories, but rather in the service sector, which creates both the business need and the opportunity for greater flexibility in hours of work. To some extent the sharp spatial and chronological separation of work and home has been broken down by telecommunications and a growth in self-employment, which permits an increasing number of workers to work from home for at least part of the time. Thus the challenge presented to the Luddites' way of life by the emergence of the factory workplace no longer dominates, but the under-lying problems of securing a satisfactory balance between paid work and other needs and responsibilities remain a perennial problem for employment law.

Employment regulation also has to be viewed in the context of chan-ging perceptions of the appropriate role of the state. In the twentieth century, the Welfare State was designed to guarantee a minimum stand-ard of living for all citizens funded through taxation. Although elements of this system remain in place, the emphasis now is much more upon steering the labour market so that it produces adequate welfare for every-one. Dependency on welfare benefits is increasingly seen as part of the problem rather than as a solution to problems of social exclusion and social cohesion. Yet the task of harnessing the labour market to produce adequate solutions involves complex challenges for governments. It requires, as we saw in the previous chapter, intensive regulation with respect to access to labour markets combined with extensive provision to enable people to acquire the education and skills that employers require. The task also requires similar measures to address problems of the work/ life balance. Perhaps the most important element in state support is the provision or subsidization of care for children, the elderly, and other

---

[33] J. Conaghan, 'Women, Work, and Family: A British Revolution?', in J. Conaghan, R. M. Fischl, and K. Klare (eds), *Labour Law in an Era of Globalization* (Oxford: Oxford University Press, 2002), ch. 3.

dependants, which enables adults to participate more fully in the labour market. In Nordic countries such as Denmark, comprehensive and affordable childcare is available, which enables full labour market participation by all adults. In Britain we are slowly imitating this expensive social agenda. What remains deeply controversial is how the costs of such provision should be shared between the worker, the employer, and the taxpayer.

This chapter has focused on the detailed regulation of terms of conditions of employment, which also can play a part in solving problems of the work/life balance. The issue of who bears the costs of this regulation lurks in the differences between the measures. Should the worker bear the cost, as in cases of unpaid leave such as the tea-break, the employer, as in instances of paid leave, or should the state subsidize the cost to the employer, as is the case for instance with respect to maternity pay? However the burden is distributed, there is a need for legal regulation, because employers prefer to preserve their discretion to fix terms of employment in the light of their perceptions of business efficiency. These perceptions do not necessarily rule out flexible working, time off, nursery care, and a living wage, for employers have to recruit and retain good workers. But too often the traditional terms of employment rest upon unconscious assumptions about the value of particular kinds of work, how work should be organized, and the limited responsibilities of employers towards their staff, which, when thoroughly examined as in equal pay claims, cannot be justified on objective business grounds. The pattern of legal regulation that may be evolving, and that may go a considerable way to improving the work/life balance for many workers and reducing problems of social exclusion, is one in which employers have a duty to consider and to accommodate the needs of workers to balance their personal lives with paid work to an extent that is compatible with carefully scrutinized business needs.

Part III

Competitiveness

5

Co-operation

In the spring of 1972, the British railway system was grinding to a halt—even more than usual. The railway workers' unions had rejected the employer's final pay offer and had instructed their members to 'work to rule'. In a legal action, the government, supported by the employers, sought an injunction commanding the union officials to withdraw their instruction until a ballot had been held. A crucial legal question was whether compliance with the instruction constituted a breach of the workers' contracts of employment. The problem was that the instruction apparently amounted to no more than a requirement that workers should comply strictly with their terms of employment and obey punctiliously the rules laid down by management for the performance of work. How could precise performance of the contractual obligations amount to a breach of contract? A glittering array of the finest legal minds argued the case before the Court of Appeal—the barristers destined to become peers included Geoffrey Howe, architect of the legislation on which the case was based and future foreign secretary, Tom Bingham, future Lord Chief Justice and Senior Law Lord, Alexander Irvine, future Lord Chancellor, and Professor Wedderburn, the eminent LSE labour law scholar. Undaunted by the subtleties of the legal submissions, and avoiding the distractions of legal authorities, Lord Denning MR held that although a man is not bound positively to do more for his employer than his contract requires, and can withdraw his goodwill, what he must not do is wilfully to obstruct the employer's business, for that amounts to a breach of contract going to the 'very root of the consideration'. The other members of the court agreed that the workers were in breach of their contracts of employment and that an injunction should be issued. In a phrase that has since become an authoritative expression of the legal construction of the contract of employment, Buckley LJ summarized the law by stating that the employees were in breach of 'an implied term to serve the employer faithfully within the requirements of the contract'.[1]

---

[1] *Secretary of State for Employment v. Associated Society of Locomotive Engineers and Firemen and Others (No. 2)* [1972] ICR 19. The Industrial Relations Act 1971 on which the legal proceedings were based was abolished in 1974.

Men are not machines, but must be induced to work. A contract creates a legally enforceable exchange of work in return for pay. Pay serves as a strong inducement to perform the terms of the contractual obligation, but it may prove insufficient to persuade employees to work hard, to maximize productivity, and to act always in the best interests of the employer. Ever since owners of the means of production discovered that in some instances it would be more efficient to make a product by employing wage labour than to purchase the product in the market, they had to confront the problem that the expected gains in efficiency could only be obtained if the workforce co-operated fully. In the early factories, employers quickly discovered the two main levers for securing co-operation: incentives in the payment system, and detailed direction and surveillance of the performance of work. The former led to the introduction of diverse payment mechanisms, which made the amount of pay contingent on variables such as production outcomes, attendance, length of service, and assessments of effort. The latter led to the subordination of workers to a managerial bureaucratic hierarchy that directed and monitored the performance of work. The history of management can be told as the unceasing search for new combinations of these two levers that will secure the most efficient extraction of labour power from the workforce. Although an infinite number of combinations may be available to management, it is worth remarking upon the presence in contemporary businesses of two competing patterns of employment relation in large businesses using skilled workforces.

A rigid system of workplace governance is often described as Fordist, since it is associated with the development of the mass production of cheap standardized goods and services such as cars or consumer banking services. The contractual exchange consists of payment for time at work performing a particular job package, as opposed to a measurement of performance or productivity. The risk of low productivity is countered by elaborate hierarchical monitoring systems and the use of conveyor-belt technology to force the pace of work. The contract provides for full-time work for an indefinite duration, though it can be terminated by notice or as a disciplinary measure. Every detail of work is regulated through a book of rules described as the 'works rules' or 'staff handbook', by which the employer issues detailed standing instructions about the content of each job and the responsibilities of employees, and specifies disciplinary sanctions for disobedience to these standing orders. Training and the acquisition of skills often occurs during performance of the job and will therefore be specific to the particular task required. Both employer and employee are likely to have made considerable investment in the success of the employment relation. The employer will have invested heavily in plant and machinery, and in the training of the workforce. The employee has also invested in those firm-specific skills, for which there will be rewards of payment based upon seniority and promotion.

The contrasting, more flexible, model lacks a conventional label, but is often associated with Japanese-owned firms. The payment system sharpens incentives for hard work by techniques such as individualized performance-related pay, commissions, or profit-related pay. The formal length of the contract often shifts to fixed term, temporary, or part time, though this is modified by policies to ensure permanent employment in fact for essential or 'core employees'. In many instances, the hierarchies of the workplace become flattened, with a greater emphasis upon collaborative group working or individual autonomy. The job packages become less determinate and fewer in number, with the expectation therefore that employees should work flexibly, thereby concentrating on the most productive use of their labour. Under the management strategy of 'human resources management', there is much greater emphasis upon training and skills at work, and also the acquisition of more generic skills through external training and education is emphasized and rewarded by the payment system. For example, in the Japanese Nissan plant in Britain, all tasks were condensed into 15 job descriptions, such as production staff or maintenance staff, with no job descriptions within these categories. Pay within each category is determined by reference to know-how, the number of tasks mastered, flexibility, co-operation with colleagues in the same working group, so that rewards track performance evaluation, rather than job descriptions.[2]

The precise features, the prevalence, and even the existence of this alternative, flexible model for the contractual and institutional arrangements governing employment remain controversial. The pressure behind this management strategy seems to come from the intensification of competition between products not only in relation to price but crucially in respect of quality and innovation. The consumer market seems to be more discriminating, so that firms need to be able to exploit technological innovations quickly, be able to offer credible commitments to quality, and to have the capacity to enter specialist niche markets.[3] The rigid model is

---

[2] P. Wickens, *The Road to Nissan* (Basingstoke: MacMillan, 1987).

[3] M. J. Piore and C. F. Sabel, *The Second Industrial Divide* (New York: Basic Books, 1984).

believed to stifle innovation and to discourage the acquisition of generic skills, which in the long run weaken a firm's ability to compete in these new market conditions of a knowledge-based economy. The more flexible model seeks to develop a commitment within the workforce to continuous improvements in quality and efficiency by giving work groups greater autonomy and responsibility for the way in which work is performed. This policy of 'human resource management' has been viewed with suspicion, of course, for the language of empowering the workforce can disguise a reality of increasing requirements for the intensification of work effort. Functional flexibility for the worker means learning everyone else's jobs, covering when they are absent, helping out everywhere when needed, being responsible for production and efficiency, and never getting a moment's break. But even if flexible production does make heavier demands on the workforce, there is evidence to support the view that it enables a transformation of the meaning of work, so that it is no longer regarded as a purely instrumental task for earning a wage and workers feel less as if they are being treated as commodities.[4]

All of these flexible kinds of contractual and institutional arrangements have been present since the Industrial Revolution. In any one enterprise it is possible to combine different elements of these strategies, so that rigid pattern of governance may be applied to a core group of employees, but a flexible pattern applied to peripheral groups, such as unskilled temporary, part-time workers hired in order to cope with fluctuations in demand, or skilled consultants brought in for particular research and development tasks. The important lesson to be learned for the purposes of regulation of employment relations is that no single pattern of employment relation is likely to predominate in the future, so that any regulation must be able to accommodate a wide spectrum of employment relations.

The employer's persistent search for more efficient systems for the management of labour has proceeded largely unfettered by the law. The legal framework of contract created a strong presumption that an employer should be permitted to offer any terms of employment that it chose, and workers were in theory equally free to accept or reject these terms. Once the bargain had been struck, however, its terms determined the scope of the legal rights and obligations of the parties. The most that the judges of the common law were prepared to do was to insert implied

---

[4] D. Gallie, M. White, Y. Cheng, and M. Tomlinson, *Restructuring the Employment Relationship* (Oxford: Oxford University Press, 1998); P. Rosenthal, S. Hill, and R. Peccei, 'Checking Out Service: Evaluating Excellence, HRM and TQM in Retailing' (1997) 11 *Work, Employment & Society* 481.

obligations into the contract of employment, which rendered explicit the 'very root of the consideration', the requirement of co-operation or performance in good faith. Lord Tucker summarized the principal elements of these implicit obligations of employees in the old-fashioned though nonetheless apt terminology of master and servant:

(1) the duty to give reasonable notice in the absence of custom or express agreement; (2) the duty to obey lawful orders of the master; (3) the duty to be honest and diligent in the master's service; (4) the duty to take reasonable care of his master's property entrusted to him and generally in the performance of his duties; (5) to account to his master for any secret commission or remuneration received by him; (6) not to abuse his master's confidence in matters pertaining to his services.[5]

The combination of the employer's selection of the express terms of the contract and the common law's implication of terms designed to reinforce an employer's implicit expectations of good-faith performance provides a legal framework that is plainly conducive to the employer's aim of maximizing productive efficiency. Given that one of employment law's principal aims is to support the efficiency of contracts for the supply of labour and thereby to enhance the competitiveness of business, the question arises whether any further legal intervention is required. Mandatory regulation of the terms of employment relations might interfere with the contractual process of negotiation for the efficient acquisition and use of labour power, thereby harming competitiveness. What has to be investigated in this chapter is whether some legal regulation can in fact be conducive to competitiveness.

1. MUTUAL TRUST AND CONFIDENCE

To understand how legal regulation of the employment relation can contribute to productive efficiency, we need to examine more closely what is necessary to achieve a co-operative working system. A contract provides a framework for an employment relation, but detailed operations must be determined on a daily basis. Both management and employees have considerable discretionary power under the contract. The employer typically has the power to direct the workforce and to set rules for operating procedures and the organization of the workplace. These rules and procedures leave gaps where management has to issue further instructions.

---

[5] *Lister v. Romford Ice and Cold Storage Co Ltd* [1957] AC 555, HL, at 594.

Even within this complex governance structure, however, there remain interstices where employees effectively have discretion about how work should be performed. Although the Fordist conveyor-belt factory system minimized this employee discretion, most workers, including the train drivers in our opening example and especially those engaged in more flexible systems of production, have some autonomy with respect to the pace of work, the methods of working, and styles of co-operation with other workers. The point of the implied term of performance in good faith is to insist that in law this discretion of employees should be exercised in the best interests of the employer. In practice, however, good co-operation in the workplace depends upon more subtle processes for building commitment, which require give and take, negotiation, and accommodation. Both managers and employees have to exercise their discretionary powers in ways that are perceived to be fair, in order to maximize co-operation and productive efficiency. For co-operation to work in the long run, there has to be mutual trust and confidence that both parties will continue to exercise their discretionary powers fairly with respect to the other.

The idea that the employment relation rests upon mutual trust and confidence has long been a cornerstone of the legal construction of the contract of employment. Once there has been a breakdown in mutual trust and confidence, the courts recognize that the contract has come to an end, whatever the wishes of the parties. In the quotation above, Lord Tucker explains that an employee has an implied legal duty to be loyal and not to abuse his employer's confidence. What has been stressed more recently by English courts is that the obligation is mutual. The implied term also requires that an employer 'shall not without reasonable and proper cause conduct itself in a manner calculated and likely to destroy or seriously damage the relationship of confidence and trust between employer and employee'.[6] This implied term functions as a regulatory tool for supporting co-operation by prohibiting unfair exercises of discretionary power by an employer. The term seeks to support trust and confidence, and therefore productive efficiency, by determining that unfair exercises of discretionary power amount to a breach of contract.

An implied term is not a very effective instrument for ensuring that neither party betrays trust and confidence. Express terms may override its requirements, so the term only qualifies the exercise of discretionary

---

[6] Lord Steyn, *Mahmoud v. Bank of Credit and Commerce International S.A.* [1998] AC 20, HL.

powers under the contract. Moreover, employees are unlikely to invoke the regulation until they feel that there is no point in continuing with the job, at which point they resign and claim compensation for breach of contract or 'constructive dismissal'. Nevertheless, the term recognizes and tries to support this necessary ingredient of efficient employment relations by compensating employees for detriment caused by misuse of discretionary power. For example, in *French v. Barclays Bank plc*,[7] having been required to relocate, an employee of the bank took advantage of a generous, though discretionary, scheme for cheap loans in order to enable him to purchase a new home before he had sold his existing house. After a while, however, the employer altered the scheme owing to its expense in a sluggish housing market. Suddenly, therefore, the employee faced severe financial difficulties from having to pay two mortgages. Although the employer was legally entitled to alter the scheme under the contract, the Court of Appeal found a breach of the implied term of mutual trust and confidence. The employer's abrupt change in the scheme that had been applied for many years and that caused financial hardship to the employee was conduct that was likely to destroy confidence and trust.

Another example illustrates how the implied term controls day-to-day managerial behaviour. In *Lewis v. Motorworld Garages Ltd*,[8] the employee worked for a garage as a service manager. Following a restructuring of the management, he was effectively demoted to a position with fewer fringe benefits and a less advantageous salary structure. Although this demotion was probably a breach of contract, the employee stayed on. Over the next few months, however, the directors of the company started complaining about his work in a way that the employee regarded as nitpicking. Despite the employee's explanations and objections, the criticisms became even harsher, culminating in a final warning that unless his work improved his employment would be terminated. The employee eventually felt that he had no alternative but to resign and claim compensation for constructive dismissal. The central legal question was whether the employer had broken the implied term of trust and confidence. The Court of Appeal accepted that a series of actions by an employer, some of them perhaps quite trivial, could, when regarded cumulatively, amount to a breach of the implied term, so the case was remitted to a tribunal to assess whether the term had been broken in fact. It is important to appreciate, however, that small acts of meanness, harsh criticism, and unfairness will not be sufficient to amount to a breach of contract. Employees are expected to

---

[7] [1998] IRLR 652, CA.   [8] [1986] ICR 157, CA.

put up with the normal incidents of a hierarchical relation, such as per-emptory orders, harsh criticism, and intrusive surveillance. When one manager told an employee, 'You can't do the bloody job anyway', that kind of trenchant criticism would not in the view of one tribunal ordinarily amount to a breach of the implied term.[9]

2. ADAPTATION

Often the crucial issue of co-operation concerns whether employees will accept new working conditions and methods. Most contracts of employ-ment, as we have noted, are incomplete by design in the sense that the performance of obligations of employees are stated at a high level of generality combined with an obligation to obey the directions of man-agement within the scope of the contract. Within this framework, an employer can instruct the worker to change working methods, to work with new technology, and change tasks. The contract places some limits on what the employer may require to the extent that it provides a job description. But employers often award themselves a free hand for adap-tation by inserting an express flexibility clause to the effect that an employee can be required to perform any duties that an employer pre-scribes. Even more remarkably, employers sometimes insert sweeping clauses that permit them to vary unilaterally even basic terms of employment such as pay: 'The Company may make reasonable changes to the terms and conditions of your employment. Such changes will be confirmed in writing.'[10] With such flexibility clauses, even the express terms of the contract provide the employee with no legal safeguards against opportunistic demands by the employer. Although the willingness to adapt is an essential ingredient in a co-operative and productive work-ing relation, our earlier analysis suggests that a fear that this discretionary power will be operated unfairly by an employer is likely to subvert co-operation. Employers appreciate the potential damage to employee relations that opportunistic use of flexibility clauses may cause, which provides some reassurance to employees. In addition, legal regulation can provide safeguards against the misuse of discretionary power, which may strengthen mutual trust and confidence and facilitate co-operation through flexibility and adaptation.

---

[9] *Courtaulds Northern Textiles Ltd v. Andrew* [1979] IRLR 84, EAT.

[10] W. Brown, right *et al.*, *The Individualisation of Employment Contracts in Britain* (London: Department of Trade and Industry, Employment Research Series No. 4, 1998), pp. 45–6.

English courts have used implied terms and other general legal principles to provide such safeguards. As a general principle of construction, the courts are likely to interpret express powers to vary obligations under the contract narrowly, against the employer. In exercising those powers, the courts require the employer to give reasonable notice of changes, so that an employee has a reasonable opportunity to make the necessary adaptation. For instance, if the employer requires the employee to transfer to a different workplace under a relocation clause in the contract, this power has to be exercised in such a way that the employee has sufficient notice to be able to arrange for new accommodation and moving dependants.[11] But none of these legal constraints on the exercise of discretionary powers insists that the power should be exercised fairly or reasonably.

The closest approximation to such a standard has evolved in connection with discretionary powers in the payment mechanism. Many contracts make provision for discretionary bonus payments or other fringe benefits. Employers use this incentive mechanism to encourage co-operation, whilst reserving a discretionary power to determine both whether and how much additional reward should be given. As a matter of construction of the contract as a whole, a court may conclude that the discretion to award a bonus is limited by reference to criteria mentioned in the contract, such as the employee's performance at work. But even if the contract appears silent on the relevant criteria, the courts have insisted that such powers should be exercised rationally or not perversely. It is unlawful to exercise such a discretionary power to make a decision that no reasonable employer would have reached in the circumstances. This principle was applied, for instance, to a decision of an employer not to award any share options to a manager on his dismissal, even though the purpose of the scheme was to reward hard work and loyalty for employees with long service, conditions which the employee amply satisfied.[12] This principle of irrationality, which is drawn from administrative law, could be applied to any discretionary power of the employer under a contract of employment, including instructions to make substantial changes in working conditions.

3. FORMALITY

Mutual trust and confidence can also be constructed through greater clarity in the reciprocal undertakings of the parties to an employment

---

[11] *United Bank v. Akhtar* [1989] IRLR 507, EAT.
[12] *Mallone v. BPB Industries plc* [2002] EWCA Civ 126 [2002] IRLR 452, CA.

relation. A written document that explains the details of the rights and obligations of the parties, together with a handbook that explains how an employer expects to exercise discretionary powers, is likely to avoid misunderstandings and to promote confidence and trust. Employment law has not, however, insisted that valid contracts of employment should be in writing. Such a rule might turn out to be a trap for casual workers, if they discovered that they could not even bring a claim for their wages without a written document. Instead, in Europe, employers are under an obligation to provide a written statement of the essential aspects of the contract or employment relationship.[13] In practice, employers often fulfil this requirement by presenting a written statement and ask the employee to sign it as a formal contract of employment.

Although greater formality is probably conducive to better co-operation, the complex rule systems that surround employment relations render this objective difficult to achieve. For example, remuneration is clearly an essential aspect of the employment relation, but when pay includes subtle incentive systems and deferred benefits such as occupational pensions, or when pay is set from time to time by other mechanisms such as collective agreements, it is not a simple or inexpensive task to formalize the system and inform the employee of all the details of the arrangement. This problem is compounded if elements of the remuneration system are subject to frequent changes. The legislation in the UK permits employers to satisfy the requirement of a written statement by referring to other documents, such as sick pay arrangements, pension schemes, disciplinary procedures, and collective agreements, provided that the documents are made reasonably accessible to the employee. An employer is also required to give a written notification of changes in the essential aspects of the contract. The statutory remedy for breach of these requirements includes a tribunal's power to issue a correct written statement and to award a small sum of compensation.[14] The common law may provide an additional remedy of compensation for breach of an implied term requiring disclosure of benefits under the contract, if an employee suffers economic loss from an employer's failure to notify the employee of a possible benefit, which in the circumstances an employee could not reasonably discover without assistance from the employer.[15]

---

[13] Directive 91/533/EC; Employment Rights Act 1996, s. 1.
[14] Employment Act 2002, s. 38.
[15] *Scally v. Southern Health and Social Services Board* [1992] 1 AC 294, HL.

4 · GRIEVANCES

One of the potential benefits of greater formality in employment relations is that disputes between employer and employee about their respective entitlements can be reduced. Indeed, as we have noted previously, because an employment relation is expected to be long term and is incomplete by design, it is inevitable that disagreements will arise about how the relationship should evolve and how discretion should be exercised. These disagreements, if left unresolved and festering, can of course destroy the necessary trust and confidence on which the co-operative relation is based. It is therefore essential for contracts of employment of longer duration to contain some kind of grievance mechanism, so that if an employee wants to challenge some decision or practice of the employer, this matter can be resolved without a breakdown in the economic relationship as a whole. Indeed, an employer's persistent refusal even to listen to reasonable complaints of employees might amount to a breach of the implied term of mutual trust and confidence.

Most employers therefore construct a grievance mechanism through which employees can air issues and perhaps receive some satisfaction. Where the employer recognizes a trade union, a collective agreement is likely to provide for a procedure for resolving disputes about its application and a method for handling individual employees' grievances. Perhaps surprisingly, until recently in the UK there was no statutory requirement for employers to provide formal grievance procedures for employees. This gap was effectively closed, however, because a court can find an employer who fails to deal with a grievance in a proper and timely fashion in breach of an implied term of the contract.[16] Legislation now imposes in every contract of employment a prescribed minimum grievance procedure. The procedure requires an employee to set out the grievance in writing, and then the employer must meet the employee to discuss the grievance and provide the employee with a right of appeal against the decision. If the employer fails to provide such a grievance procedure or fails to follow it, however, it is unclear whether an employee has an independent right to claim compensation for breach of this legal requirement. But in other proceedings brought by an employee, such as a claim for unfair dismissal, the tribunal will increase the employee's compensation if the employer has not complied with the grievance procedure,

---

[16] *W. A. Goold (Pearmak) Ltd v. McConnell* [1995] IRLR 516, EAT.

though equally the employee's compensation will be reduced if the employee has failed to avail himself of the procedure.[17]

These novel statutory procedures will no doubt cause unexpected difficulties initially, but the general aim of promoting informal dispute resolution in the workplace is clearly an important ingredient in helping to establish and preserve mutual trust and confidence. The underlying regulatory strategy of providing incentives for the parties to go through an internal dispute resolution mechanism before resorting to legal claims seems correct, though it could be improved by encouraging collective self-regulation of such grievance procedures, with a view to obtaining the advantages of reflexivity and high levels of compliance usually achieved through this technique of procedural regulation.

5 . HUMAN CAPITAL

An important dimension of the benefits that an employee receives from work is the opportunity to acquire skills, technical knowledge, management experience, contacts, and knowledge of the business. These benefits or 'human capital' enable the worker to command higher wages in the labour market, improve the employability of the worker, and can provide a springboard for the worker to set up a small business. An employer also stands to gain from investing in the human capital of its workforce, because improved skills in the workforce may contribute to productive efficiency, flexibility, and innovation. In a knowledge-based economic sector, where the value of work depends almost entirely on the skills, experience, and knowledge of the employees, these benefits to employers arising from investment in human capital become augmented. Some of this knowledge is acquired through the process of 'learning by doing', but employers also bear the costs of workplace training and may share the cost of more formal education outside the workplace. Despite this significance of investments in human capital to the employment relation and the potential benefits for competitiveness, contracts of employment rarely pay much attention to the issues involved, and the relevant legal regulation appears unclear about its objectives. What seems to be missing is a clear framework of incentives for employers and employees to improve the human capital of the workforce and to promote innovations in products and processes.

---

[17] Employment Act 2002, ss. 29–33.

TRAINING

Should an employer be under a legal duty to invest in the human capital of its workforce? Such a duty might imply an obligation to provide training, to give opportunities in the workplace to improve skills, and to permit employees to have a right to flexibility with respect to hours of work so that they can take up formal education outside the workplace. Many employers provide such benefits on the basis of a rational calculation that these investments in human capital will benefit the business in the long run by improving productivity and helping to retain staff. Where the necessary skills can be acquired by on-the-job training, a standard pattern in large firms is the provision of this training with the incentive that, provided the worker remains with the business, the improvement in skills is likely to lead to better wages through internal promotion and enhanced job security. Although this model can apply in many contexts, economic forces tend to undermine this incentive system for investments in human capital. Only about 15 per cent of the UK workforce receive regular job-related training provided by their by employer.[18] There is a 'freerider' problem among employers, for it may be cheaper for an employer to hire workers with the requisite skills than to incur the costs of training. The presence of freeriders threatens to undermine the incentives for employers to make investments in human capital because, once trained, a worker may leave for another employer. Furthermore, in a rapidly changing economic environment, the employer may no longer be able to keep the implicit promise of job security in return for the employee acquiring particular skills, so workers may not want the job-specific training offered by an employer, but rather seek an improvement of general transferable skills that will enhance their employability in the labour market as a whole. Both the 'freerider' problem and the inability of employers to realize the implicit promise of job security and internal advancement tend to undermine the incentives for investments in human capital in the traditional form of on-the-job training. There arises a danger that these economic forces will tend to block improvements in human capital, with a consequent loss of productive efficiency and higher levels of unemployment. Can legal regulation help to overcome these economic forces that discourage investments in human capital?

Such interventions commonly comprise subsidies for education and training, either through the state's educational system or by relieving the

---

[18] Labour Force Survey, (1997) 105 *Labour Market Trends* October No. 10, 54.

employer of part of the cost of workplace training by providing subsidies for apprenticeship schemes.[19] Our question is whether in addition employees should have legal rights to training and educational opportunities as part of a government's strategy for 'life-long learning'. The emphasis so far in the UK has been on young workers, who through lack of work experience and relevant skills may find themselves excluded from the labour market. The government provides subsidies to employers to take on young workers for a limited period of time, so that they can acquire work experience and learn some skills. In addition, young workers have a right to time off work to pursue formal educational qualifications.[20] These statutory rights might be extended to give all workers the right to time off in order to pursue training and educational opportunities, the cost of which could be subsidized by the employer or the taxpayer.

The contract of employment may provide for training and educational opportunities. Contractual rights may be difficult to enforce in practice, however, since the employer's obligation to provide training may be unspecific in content and timing, and employees may be unwilling to press their claim against their employer. A typical term in a contract may comprise a statement such as, 'The most important asset in any business is its employees and the employer is prepared to invest in its staff to ensure that they have every opportunity to develop their skills'. Although this statement suggests that the employer will devote considerable resources to staff training and development, it would be hard for employees to rely on this vague promise in order to claim breach of contract by a refusal to provide some opportunity for improvement in human capital. The common law has not recognized a general implied term to provide training, though there may be an implied term that requires the employer to offer training for workers when introducing new technology, as in the case where the tax authorities introduced computerized records. In return for the tax officials adapting to computers instead of paper files, the employer was under an implied legal obligation to provide staff with the necessary training in the new technology.[21]

An important part of the potential human capital acquired by a worker stems from work experience itself. By participating in production, an employee learns about current techniques and innovations, and establishes a network of contacts. The contract of employment places an

[19] C. Crouch, 'Skills-based Full Employment: the Latest Philosopher's Stone' (1997) 35 *British Journal of Industrial Relations* 367–91.

[20] Employment Rights Acts 1996, ss. 63A and 63B.

[21] *Cresswell v. Board of Inland Revenue* [1984] ICR 508, HC.

obligation on an employee to be ready and willing to work, but does it also impose on the employer an obligation to provide work? The common law limited the employer's obligation to pay wages for the time that the employee was willing and able to work, without imposing a duty to provide work to be done. Since the employee needs to be able to attend the workplace in order to establish this right to wages, the common law also insisted that the employer could not lawfully exclude an employee from the workplace without an express contractual term to that effect. Many contracts of employment therefore provide for the right of the employer to suspend the worker on full pay, usually pending the outcome of a disciplinary enquiry. On termination of the contract of employment, the employer may also exclude the worker by paying compensation equivalent to the wages to be earned during the notice period, that is 'pay in lieu of notice'. If an employee is excluded from the workplace in breach of contract, can the employee claim compensation for the loss of an opportunity to acquire or retain skills and knowledge in addition to the claim for wages? Subject to the express terms of the contract, some categories of workers have persuaded the court that they have lost a valuable benefit by being prevented from actually working. Actors have successfully claimed court injunctions ordering an impresario to refrain from steps such as hiring another actor that put a promised theatrical engagement beyond the actor's reach on account of the actor's loss of a chance to enhance his or her reputation.[22] In principle, if an employee can demonstrate that an employer's breach of contract in failing to provide work or training has damaged the employee's chances of future employment, a claim for compensatory damages in addition to any payment of wages due under the contract should be available.

INNOVATION

One of the principal advantages flowing from the augmentation of human capital includes the facilitation of innovation in products and services which give businesses a competitive advantage. Many companies in fields such as pharmaceuticals depend upon research and innovation for most of their profits. The innovations usually come from employees, so the question arises whether the employment relation provides a framework that encourages workers to suggest inventions, improvements, and efficiency savings. Employers can link remuneration incentives to

---

[22] *Herbert Clayton and Jack Waller Ltd v. Oliver* [1930] AC 209, HL.

suggestions for innovations, either directly by paying for ideas, or indirectly through career opportunities for promotion.

In the field of patents, the Patents Act 1977 in the UK provides a mandatory system of profit-sharing. The employer is entitled to the patent rights if the invention was the product of work within the employee's duties or resulted from the carrying out of his or her duties, but otherwise the normal presumption operates that the employee controls the rights from the invention. In cases where the employer owns the invention, the employee can claim compensation where is it just, and the amount of the compensation will take into account both the effort and skill of the employee as well as the amount of benefit which the employer has derived from it. Where the employee retains the rights to exploit the invention, these rights can be assigned to the employer, and then the employee can claim in addition to any initial fee paid for the assignment a further sum in just compensation.

Apart from this special statutory regime, the law does not provide a compulsory framework for profit-sharing with respect to innovations. The law seems to assume that performance in good faith of the contract of employment requires employees to produce innovations and not to receive any rewards other than those provided under the express terms of the contract. These terms may not offer much incentive, however, since implicit promises of promotion or bonuses appear vague and too discretionary. It is unclear that any general legal regulation might help to establish a better incentive structure, however, because the particular circumstances and needs of different business differ so widely. Moreover, the crucial incentive system that operates in practice is that employees who have a good idea tend to leave their jobs and set up a business themselves, perhaps as a joint venture with their former employer. The absence of profit-sharing in employment forces workers to become entrepreneurs by setting up their own small business. In the long run, this promotion of entrepreneurial activity may serve the end of competitiveness in business better than a clearer system of profit-sharing for innovations within employment.

6. FLEXIBILITY AND FAIRNESS

Better productivity, innovation, and closer attention to quality and customer service—all these key features of a competitive business require co-operation from the workforce. Freedom of contract permits employers to construct employment relations that award management the power to direct the workforce efficiently and to sanction those employees who do not perform the contract in good faith. But to achieve a higher level of competitiveness, especially in business sectors where the success of the business depends heavily on the knowledge and ideas of the workforce, this command and control strategy of a hierarchical employment relation does not function so well. Employers require a greater degree of co-operation from the workforce, a willingness to adapt, to innovate, and to assume the responsibilities entailed by flexibility in the performance of tasks. To achieve this level of co-operation, employers need to make a credible commitment to treat the workforce fairly and perhaps to share the profits arising from better co-operation.

In this chapter we have considered how employment law has evolved rules governing the contract of employment that begin to meet this need for matching high levels of co-operation with protections for fair treatment and profit-sharing. Implied terms concerning trust and confidence protect implicit expectations, and formal documents protect the diverse express expectations of employees. A reliable informal system of dealing with grievances about these matters can reduce conflict and promote co-operation. Legal regulation may also help rather more than it does at present to ensure that workers enjoy reliable assurances of improvements to their skills and employability. But such measures form only part of the legal framework designed primarily to improve the competitiveness of business by ensuring the fair treatment of workers, thus leading to better co-operation. The next four chapters examine other essential ingredients in this strategy of improving competitiveness through the regulation of employment relations. Employment law can help to create rules and institutions that enable employers to make credible commitments to treat their workforce fairly in return for better co-operation.

6

Partnership

In the opening chapter, we observed how in the early part of the twentieth century, most industrialized countries reached a political settlement between capital and labour. Laws granted organizations of workers the right to bargain collectively on behalf of their members and to take industrial action to reinforce their demands. In return, however, trade unions accepted limits on their activities, which confined the scope of strike action, and in particular prohibited political strikes. Although the spectre of the red flag we observed being raised by the Luddites always hangs over employment law, with its threat that organizations of workers will engage in a more profound challenge to the legitimacy of the market order and the parliamentary system of government, the industrial pluralist settlement has, at least in its broad outline that separates industrial from political action, remained remarkably constant and robust.

With hindsight, however, we can see that this settlement, though successfully partitioning industrial conflict from broader political conflict, created a new set of problems. By confining the legitimate activity of workers' organizations to bargaining about terms and conditions of employment, these institutional arrangements suffered from three weaknesses. First, the emphasis on collective bargaining over terms of employment set trade unions out on a path where industrial conflict or the threat of it was their normal operational method to secure their goal. Second, unions and their members were unable to use collective bargaining to obtain broader discussions with employers about every aspect of the workplace and the future direction of the business. Third, the trajectory of conflict created distrust between the parties, so that rarely was an employer able to harness collective bargaining to establish better cooperative relations with the workforce. In other words, the British legislation blocked the perceived radical threat of trade unions, but in so doing created a recipe for permanent conflict in industrial relations, which both damaged productivity and prevented employees from gaining a voice in the running of every aspect of the business. When the economy was strong, these inherent problems of the British system of industrial relations could be ignored. In the long run, however, the damage to competitiveness caused by conflictual, low-trust, working relations had to be addressed. Trade unions were often blamed as the source of the problem, which was hardly fair, since they had had to operate within the legal constraints that set them off down this path. Employers pressed governments to enable them to get rid of trade unions from the workplace and to weaken their powers. Although legislation responded to these demands to some extent, the elimination of trade unions and collective bargaining could not provide a stable solution to industrial relations.

Most employers may not want trade unions and collective bargaining, but they certainly require industrial relations mechanisms for securing collective co-operation from the workforce. Just as the individual employment relation only achieves maximum productive efficiency through co-operation based upon mutual trust and confidence, so too these conditions have to be satisfied at a more general level for the workforce as a whole. Indeed, consultations and negotiations with representatives of the workforce can provide an efficient mechanism for securing co-operation and improving trust and confidence for the entire workforce. The need for such collective mechanisms of workforce consultation varies according to the method of production. Where a business or a service depends heavily for its success on its employees exercising their discretion intelligently, using all their skills and knowledge, the advantages of achieving co-operation through consultation and management by agreement become greater. Co-operation from the workforce can be secured by negotiating with them about the terms and conditions of work, discussing how work should be performed, and planning how the organization should be managed. This model of securing co-operation through power-sharing challenges profoundly the notion that labour can be purchased like any other commodity. It also undermines an employer's assumption that ownership of the means of production entails the exclusive right to manage the enterprise. Nevertheless, employers cannot ignore the business need to secure co-operation through some kind of partnership with the workforce.

This metaphor of partnership has been widely used to attempt to describe this objective of securing better co-operation and therefore competitiveness through power-sharing. Prime Minister Blair, for instance, has described his government's programme as one 'to replace the notion of conflict between employers and employees with the promotion of partnership'.[1] But what is meant by partnership, and how can conflict be avoided? Far from denying that there is a conflict of interest between employers and employees, the notion of partnership in fact presupposes that conflicts of interest lie at the heart of productive organizations. This conflict operates, however, on several dimensions. A central conflict in the private sector no doubt concerns the distribution of profits from the business as between investors and the suppliers of labour. But many other sources of conflict may prove equally intense, such as resistance on the part of the workforce to authoritarian command structures of management, disagreements about the timing and pace of work, and objections to particular definitions of the goals of the organisation. Yet the principle of partnership does not regard the problem of conflict in the workplace as the central problem to be addressed. Conflict that disrupts the productive operations of the organization is regarded rather as a poisonous side-effect of inadequate solutions to the problem of co-operation. The principle of partnership supports measures designed to overcome through agreement and dialogue the problems presented by the need for constant adaptation and revision of business goals and methods. The implementation of partnership requires institutional arrangements designed to avoid permanently any outbreak of open conflict such as strikes and other forms of industrial action by creating a co-operative relationship. But the metaphor of partnership leaves unanswered such questions as what power needs to be shared, through what kinds of institutional arrangements, and to what extent must the law become involved in building these co-operative mechanisms for the governance of the workplace.

At the outset, it must be doubted whether legal regulation is either necessary or likely to be efficacious in the pursuit of the goal of partnership between management and the workforce. No doubt the most effective form of partnership will evolve through experimentation within the organization, by the invention of institutional arrangements designed to secure co-operation through dialogue. Such institutional arrangements produced by discussion and negotiation respond to the interests and aspirations of both the employer and the employees. No doubt different views about the appropriate partnership institutions will emerge. Employers typically seek arrangements that will clearly augment productive efficiency. For example, the Rover car plant collective agreement in

---

[1] Department of Trade and Industry White Paper, *Fairness at Work*, Cm. 3968 (London: HMSO, 1998), Foreword by the Prime Minister; D. E. Guest and R. Peccei, 'Partnership at Work: Mutuality and the Balance of Advantage' (2001) 39 BJIR 207.

the early 1990s expanded the field of consultation and negotiation far beyond the traditional subject matter of the collective agreement. At the local workplace level, the agreement involved devolution and account-ability to cells consisting of 40–50 employees with a team leader; each cell becoming responsible for the quality of its work, routine maintenance, process improvements, cost control and control of consumable tools and materials, work allocation, job rotations, and training. There were also discussion groups, quality action teams, and suggestion schemes. At the same time, consultations with recognized trade unions expanded in a strategic direction to include company performance, products, and long-term corporate plans. These initiatives by management to expand the scope of participation were not presumably made in order to support some abstract ideal of industrial democracy but rather were perceived to enhance the productive capacity of the business by promoting flexibility, efficiency, and improvements in the quality of the product. Trade unions could accept these new arrangements, however, because whilst motivated by considerations of efficiency, they also empowered the workforce by enabling them to participate in strategic and organizational decisions.

The danger posed by the legal imposition of a favoured institutional model, whether it comprises workers on the board of directors, compul-sory union recognition for the purposes of collective bargaining, or works councils with rights to be consulted on a particular set of issues, is that it imposes a straitjacket upon the systems of representation. A rigid insti-tutional framework may inhibit employers and the workforce from evolv-ing patterns of dialogue best suited to the promotion of co-operation within the context of the particular productive activities of the firm. Furthermore, we must always doubt the capacity of legal regulation to compel fruitful dialogue for the purpose of solving the problems of co-operation. The law may be able to force employers and workers represen-tatives to establish formal institutional arrangements, and it may even be able to compel attendance and discussions at such meetings, but it is beyond the capacity of legal regulation to compel the parties to use these institutional forms productively in order to resolve problems of co-operation.

Against these considerations that point in the direction of legal absten-tion, we should recognize nonetheless that a legal model can provide a framework for human interaction, one that becomes a familiar and trusted institutional arrangement. A legal institution, such as an incorporated company or the contract of employment, articulates the implicit expectations of the parties, and safeguards those expectations by prohibiting misuse of the institution.[2] The problem for legal intervention is how to balance this potential advantage of institution building against the need to permit the parties to adapt their arrangements to meet the needs of their particular business activities and workplace relations. In short, it is a problem of constructing trust whilst respecting the need for reflexivity.

1. PROMOTING COLLECTIVE BARGAINING

Whatever stance the law takes, workers will attempt to improve their terms and conditions of employment. We have already noted that in the twentieth century most industrialized countries adjusted the law in order to permit collective bargaining to take place. This involved dismantling of prohibitions against trade union organizations and collective industrial action. Our concern here, however, is with the extent to which the law should promote the institution of collective bargaining.

Such positive action giving legal support to mechanisms for collective representation can assume many different forms. Legislation may require an employer to recognize a trade union as a representative of the work-force and to negotiate terms and conditions of employment with these representatives. Another means for giving legal support to collective bargaining is the use of wages councils, which we considered above, as an institutional support for the promotion of bargaining at the industrial sector level. Another type of regulation, which has been abolished in Britain, provides indirect support for collective bargaining by requiring employers to pay a collectively agreed minimum rate for the industrial sector, whether or not a particular employer negotiates directly with the union itself. This mechanism extends the results of collective bargaining on the terms and conditions of employees to a larger group, such as a region, an industrial sector, or even, as in Australia, to the nation's workforce as a whole.

These different techniques of legal intervention reveal divergent goals behind statutory support for collective bargaining. One aim may be to tackle low pay and to establish through a peaceful process basic terms and conditions for an industrial sector or an occupational group. That aim is sometimes linked to the use of national-level bargaining as a mechanism to steer the level of wage increases with a view to management of the

---

[2] J. Rogers and W. Streek, 'Workplace Representation Overseas: The Works Council Story' in R. B. Freeman (ed.), *Working Under Different Rules* (New York: Russell Sage, 1994), p. 97.

health of economy as a whole. A rather different aim is to try to promote the use of collective bargaining as an institution to support partnership in each workplace. In Britain, legal support for collective bargaining, to the extent that it existed at all, switched after the 1960s from the former to the latter aim. The emphasis in public policy shifted from the promotion of industrial–sector–level bargaining about terms and conditions of employment to the legal regulation of enterprise or workplace bargaining, with a view to establishing a partnership institution at a local level.

The National Labour Relations Act 1935 in the United States provided an early and influential model of legal support for workplace collective bargaining. Against a background of bitter disputes between employers and unions about whether a union would be recognized for the purpose of collective bargaining, this legislation attempts to provide a peaceful procedure for the establishment and conduct of collective bargaining at a local level. The key elements of this institutional paradigm, which are imitated in other legal systems, including the United Kingdom, are, first, a determination that the workforce or a particular group within the workforce desires to have a particular union to represent them, and second, the enforcement of an obligation on the employer to bargain seriously or in 'good faith' with the approved union representatives. The existence of such a legal procedure no doubt induces some employers to concede collective bargaining agreements without going through the legal process. Where employers remain intransigently opposed to any collective bargaining relation, however, the operation of a statutory procedure becomes a source of controversy itself, and may generate extensive, lengthy, and complex administrative and legal problems. In the United States, the procedure has earned the reputation of providing employers with numerous opportunities to block or obstruct union recognition claims. The current UK legislation,[3] learning both from the American and Canadian experience, as well as from earlier largely unsuccessful experiments in the UK,[4] tries to minimize such procedural obstacles and sticking-points, mostly by facilitating agreements between an employer and a union to limit the extent of recognition for the purposes of collective bargaining.

---

[3] Trade Union and Labour Relations (Consolidation) Act (TULR(C)A) 1992, Sched. A1, inserted by the Employment Relations Act 1999.
[4] Industrial Relations Act 1971; Employment Protection Act 1975.

RECOGNITION

The British statutory procedure can only be used by a trade union that has been certified as independent, in the sense that a government official, the Certification Officer, has determined that the organization is not under the domination or control of an employer and is not liable or vulnerable to interference by an employer.[5] An independent union can request recognition from an employer, and if the request is refused, the procedure has to address the first difficult issue of whether the workforce wants union representation. Although the potential benefits of collective bargaining might be expected to lead workers to support union representation, this issue is sometimes complicated by rivalry between unions to become the representative, and divergence of interests between different groups of workers. The statutory procedure protects an incumbent union from poaching by another, and the TUC operates an informal disputes procedure that arbitrates between affiliated unions in cases of rivalry. The divergence of interests between groups of workers can be accommodated by limiting the proposed bargaining unit to a group of workers with common concerns. If the union and employer cannot agree upon a bargaining unit, an autonomous public authority, the Central Arbitration Committee (CAC) has to decide the question, taking into account, however, both the characteristics of the workers and, what is often in sharp opposition, the need for the unit to be compatible with effective management.

Disagreements about the scope of the bargaining unit are often entwined with the next issue. In order to invoke this statutory recognition procedure, the union has to demonstrate that it has the support of the majority of the bargaining unit and that 10 per cent of the workers are already members of the union. The greater the size, diversity, and geographical dispersion of a bargaining unit, the harder it becomes for a union to satisfy these conditions. At this point in the process, therefore, employers have an opportunity to try to block recognition by insisting on a wide bargaining unit in which the union lacks sufficient density of membership.

Once these preliminary skirmishes have been resolved in the union's favour, and the employer still declines to recognize the union, the question becomes whether the union's demonstration of likely support from a majority of the bargaining unit suffices to persuade the CAC to order the

---

[5] TULR(C)A 1992, s. 5; *Squibb UK Staff Association v. Certification Officer* [1979] ICR 235, CA.

employer to recognize the union. Even when the union membership amounts to a majority of the workforce, the CAC may decline to make a recognition order and instead order a ballot of the workforce, either if it finds evidence to doubt whether a significant number of the union members want the union to conduct collective bargaining on their behalf, or if it believes that a ballot should be held in the interests of good industrial relations. In some instances, for instance, members may have joined a union for other purposes, such as legal advice and support for other consultation mechanisms. Once the CAC has decided to order a ballot, both sides are likely to conduct a vigorous campaign to persuade the workforce. Employers often try to deter workers from supporting a union by allegations that their support will damage their personal prospects with the firm and perhaps lead to loss of jobs and even plant closure. In the United States lawyers specialize in managing anti-union campaigns for employers, and no doubt similar practices emerge wherever recognition depends on a ballot.

The crucial issue at the balloting stage becomes what tactics an employer can use to persuade the workforce not to vote in favour of union recognition. The employer cannot be permitted to block the union's access to the workforce during the campaign, so the employer is placed under a duty to co-operate and to provide the names and addresses of workers in the bargaining unit. Failure to do so may result in cancellation of the ballot and an order for recognition. Can the employer threaten to discipline or dismiss supporters of the union? Action against union members simply by reason of their membership will be unlawful in violation of the basic right of freedom of association.[6] Furthermore, detrimental action against individuals by reason of their support for recognition and collective bargaining and for voting in the ballot is also unlawful. But when, in response to the recognition claim, an employer simply dismisses a proportion of the workforce regardless of their union membership or support for recognition, these dismissals are not automatically unfair, though an employer will have to justify them before a tribunal.[7] How far can an employer use threats and warnings to discourage support for the union? The rules in the United States try to steer a path between, on the one hand, respecting freedom of speech for the employer, which permits the employer to communicate its opinions and to predict the effect of recognition on its business, whilst on the other hand forbidding

---

[6] See below, Chapter 11.
[7] *Carrington v. Therm-A-Stor Ltd* [1983] ICR 208, CA.

the employer to destroy the integrity of the balloting procedure by making threats of reprisals against the workforce for supporting the union.[8] No equivalent rules apply in the UK, though it is possible that some threats of retaliation could be considered as constituting unlawful detrimental action against an individual worker for supporting recognition. Employers do not need to persuade workers to vote against the union. The union wins the ballot under UK law only if the union is supported by a majority of those voting and at least 40 per cent of the bargaining unit vote in favour of the union. An employer can therefore defeat a recognition claim, if it creates a sufficient atmosphere of intimidation against voting at all. In view of this danger to the integrity of the election process, it seems unfortunate that the UK legislation does not emulate the Canadian rules that forbid certain election campaign practices, such as threats to close the business, unilateral alteration of existing terms of employment such as pay increases, the use of spies and infiltrators, and interrogation or counselling of employees, all backed up by the ultimate threat that the legal sanction is an award or certification of recognition.[9]

THE DUTY TO BARGAIN

Assuming that the union wins the ballot despite fierce opposition from the employer, the CAC will order the employer to recognize the union for the purpose of collective bargaining. The second major problem then arises that the employer may still decline to attend a meeting with union representatives, or, more likely, may agree to meet, but refuse to discuss important matters such as pay. In the United States, the employer is placed under a duty to bargain in good faith on 'mandatory issues' such as pay and hours, but this duty can be satisfied by the employer making proposals and then remaining intransigent. To avoid this practice and to promote co-operation through collective bargaining, the UK approach encourages the parties to reach an agreement about the procedures and scope of collective bargaining. The incentive for the employer to reach such an agreement is that it may confine collective bargaining to certain topics. For instance, the agreement may exclude pay from negotiations.

If the parties fail to reach an agreement about the procedures and scope of collective bargaining, the CAC orders a standard method for conducting bargaining, which requires annual negotiations on pay, hours,

---

[8] *NLRB v. Gissel Packing Co.*, 395 US 575, S Ct US.
[9] T. Thomason, 'The Effect of Accelerated Certification Procedures on Union Organizing Success in Ontario' (1994) 47 *Industrial and Labor Relations Review* 207.

and holidays.[10] This order becomes a legally binding agreement between the employer and the union, which can in principle be enforced by a court order for specific performance. In addition, trade union representatives have a legal right to information from the employer without which they would be to a material extent impeded in carrying out collective bargaining.[11] The question that arises in connection with these compulsory orders to follow a procedure for collective bargaining is whether the law requires an employer to do much more than listen to what union representatives have to say about pay, hours, and holidays. An employer has to respond to proposals, but provided that the employer goes through this procedure of proposals and counter-proposals, it can ultimately impose its preferred terms on the workforce without the union's agreement. In the final analysis, therefore, the legal system seems unable to force an employer to enter into serious discussions and negotiations of the kind envisaged by the metaphor of partnership.

PROSPECTS

Trade unionists may be disappointed with that conclusion, but there are reasons to be sceptical about whether the law can usefully play a role in any further development of collective bargaining as a partnership institution. If the objective is to promote co-operation in the workplace through building mutual trust and confidence at a collective level, the launching of a legal process that may prove lengthy and acerbic is unlikely to achieve its goal. A more constructive aim for the legislation is to seek to induce an employer to use collective bargaining as a method for securing better co-operation, if it can be convinced that the workforce favours this kind of institutional framework. The current UK legislation emphasizes this approach by giving the employer many opportunities to negotiate with the union for an acceptable institutional arrangement. In particular, if the union has overwhelming support or wins a ballot, the employer has considerable freedom to negotiate a recognition agreement that confines the scope of collective bargaining to topics where the employer can perceive advantages in more co-operation and consultation, whilst avoiding topics such as pay in relation to which the employer may seek greater discretion. In order to keep the support of its members, a trade union may be reluctant to concede the employer's

---

[10] Trade Union Recognition (Method of Collective Bargaining) Order 2000, SI 2000/1300.
[11] TULR(C)A 1992, s. 181.

preferences for the scope of collective bargaining topics, but the alternative available through the law of a compulsory process that need not produce serious negotiations may prove even less attractive. Furthermore, the union may discover that an employer may be seeking discussions over a broad range of issues concerning working methods, the working environment, fringe benefits, strategic plans, and other dimensions of workplace relations that may contribute to better co-operation. Once collective bargaining is conceived by management as a potential partnership institution rather than a mechanism for fixing the price of labour, there is no limit to the potential scope of management by agreement.

2. CONSULTATION MECHANISMS

Although most employers may be sceptical of the potential of collective bargaining as a partnership mechanism, they are certainly not opposed to other consultation mechanisms with employees. The potential advantages of affording workers a voice in the management of the business include improvements in motivation and co-operation, and better tapping into the knowledge and skills of the workforce with a view to improvements in efficiency and the quality of products and services. Consultation through various kinds of committees, 'quality circles', and open meetings with managers is therefore a normal feature of management in larger businesses. These consultation mechanisms are likely to discuss details of working methods, aspects of the working environment, and perhaps the long-term plans for the business. Linked to local consultation with groups of workers is likely to be the employer's requirement that the groups should accept some responsibility for such matters as the quality of work, allocation of tasks, and cost control. Some of these consultation techniques may grow out of collective agreements, but they can also be created as independent mechanisms.

In many European countries, most notably Germany, the law provides a statutory framework for workplace consultation alongside, but separate from, regulation of collective bargaining. The Charter of Fundamental Rights of the European Union 2000 declares a collective right of workers to information and consultation at the appropriate levels of an enterprise. This right has been implemented by two principal Directives, one requiring a consultation mechanism known as European Works Councils in large multinational enterprises operating in two or more Member States, and the other requiring a similar mechanism in all undertakings with more than 50 employees.[12] The justification for this compulsory information and consultation system is explained in the Preamble to the latter Directive in terms of supporting partnership:

There is a need to strengthen dialogue and promote mutual trust within undertakings in order to improve risk anticipation, make work organisations more flexible and facilitate employee access to training within the undertaking while maintaining security, make employees aware of adaptation needs, increase employees' availability to undertake measures and activities to increase their employability, promote employee involvement in the operation and future of the undertaking and increase its competitiveness.

The UK government, though concerned not to impose a legal straitjacket on employers, shares the view widely held in management circles and among workers' organizations that 'high-performance workplaces' require extensive employee involvement in decision-making.[13]

Although consultation mechanisms in the workplace may take many different forms, the central idea is that before a decision on a particular matter, management should both inform the affected workers of its plans and the reasons behind them, and give the workforce a chance to criticize the plans and to propose alternatives. A consultation mechanism, unlike a collective agreement, does not require the agreement of the representatives of the workforce, but the process can be structured to encourage agreements. Nor does a consultation mechanism necessarily require a role for trade unions. Consultation arrangements usually involve elected representative workers drawn from the workforce. Of course, union members can be selected, and a trade union can often help representatives by sharing experience and advice. In the past trade unions in Britain were suspicious of consultation mechanisms, fearing a threat both to collective bargaining and to their independent representation of the workforce. Trade unions have in the past pressed for priority to be given to collective bargaining as the appropriate mechanism in any legislatively mandated information and consultation requirements, as for example is the case in

[12] Respectively Directives 94/45/EC and 2002/14/EC. In addition there are consultation and information requirements for economic dismissals of more than 20 employees (Directive 98/59/EC, implemented in the UK by TULR(C)A 1992, s. 188); on transfers of undertakings (Directive 2001/23/EC, implemented by Transfer of Undertakings (Protection of Employment) Regulations 1981 SI 1981/1794); for health and safety in the workplace (Directive 89/391/EC, implemented by Health and Safety at Work etc., Act 1974, the Safety Representatives and Safety Committees Regulations 1997, SI 1997/500, and the Health and Safety (Consultation with Employees) Regulations 1996, SI 1996/1513.

[13] Department of Trade and Industry, *High performance workplaces: The role of employee involvement in a modern economy* (London: DTI, July 2002).

the regulation of consultation with respect to employers' proposals to make economic dismissals of 20 or more employees.[14] But this attitude is changing, because it is appreciated that a consultation mechanism can provide an avenue through which unions can help their members in matters not dealt with in any collective bargaining arrangements, and furthermore this involvement may assist a union in building its membership base sufficiently to ask for recognition for the purposes of collective bargaining. This change in attitude is reflected in recent legislation in the UK, such as 'workforce agreements' that modify working time standards, which permit an employer to choose between consultation through collective bargaining or the creation of other mechanisms for consultation with the workforce.[15]

There remains the difficult question of what contribution that legal regulation may make to the development of consultation between employers and representatives of the workforce. It seems clear that any legislation should merely provide a default model for the parties to adopt, for partnership is likely to be fostered if the employers and workforce devise their own scheme for consultation that accommodates the intricacies of production methods and responds to their needs and interests. The legislative technique adopted for multinational enterprises to compel them to introduce what are known as European Works Councils follows this pattern. Although it provides a default model for a consultative mechanism, it encourages employers to introduce their own scheme instead, an invitation that was widely accepted. Nor does it seem likely that any default model could be applicable to the wide variety of businesses that exist. For this reason the UK insisted that the Directive on consultation inside national companies should only apply above a threshold of 50 employees, which limits its impact to 1 per cent of companies (though it thereby encompasses about 75 per cent of employees). In other European countries, it is clear that whatever the threshold size (which drops as low as 5 in Germany), whether consultation actually occurs depends much more on the commitment of managers and worker representatives (often in practice union organizers) than on the formal legal requirements.

Although this default model for regulation may have little impact in compelling serious consultation, it can serve two vital purposes. As we have observed before, the existence of a legal institution such as a works council, which can be adopted, with or without modifications, provides

---

[14] Above n. 12.   [15] Working Time Regulations 1998, SI 1998/1833.

the parties with a framework of normative expectations on which can be built trust and confidence. In Germany, for instance, works councils in larger enterprises perform a distinct role from collective bargaining, and within that province of activity the council receives legal guarantees that it will be consulted, whilst at the same time the employer is given legal assurances that the council can be forbidden to stray outside its defined role. As well as helping the parties to establish workable and high-trust consultation arrangements, the default model may help to steer discussions towards the kind of partnership model that governments seek to promote for the sake of competitiveness. The legal framework can indicate the topics on which consultation should ideally take place, and perhaps also those on which it is forbidden or not required. The EC Directive indicates that the principal topics should be the future of the business enterprise, security of employment in the undertaking, and possible changes in work organization and terms of employment. This brief guide could be supplemented by other topics conducive to building better co-operation, such as matters concerning flexible working and other aspects of the work/life balance, the development of training and educational opportunities, and equal opportunities practices.

In Britain we are still at the early stages of discovering how legal regulation may assist the building of such consultation and information mechanisms. As well as domestic regulation on European Works Councils,[16] there is a patchwork of legal provisions that require information and consultation on particular issues, such as health and safety, collective dismissals for economic reasons, sales of a business, and modification of standards in relation to working time and maternity and parental leave. It seems likely that a more comprehensive institution like a works council will have to be invented, in order to consolidate and facilitate these diverse obligations for consultation. Elements of such an institution will have to include provisions regarding the integrity of the election of worker representatives, the protection of the freedom of representatives to speak their mind without retaliation by an employer, the extent to which agreements with a works council bind both parties, and how the institution can be protected against abuse by both sides. But what is clear is that partly through legal requirements and partly through employer initiatives, these consultation mechanisms will become an increasingly significant part of the experience of workers. They will add to an

---

[16] Transnational Information and Consultation of Employees Regulations 1999, SI 1999/3323.

employee's feeling of having a 'voice' at work, and not simply being treated like a commodity.

3. STAKEHOLDER ORGANIZATIONS

The legal framework for companies in the UK adopts a simple model that the shareholders own the capital, which entitles them to appoint directors to manage the company in their best interests. Whether or not this model accords with the reality of passive, widely dispersed share-holdings in large companies, and boards of directors that may look after their own interests rather than the shareholders', is much debated. In addition, the huge wealth and economic power of many large companies raises the question of whether the shareholders should have sole ultimate control over the management of the company. In a world where many enterprises have assets larger than those of small countries, and where global financial markets permit the directors to move capital investments across regions, countries, and economic blocs with ease, the question is posed whether companies should be required to consider the social responsibilities of their powerful economic position. The issue of corporate social responsibility could take us deep into the intricacies of the corporate governance debate, but here we need only pay attention to one strand in that debate, which concerns the participation of worker representatives in the managing institutions of the business, in particular their possible role on the board of directors.

A company can be regarded as an organization in which many groups have a stake in its survival and prosperity. As well as capital investors such as shareholders and banks that lend it money, the workforce, other contractors to the company, and the local community have a vital economic interest in the strategic decisions of the board of directors. In reaching such decisions no doubt directors may bear these interests in mind, but as long as their legal duty is to give priority to the interests of shareholders, the interests of other stakeholders are unlikely to be given much weight unless the stakeholder can secure strong contractual rights against the company, such as the proprietary charge usually taken by a bank. To compel directors to give greater weight to the interests of other stakeholders, such as the interests of employees in employment security, requires a modification of the legal framework, but it is unclear what mechanism might achieve this goal. The law might instruct directors to consider the interests of other stakeholders in reaching their decisions,[17]

---

[17] Companies Act 1985, s. 309.

but given the position that directors are appointed by the shareholders, they are unlikely ever to reach a conclusion that sacrifices the value of shares for the benefit of some other group. An alternative mechanism is to insert representatives of other stakeholders into the management of the company, so that these groups can voice their concerns and participate in strategic decisions.

In Germany this second mechanism has been created for large companies, where a second, supervisory board reviews strategic decisions of the managers. Workers are represented on the supervisory board, and have the chance to influence the direction of the business. The European Company Statute, under which companies may be incorporated after 2004, also envisages the possibility of worker representation on the board of directors. These mechanisms for worker participation at board level share with consultation and information legislation the ambition of securing partnership between the employer and the workforce, but attempt to enhance mutual trust and confidence by enabling representatives of the workforce to participate in and influence the strategic thinking of the company.

Similar ideas have been floated in Britain, but never implemented.[18] Employers object that stakeholder representation would undermine the major role of business corporations to enhance wealth and make boards of directors less effective in making strategic decisions. Trade unions question whether a worker representative on a board can represent faithfully the interests of the workforce and at the same time agree to decisions that maximize the profitability of the company. There is also doubt whether mutual trust and confidence could be enhanced by this mechanism if worker representatives are required to respect the confidentiality and commercial sensitivity of board discussions, and therefore would not be in a position to disseminate their knowledge and expertise to the workforce. Although it may be possible to find practical ways to overcome these obstacles to worker participation at the level of the board of directors of a company, the difficulties are certainly daunting, and it may be concluded that almost equivalent contributions to building partnership can be achieved through other consultation mechanisms such as works councils.[19]

---

[18] Report of the Committee of Inquiry on Industrial Democracy, Cmnd. 6706 (1977); O. Kahn-Freund, 'Industrial Democracy' (1977) 6 ILJ 65; P. Davies and Lord Wedderburn, 'The Land of Industrial Democracy' (1977) 6 ILJ 197.

[19] P. Davies, 'Employee Representation and Corporate Law Reform' (2000) 22 *Comparative Labor Law & Policy Journal* 135; and recognizing though disapproving of this trend, Lord Wedderburn, 'Employees, Partnership and Company Law' (2002) 31 ILJ 99.

4. INDUSTRIAL DEMOCRACY

This chapter has examined the contribution that the law can make to the building of co-operation between employers and workers at a collective level through partnership institutions. We have observed that the law cannot successfully impose such institutions on unwilling parties, but it can help the evolution of such institutions through requiring employers and workers to follow certain procedures and by providing institutional arrangements through which mutual trust and confidence can be built. In the course of this analysis of the legal contribution to partnership, however, we have observed that legal support for collective arrangements to share power in the organization have been motivated not only by considerations of competitiveness. As well as such economic motives, there has been at times an aspiration to give employees a 'voice' in the workplace. This ambition views the workforce as members of an organization, who should have, by virtue of their membership and subjection to its rules and authority structure, a say in how the organization is managed. An analogy can be drawn between the rights of a citizen to a democratic system of government in the state, and equivalent rights of workers as members of the enterprise to participation in its system of government.

The notion of industrial democracy has certainly formed an important element in workers' claims to participate in management decisions. Collective bargaining has been frequently presented as a form of industrial democracy, which provides an equivalent respect for the dignity and freedom of individuals to the rights of citizens to influence the policies of governments. Drawing exact analogies between state government and business management is, of course, unconvincing. A trade union recognized for the purpose of collective bargaining does not aspire like a political party to replace the government of managers, nor does it usually seek to influence or participate in all decisions, but merely those that affect the workforce directly. But exponents of industrial pluralism could argue that collective bargaining was a mechanism in which two powerful interests groups, capital and organized labour, could negotiate the joint regulation of workplace relations in a way that was similar on some occasions to a legislative process that responds to powerful pressure groups.

Arguments in favour of industrial democracy apply with particular force to public sector workers. The absence of the brooding presence of the need to maximize the value of shares permits managers in the public sector to consider a wide range of interests, especially of course the interest of the general public in receiving a good service. Workers in the public sector can claim to wear two hats, both employees committed to providing a service to the public and members of the public themselves who understand what kind of service is required. Although bureaucratic hierarchies permeate the public sector, it is also true that many employees such as teachers, doctors in public hospitals, and senior civil servants have a significant say in the nature of the service provided. Furthermore, western governments have typically supported the policy of industrial pluralism by recognizing trade unions in the public sector, so that public sector workers tend to comprise the most densely unionized part of the economy. This tendency towards greater industrial democracy in the public sector has, however, come under increasing challenge. In order to control costs and to secure better implementation of their policies, governments have sought both to privatize public services by contracting out services to the private sector and to introduce stricter management controls in the search for better value for money and more effective service delivery. One result of these reforms of the public sector is the reduction of the power of workers to influence the content of the service they produce and how they deliver the service. In this new culture for the public sector, workers who protest against cuts in services and new priorities imposed from above are no longer presented as spokesmen for the interests of the public but rather as self-interested groups who are unreasonably obstructing the democratic wishes of the majority. The exception in favour of greater industrial democracy provided by public ownership has become greatly diminished.

These analogies between democratic government and employee involvement in the management of business should not be pressed too far. Nevertheless, the idea underlying the rhetoric of industrial democracy is surely appealing. It is a liberal idea that individuals should be accorded sufficient respect and autonomy so that they may influence the operation and composition of the social and political structures through which they experience their lives. These structures, whether they are institutions of public government or private enterprise, enable productive co-operation through their processes and constraints, but at the price of diminishing individual liberty and confining social practices. Whilst acknowledging the necessity of such bureaucratic constraints, we can nevertheless press in every location for the maximum degree of autonomy that is compatible with the successful functioning of the institution. In the workplace, giving workers a voice in how the business or service is run not only satisfies that ideal, but also may enable the organization to function more competitively and efficiently by fostering co-operation through partnership institutions.

7

Competition and Industrial Action

We were on strike in Weld and Boulder Counties, and they secured an injunction
from Judge Greeley Whitford in Denver County, an injunction that forbade us to
do anything, in fact, but eat or sleep. We couldn't fly banners, post notices, hold
meetings, talk to a neighbour or to strangers, and you would say a word about it he
could pronounce you guilty . . . [O]n the 17th of December, 1910, a fight was
supposed to have taken place on the streets of Lafayette . . . and about the 20th 16
miners from Lafayette were arrested, charged with violating the injunction and
brought to Denver for a farcical trial without a jury and were sentenced to jail . . .
We didn't know what we were arrested for and couldn't find out until the day
before the trial. We were released on bonds . . . and when we returned to Lafayette there was a great crowd at the station when we got back to welcome us, and
that was used as evidence against us for being congregated at the depot. That was
evidence in our trial . . . And after two days of a farcical trial . . . we were sentenced to one year in the county jail in the city of Denver . . . [W]e were tried in
the courthouse down here in Denver and the goddess of justice is standing up
there on the dome holding the scales of justice in her hand . . . and when we were
sentenced to jail—after we were sentenced she throwed the scales on top of the
roof and they are there yet.[1]

This story, though emanating from the Wild West, could, in its essen-
tials, be retold about countless strikes in many other countries. To this
day in Britain, whenever a major strike is called, the employer usually
scurries off to the High Court just hours before to seek an injunction
against the industrial action on the ground that the union officials have
breached some legal technicality that removes their protection or immunity from competition law. Organizations of workers have always confronted head-on the maxims of competition law that forbid combinations
and abuses of a dominant position that interfere with the operation of
competitive markets. These legal principles have been regarded as so

---

[1] Testimony of Edward Doyle, a mine worker and union official, before the US Commission of Industrial Relations 1915, 38819 S. Doc. 415, 64–1, Vol. 7–31, quoted (at greater
length) in J. G. Getman and J. D. Blackburn, *Labor Relations*, 2nd edn (Mineola, NY:
Foundation Press, 1983), p. 14.

important that they have been sanctioned by the strongest weapons of the legal system—criminal punishment and injunctions backed by the threat of contempt of court. Competition law has cast a long shadow over employment law.

In a sense, employment law was conceived within the womb of competition laws. The earliest legislation applicable to employment relations was principally motivated by a concern either to suppress or to protect competition in the labour market. Rules that prevented servants from leaving their masters without permission aimed to restrict competition in wages in times of labour shortage. Laws against conspiracies and combinations of workers sought to prevent cartels of workers from forcing up wages.[2] A central controversy in employment law has always been whether and to what extent the labour market and the employment relation should be subject to ordinary competition rules.

In exploring answers to that question, we will examine four contemporary flashpoints between competition law and employment law. The first concerns the freedom of workers to move around the labour market at will, seeking the best available jobs wherever and whenever they find them. The second concerns the extent to which employment law and other government measures of social policy designed to combat unemployment and social exclusion may violate competition laws. The most heated issue remains the conflict at the heart of the Denver case above: whether trade unions that seek to improve the bargaining position of their members through threats of collective industrial action should be regarded as a form of unfair and unlawful cartel that restricts competition in the labour market. The final flashpoint to be considered is to what extent, if any, should businesses be permitted to prevent their employees from setting up in business for themselves in competition with their former employer? In each of these areas, the recurrent question is whether or not the general rules that proscribe anti-competitive practices should be modified to accommodate the special features of the employment relation and the labour market.

I. MIGRATION

The idea that workers should be free to travel and to take up any occupation where they can earn a living arose in conjunction with the economic processes of industrialization. In earlier agricultural systems, workers

---

[2] Above p. 18.

were bound as serfs or peasants to the lord of the manor, and vagrancy laws prohibited their departure to seek their fortune elsewhere. Although these laws were gradually dismantled as industrialization attracted workers to the factories and the new towns that sprang up around them, they survived long into the nineteenth century in modified form, since they could be manipulated to combat strike action. In the middle of the nineteenth century in Britain, there were about 10,000 prosecutions a year under these Master and Servant laws that prohibited workers from stopping work without permission. In France, the law required workers to have a 'carnet', which had to be signed by an employer before the worker could leave to find another job. These laws served the interests of employers by restricting competition in the labour market. As a result of pressure from trade unions and an acceptance of the idea of a free market in labour, these laws were dismantled in Europe by the last quarter of the nineteenth century.

Although nation states generally permit free movement of workers within their borders, the entry of foreign workers remains intensely regulated by immigration laws. The carnet has been replaced by the work permit. Governments can use immigration laws to control the supply of labour, restricting migration in times of high unemployment, and relaxing it to meet labour shortages. From its inception, however, the EC decided to eliminate controls over economic migration between Member States as part of its mission to liberalize trade within the economic bloc. Article 39 of the Treaty Establishing the European Community ('the EC Treaty') proclaims: 'Freedom of movement for workers shall be secured within the Community'. Of course workers find this freedom difficult to exercise, because finding a job in another country involves learning a different language, uprooting their families, and acclimatizing to a different culture. Although the law cannot assist in dealing with those problems, it can remove more subtle obstacles to migration. Complex regulations of the EC establish the right of a worker not to be disqualified or excluded by nationality from the social security, welfare, education, and health systems of the state in which the worker and any dependants are resident.[3] National rules governing vocational qualifications, such as those of a doctor, lawyer, or skilled craftsman, prove a more intractable obstacle to free movement of workers. The general principle applied is that states must recognize the professional qualifications obtained in another state if they are the result of the successful completion of at least three years'

---

[3] Regulations 1612/68/EEC; 1408/71 EEC.

study or the professional has been in practice in his home state for ten years.[4]

Although these mutual recognition rules assist free movement of workers, more subtle impediments found in informal practices and conventions in recruitment continue to produce much less internal migration in Europe than in the United States. These conventions can be challenged, however, under the general principle of free movement of workers. For example, Jean-Marc Bosnan, a Belgian professional footballer, claimed successfully that the insistence by his club on payment of a substantial transfer fee effectively prevented him from obtaining a job with a French club. The ECJ held that the transfer fee system between football clubs constituted an obstacle to free movement of workers, which could only be permitted if the rules pursued a legitimate aim compatible with the European Treaty, that they were proportionate to the achievement of that aim, and that they were justified by pressing reasons of public interest.[5] Furthermore, the rules of the union of European Football Associations, which restricted how many foreign nationals could play for a club team, were also held to be contrary to Article 39 of the Treaty.

When a worker takes a job in another Member State, the general rule is that the local national employment laws apply to the contract of employment. But more complex legal issues arise when the employee is transferred across national borders to a different location with the same employer. The contract of employment may select as the choice of law the employment laws of the original residence of the worker. This choice of law may not be binding in two circumstances. An employee may be able to rely upon mandatory employment rights of the country where work is being performed, unless perhaps where the posting is temporary and a court concludes that in the circumstances as whole the employment relation is more closely connected with the original place of residence of the worker.[6]

Under EC law, employers also have freedom of movement, and in particular the freedom to offer services in other Member States. If an employer wins a contract to provide services in another state, it may seek to send its own workforce abroad to perform the commercial contract. These workers would normally be employed under terms and conditions

---

[4] Directive 89/48/EEC; special rules apply to lawyers.

[5] Case C–415/93, *Union Royal Belge des Societes de Football Association v. Bosman* [1995] ECR I-4921, ECJ.

[6] Rome Convention 1980, given effect in the UK by the Contracts (Applicable Law) Act 1990.

governed by the laws of their ordinary place of residence. This arrangement permits some foreign businesses to achieve a competitive advantage, because they can avoid the minimum labour standards, such as a minimum wage law, in the country where the work is to be performed. In an exception to the normal principle of the freedom of businesses to offer services in other Member States, an EC Directive requires that such 'posted workers' should be employed on terms which respect the minimum standards regarding working conditions, pay, safety, and discrimination that apply in the state where the work is performed.[7] The purpose of this Directive is to protect businesses and their employees from foreign competition that involves undercutting basic labour standards, and it also entitles the posted workers to claim any superior rights in their place of work. It represents an exception to the general competition rule that employers should be permitted an unrestricted right to compete for business throughout the European economic area.

2. STATE AID

This right for businesses to enjoy free competition in the single market of the EU is protected not only by the freedom to trade, the freedom to move capital, and the freedom to supply services, but also by prohibitions on protectionist and anti-competitive measures by States. European competition law prevents Member States from subsidizing businesses,[8] because these measures may give their national businesses an unfair competitive advantage. The issue of what amounts to a state aid to business for these purposes and the extent to which states should be permitted to help the competitiveness of national enterprises will always prove a thorny issue for the EC. For example, a low taxation rate on businesses is arguably a form of state subsidy, though the Community does not have powers to prevent different national tax rates. It has also been argued, though unsuccessfully, that the exclusion of small employers from national employment laws in effect amounts to a state subsidy by reducing the labour costs of small businesses.[9]

The principle followed by the ECJ is that measures of general application, such as employment and taxation laws, cannot amount to state aids, but discretionary special measures, such as public financial support for a business threatening closure and widespread economic dismissals, must

---

[7] Directive 96/71/EC.   [8] EC Treaty, Art. 87.
[9] Case 189/91 *Kirshammer-Hack v. Sidal* [1994] IRLR 185, ECJ.

be subjected to scrutiny.[10] Such a state aid has to be notified to the EC Commission, which decides whether it can be justified under one of the exceptions, such as financial support to facilitate the development of certain economic activities or of certain economic areas, where such aid does not adversely affect trading conditions to an extent contrary to the common interest.

The boundaries between, on the one hand, state aids through discretionary subsidies, and on the other, general measures designed to promote investment in business and more particular, active employment policies designed to stimulate jobs in a particular region or industrial sector cannot always be drawn easily. But these active employment policies are certainly permitted under competition law. Indeed, the EC, through its Social Fund, dispenses substantial grants to stimulate economic growth in particular regions of the Community. This Social Fund is intended to counteract the possible detrimental effects of unrestricted transnational business competition on local economies.

3. INDUSTRIAL ACTION

To improve the bargaining position of their members, trade unions had to be able to make a credible threat that they could control the labour supply to the employer by instructing their members to cease working and by deterring others from taking their place. But this threat immediately falls foul of competition law, because it involves the creation of a cartel of workers and the prevention of others from exercising their freedom to take the jobs of strikers. For collective bargaining to operate at all, therefore, exceptions had to be created to the ordinary competition laws, such as the exclusion of trade unions from the common law rules that prohibit combinations in restraint of trade.[11] The philosophy of industrial pluralism, with its commitment to restoring equality of bargaining power between capital and labour by means of permitting or promoting collective bargaining, argued strongly for the creation of immunities from competition law for industrial action. Even if governments of industrialized countries did not embrace the desire to promote collective bargaining, most accepted that legal prohibitions on industrial conflict might only serve to exacerbate labour disputes, and might ultimately undermine the legitimacy of the courts and the legal system by placing them in direct

---

[10] Case C–241/94 *French Republic v. Commission* [1996] ECR I-4551, ECJ.
[11] TULR(C)A 1992 s. 11.

conflict with organizations of workers. What has always remained controversial, however, is the precise scope of the exemption or immunity from competition laws that ought to be granted to collective industrial action.

LABOUR INJUNCTION

The precise legal rules governing the scope of the immunity for industrial action form a complex body of law in every country, but in practice these rules are less important than a court's exercise of its discretion to issue a labour injunction. When faced by the threat of industrial action, an employer that chooses to try to use the law to counter the threat usually seeks an order from a court directed against the union and its officials to withdraw the strike call. Such an order can be obtained in civil proceedings as a measure of interim relief pending a full trial of the issues. The employer therefore issues proceedings that allege that the strike is unlawful in some respects, and seeks immediate interim relief by way of an injunction against the strike pending an outcome of the case. If the court issues an injunction, a union has little option but to obey and to withdraw the strike call. Disobedience to a court order is usually accompanied by fierce sanctions, such as the year's imprisonment in the Denver miner's case. In the event of a breach of an injunction in Britain today, the union leaders can be imprisoned for contempt of court, the union can be fined to an unlimited extent, and all its assets can be seized or sequestered by the court until the union obeys the order. In practice, therefore, a labour injunction, as this procedure is traditionally described, effectively stops industrial action dead in its tracks.

The crucial legal question is how a court exercises its discretion to issue a labour injunction. Unlike Judge Greely Whitford of Denver county court, modern judges appreciate that this is a sensitive question, because by issuing interim relief they appear inevitably to side with the employers against the workforce, thus calling into question their neutrality and impartiality. Nevertheless, the legal hurdles that the courts place before the employer can obtain an injunction frequently present no serious obstacle. In the first place, the courts permit the employer to seek an injunction *ex parte*, which means that it is not a requirement that the union should have a chance to respond before the injunction is issued. The employer merely has to present evidence to the court in support of its claim that there is a serious issue to be tried, and unless the evidence shows that the employer has no real prospect of success at full trial of the issues, the court considers whether the 'balance of convenience' lies in

favour of granting or refusing an injunction.[12] The balance of convenience test turns largely on whether damages awarded against the union in
the event of a full trial of the issue would provide the employer with an
adequate remedy in the sense that the employer would be fully compen-
sated for all losses and the union would have the resources to pay the
damages. This balance of convenience usually favours the employer,
because, even assuming that the union has sufficient funds to pay in full,
damages may not fully compensate the employer for all consequential
losses, and there are statutory limits on the potential extent of liability of
a trade union.[13] In truth, there can never be a balance of convenience,
because the 'conundrum is which side should bear the risk of unavoidable
irreparable damage'.[14] The other hurdle for the employer, that there is a
serious issue to be tried, depends on whether or not the employer can
point to possible torts and other illegalities committed by the union. The
more complex the rules governing the immunities for industrial action,
the easier it is to raise such questions. A court is required to consider the
likelihood of the union establishing a defence under the legal immunities
for industrial action,[15] which means that the union, if it manages to reach
the court in time before the injunction is issued, needs to show that it is
more likely than not that the industrial action is within the legal
immunity.[16]

Once the employer has obtained an injunction, the case is effectively
over. The employer only rarely proceeds with the action, in part because
the injunction may have prevented any economic loss, and in part because
further legal proceedings may make it harder to achieve a settlement with
the union on the issues that provoked the strike call. The only reason for
returning to court is to initiate contempt proceedings if the union and its
members fail to obey the order. Obedience requires strict conformity to
the terms of the order, which is likely to require an instruction communicated to members of the union to refrain from industrial action and
observance of that instruction. If the union disobeys, the court will
impose a substantial fine, and appoint officials to sequester the assets of
the union to pay the fine. Notice how the judge in contempt proceedings
becomes the adjudicator over the court's own complaint of disobedience

[12] *American Cyanamid Co v. Ethicon Ltd* [1975] AC 396, HL.
[13] TULR(C)A 1992 s. 22.
[14] F. Frankfurter and N. Greene, *The Labour Injunction* (New York: Macmillan, 1930)
201.
[15] TULR(C)A 1992, s. 221.
[16] *NWL Ltd v. Woods* [1979] ICR 867, HL.

to its order, a position in which the judge is likely to give short shrift to excuses.

This discretionary power of the courts to issue injunctions thus effectively determines the scope of the union's immunity from competition laws that render calls for industrial action unlawful. Whether the judges, who as a class may be inexperienced in industrial relations issues and unsympathetic to the claims of organizations of workers, should be vested with such a discretionary power is much debated. Many countries try to divert issues of labour injunctions into specialist courts and tribunals, whose members may be more sensitive to the importance of industrial action as a necessary incident of the system of collective bargaining. US federal law tightens up the court's discretion considerably by largely blocking *ex parte* proceedings, and requiring a full hearing of witnesses in open court, proof from the employer that substantial and irreparable injury to property will occur, and proof from the employer that it has made every reasonable effort to settle the dispute by negotiation or with the aid of governmental mediation services.[17] This ban on the use of labour injunctions has been more effective than its British counterpart in keeping competition laws out of industrial relations, though American employers can use other grounds for obtaining an injunction.

The idea that the parties to industrial conflict should be required to go through compulsory mediation or arbitration prior to calls for industrial action and legal proceedings, which is at the centre of US labour relations policy, plainly has the potential merit of reducing disruptive industrial conflict and assisting collective bargaining to achieve stable industrial relations. But British trade unions have resisted such measures, because of the fear that such compulsory proceedings might weaken considerably the credibility of the threat of industrial action by causing lengthy delays. Except during wartime, the British system has been a voluntary system of optional mediation or arbitration provided by a government service, the Arbitration and Conciliation Advisory Service (ACAS). In practice the parties to many industrial disputes seek the help of ACAS mediators and arbitrators.

ECONOMIC TORTS

The competition laws that provide the basis for employers' claims for labour injunctions have been created in common law systems by the courts as part of the law of tort. These economic torts permit recovery for

---

[17] Norris–La Guardia Act (1932), 29 USC, s. 101.

economic loss caused by intentional acts that damage another's business. The precise boundaries of these torts remains uncertain for two reasons. The first reason for this lack of clarity is that lawyers often argue about the scope of the economic torts in the context of interlocutory proceedings, during which it is unnecessary for a court to reach a final conclusion about the unlawfulness of a course of action. A court merely has to decide that there is a 'substantial issue', which means that there is the possibility that the industrial action involves the commission of a tort. Whether or not the court considers, on reflection and after full argument, that such a tort exists, is an issue that is never resolved.

The second reason for the uncertain boundaries of the economic torts concerns a structural obscurity in competition laws. In an economic system that encourages economic rivalry between businesses, it is inevitable that efforts to improve one's own position in the market, by for example gaining new customers, are almost certain to cause damage to competitors. The law must draw an almost impossible distinction between, on the one hand, actions that seek to improve one's own market position, which have to be regarded as lawful in a market society, and, on the other hand, actions that are merely intended to damage the position of a competitor, which amount to a tort. In the tort of conspiracy, which was the first tort that the courts used to control industrial action, the question became whether the predominant purpose of the union's call for industrial action was to damage an employer's business or to improve the terms and conditions of employment of its members.[18] Such a test leaves a great deal to the discretion of the courts to determine the motives or purpose of industrial action, though in practice the courts tend to accept that trade unions are usually motivated by the desire to better the interests of their members. To avoid this uncertain boundary based on motive, the common law of economic torts now focuses on the question whether unlawful means were used.

Under this latter approach, the principal question is whether the union's call for industrial action involved the intentional interference with an employer's business by unlawful means. Since industrial action, if it is to be effective, must interfere with an employer's business in some respects and be deliberate in so doing, the crucial question becomes whether or not the actual or threatened industrial action involves the use of unlawful means. The unlawful means for this purpose might involve a breach of contract, another tort, or the breach of some other statutory

---

[18] *Crofter Hand Woven Harris Tweed v. Veitch* [1942] AC 435, HL.

duty. In the context of industrial action, subject to statutory immunities, the unlawful means would normally be constituted by the tort of inducing breach of contract. This tort is typically committed by unions when calling for industrial action, since the union officials thereby induce workers to break their contracts of employment. The tort of inducing breach of contract was developed by the courts to prevent one employer from seeking to persuade an employee of another employer to quit without giving notice in breach of contract and to join the first employer's business.[19] Its origin lay in times before the right to free movement of workers was recognized, and from its inception it fitted ill with a competitive market economy. Applying the tort to industrial conflict, however, served the employer's purpose of establishing that calls for strike action by a union constituted unlawful means for the purpose of satisfying the general competition tort of interference with business by unlawful means.

IMMUNITIES

The evolution of the economic torts followed a convoluted path in Britain, because frequently Parliament sought to restrict the use of labour injunction by conferring immunities in tort on unions. But no sooner had one immunity been conferred, than lawyers sought to circumvent the protection for industrial action by suggesting the existence of a variant tort that was not covered by the statutory words. In *Rookes v. Barnard*,[20] for instance, the union's threat to call a strike was labelled not as the tort of inducing breach of contract, but as the obscure tort of intimidation, which was not covered by the statutory provisions until Parliament made a hasty amendment to plug this artificial gap. The current scope of the statutory immunity includes the tort of inducing breach of contract (and interference with the performance of a contract) and threats to do so.[21] Thus unions have immunity from the general tort of interference with business by unlawful means, since an ordinary strike call will not amount to the commission of the tort of inducing breach of contract, owing to the statutory protection, so the element of unlawful means will not be satisfied. But it is always open to an employer to try to find a loophole in the statutory immunity by pointing to some other ground for the unlawfulness of the strike call.

One other loophole that often proves useful for employers is the requirement that the call for strike action is 'in contemplation or

---

[19] *Lumley v. Gye* (1853) 2 E&B 216, QBD.   [20] [1964] AC 1129, HL.
[21] TULR(C)A 1992, s. 219.

furtherance of a trade dispute'. This formula restricts lawful industrial action to disputes between workers and their employer that relate wholly or mainly to terms and conditions of employment, union membership, recognition, and similar matters.[22] Its objective is to render unlawful any strikes with strong hints of broader, political objectives. In recent years public sector unions have encountered this barrier to lawful industrial action when they organize protests against proposals for privatization and the transfer of their jobs to private sector employers. In *University College London Hospitals NHS Trust v. UNISON*,[23] the employer was planning to enter a private finance initiative for the construction and operation of a new hospital. The union was opposed to this scheme in principle, but also tried unsuccessfully to obtain an assurance from the employer that for 30 years all employees transferred to the new private operators of the hospital and any new employees of the operator would receive equivalent terms and conditions to those negotiated by the union for the remaining public sector workers. The employer obtained an interim injunction against proposed strike action because there was no 'trade dispute'. Lord Woolf MR accepted in this case that although the union did have a political objective, that was not necessarily fatal because the union also had a predominant and legitimate objective of alleviating the possible adverse consequences of the private finance initiative on its members. Nevertheless, the strike was unlawful because it did not relate exclusively to a dispute between workers and their employer, for it also included the position of future workers of another private sector employer whose identity was not yet even known.

Unions complain that this legal regime of statutory immunities renders them vulnerable to a cat and mouse game in the courts when employers seek labour injunctions by inventing some new source of unlawful means or by restrictive interpretations of the statutory immunity. Furthermore, it is objected that the basic social right to take industrial action is falsely presented in the law as some kind of exceptional privilege, whereas the ordinary competition laws should not be applicable at all to the actions of workers' organizations. Perhaps the correct analysis of the problem here is rather that the tort of inducing breach of contract is too broad and undiscriminating for a competitive market economy. Persuading another person to break his contract because it is to his economic advantage to do so should surely not constitute a tort if the market is to be competitive. The contract breaker may have to pay compensation for

---

[22] TULR(C)A 1992, s. 244.   [23] [1999] ICR 204, CA.

losses, but wealth-maximizing breaches of contract need to be permitted, in order to allow businesses to find the best opportunities for profit in a constantly changing marketplace. The idea that every inducement to breach a contract should be unlawful under competition laws is too sweeping, because, unlike the law of conspiracy, it does not distinguish between actions designed merely to damage a business and those that serve a competitive purpose. Thus the underlying problem for unions is perhaps best understood as the over-extended competition laws as much as the complexities of the system of statutory immunities. Even if the relevant torts are fully excluded by a statutory immunity, however, most legal systems in industrialized countries place two further significant limitations on protection from labour injunctions. The first removes the immunity from 'secondary action', and the second places procedural requirements on unions before they make a strike call.

SECONDARY ACTION

In order to increase its bargaining power, a union may attempt to close or interfere with a target employer's business by indirect means that hit the suppliers or customers of the employer. The suppliers may become a target if the employer is managing to continue production with part of the workforce. To break the supply chain, the union may try to persuade the employees of the suppliers to boycott supplies to the target employer, or union members may patrol the employer's premises with a view to blocking any deliveries. Such picketing may also be used to discourage other employees at the target employer from ignoring the strike call and tend to discourage customers of the target employer. In most legal systems the statutory immunities for industrial action are typically restricted with respect to many of these strategies that are known as 'secondary action'. The main justification for this restriction is the protection of the secondary employer, who asserts its neutrality in the dispute. The secondary employer claims the law's protection against economically damaging interference with its business as a result of a dispute to which it is not a party and cannot resolve. Although the secondary employer is not always strictly neutral, being perhaps an associated company in a group of companies, governments are sympathetic to the aim of stopping the spread of industrial action.

For this reason, the statutory immunities have been qualified to exclude secondary action. A secondary employer, who is not a party to the dispute about terms and conditions of employment, can obtain a labour injunction against the union to stop it from inducing its own employees from breaching their contracts of employment.[24] This restriction on the legality of secondary action is especially irksome to unions where the primary employer refuses to recognize the union for the purpose of collective bargaining. Secondary action has the potential to force the primary employer to the bargaining table with the union. This strategy is not permitted, however, not only because it involves secondary action, but also because the statutory procedure for recognition provides unions with a peaceful alternative towards obtaining recognition. Trade unions also find secondary action a valuable strategy in seeking to ensure that all employers in an industrial sector pay the rates agreed with some of the employers through collective bargaining. The prohibition on secondary action prevents a union from using the threat of industrial action that interferes with suppliers to persuade the target employer not to undercut the collectively agreed rates. In the absence of any immunity for secondary action and any statutory procedure for extending collectively agreed terms and conditions across an industrial sector, unions cannot prevent employers from undercutting rates of pay unless the union can present a credible threat of industrial action by the employer's own workforce.

This prohibition of secondary action does not apply, however, to peaceful picketing outside the primary employer's premises. Employees of the primary employer and their union representatives are permitted to attend at or near their place of work for the purpose only of peacefully obtaining or communicating information, or peacefully persuading any person to work or to abstain from working.[25] It is extremely difficult, however, for pickets to be effective within this legal framework. As soon as the police regard the pickets as threatening a breach of the peace or as creating an obstruction to the highway, the police can ask the pickets to move away or be arrested. Furthermore, since most deliveries come by lorry and workers often arrive by car, there is little chance to communicate any information except through placards as the driver speeds past. The effectiveness of pickets therefore depends entirely on a sense of solidarity of the driver with the workers in dispute.

This sense of solidarity certainly exists within the union movement. Many union members are reluctant to cross a picket line, even though the dispute is of no direct concern to themselves. In so doing, these workers taking sympathetic industrial action run the risk of discipline from their employer for breach of contract. Furthermore, a union that promotes sympathy action, other than by way of peaceful picketing, will be

---

[24] TULR(C)A 1992, s. 224   [25] TULR(C)A 1992, s. 200..

committing prohibited secondary action. The unity of workers around the world may be part of the ethos of the trade union movement, but the law regards such solidarity as an unlawful interference with competitive markets.

PROCEDURAL RESTRAINTS AND BALLOTING

Most industrialized legal systems also seek to impose procedures on unions as a condition for lawful industrial action. In countries, unlike Britain,[26] where the collective agreement is a binding contract, as in the United States, a union and its members will be required by injunction to comply with the provisions of the agreement, which typically impose compulsory arbitration during the lifetime of the agreement.[27] It is also a popular view among governments and employers that union leaders adopt a more aggressive stance than their members, so that if the members were properly consulted they would indicate that they do not wish to take industrial action. Although this view rarely has any basis in fact and ignores the need for elected union officials to retain the support and confidence of their members, it has been used as the justification for imposition of compulsory balloting procedures prior to industrial action in the UK. Not only do these unusual provisions give members of the union the legal right to call for a secret ballot prior to industrial action, but also a failure to follow statutory balloting procedure removes the union's immunity from labour injunctions.[28]

Without going into all the details of the prescribed balloting procedure, it is important to observe that the legislation goes much further than requiring the union to hold an independently scrutinized, secret postal ballot at its own expense of its members in every workplace that will be involved in the proposed industrial action. The legislation in addition requires the union to provide extensive information to the employer. Prior to the holding of the ballot, the union must inform the employer of the intention to hold a ballot and sufficient details about the employees who will be balloted so that the employer can ascertain who they comprise. This duty to inform the employer is designed to enable the employer to wage its own campaign against strike action by communicating directly with the workers to be balloted, no doubt stressing the potential adverse effects on employees of industrial action. If a majority of

---

[26] TULR(C)A 1992, ss. 179–80.
[27] *Boys Markets, Inc. v. Retail Clerks Union, Local 770*, 398 US 235 (1970).
[28] TULR(C)A 1992, ss. 228–35.

members support the industrial action in the ballot, again the union is under a duty to inform the employer when the industrial action will commence, who will be involved, and whether it will be continuous strike action or shorter stoppages. This measure gives the employer further time to take steps to reduce the potential damage from industrial action, though of course the cumbersome balloting procedure will already have given the employer plenty of time to prepare. There is a vivid contrast between these procedural rules, which in effect prevent a union from taking quick action even in response to an employer's adverse decision such as closing down a plant, and the procedural rules requiring employers to give notice to the workforce about its plans, which only apply to sales of the business and mass economic dismissals, and are merely enforced by a small compensatory remedy as opposed to the labour injunction wielded against the union. Indeed, a union has to distance itself and repudiate any spontaneous industrial action by its members, or else it will be become subject to an injunction and liability for damages.

The sheer complexity and expense of a balloting procedure in any large workforce no doubt deters unions from calling for strike action on many occasions. When the union decides to take this step, unsurprisingly a majority of members usually vote in favour. Employers can then pick through the process, trying to find errors such as a failure to send a ballot paper to every member of the union who will be involved in the industrial action or some other irregularity in the voting process. Although the law forgives the union minor accidental mistakes, every error can be seized upon by an employer as an opportunity to ask for an interlocutory injunction. Major strike actions are often plagued by an employer's resort to legal proceedings, which in turn vests the courts once again with considerable discretion in interpreting the balloting rules to issue labour injunctions. What is so noticeably absent from these procedures is a corresponding obligation on the employer, when confronted with a solid majority in favour of industrial action, either to meet with the union and negotiate in good faith or to refer the matter to independent arbitration. Instead, the employer is entitled to hold out and take counter-measures.

4. CONTRACTUAL RESTRAINTS ON COMPETITION

The final area where competition law intersects with employment law concerns the freedom of any person to work using all his or her talents and human capital. This freedom is closely guarded by competition law, for not only does this right to work ensure that everyone has access to the labour market, but also it is likely to maximize the wealth of the nation if everyone can use their skills and knowledge. Recall how Lord Denning used this idea to compel the Jockey Club to license a woman as a trainer of horses.[29] Yet many employers seek to interfere with this freedom in order to protect what they regard as their legitimate business interests. They fear that employees, having learned the business and technical processes, and established a network of contacts among customers and suppliers, may then set up in business in competition with their former employer or work for a rival business, using this knowledge to damage the profits of their former employer. The law recognizes that to a limited extent the employers may have in such circumstances an interest in restraining competition, though the courts scrutinize very carefully whether any restriction is necessary and reasonable.

LOYALTY

To appreciate the application of competition law to human capital, we should first understand how the law conceives the obligations of the employee during the currency of the employment relation. An employee owes an implied duty of loyalty or fidelity to the employer during performance of the contract. This duty overlaps with the implied duty to perform the contract in good faith, but appears to add some further obligations concerned with competition. For example, can an employee work for a competitor during non-working hours? In general the law permits the employee to take a second job with another employer provided that there is no interference with performance of the first job. But there may be cases where performance of the second job harms the employer's business directly, as where the second employer produces goods and services in direct competition.[30] In such a case the employees may breach the implied duty of loyalty to their main employer. This obligation of loyalty or fidelity also requires the employee to respect the confidentiality of information concerning the employer's business by not making unauthorized disclosures to others.

It is sometimes suggested that the implied duty of loyalty amounts to a fiduciary duty placed upon the employee. Certainly there can be equivalent obligations. For example, an employee is under a duty to account to an employer for property and money belonging to the employer. If the

---

[29] Above p. 53.
[30] *Hivac Ltd v. Park Royal Scientific Instruments Ltd* [1946] Ch 169, CA.

employee makes an unauthorized disclosure of confidential information, the employer may be able to obtain an injunction against the use of the confidential information and demand an account of profits made through the use of confidential information. This remedy was applied, for instance, to the case of the spy Blake, who was required to relinquish all the royalties from his memoirs. This decision, though, seems to extend the employer's right of recovery because after 50 years had elapsed all the information in the memoirs was in fact in the public domain.[31] In another similar feature to fiduciary duties, if an employee learns of a business opportunity in the course of employment, and instead of permitting the employer to benefit from that opportunity, takes it for his own benefit, this kind of 'secret profit' is likely to be regarded as a breach of the duty of loyalty. Nevertheless, the position of an employee is not governed by the strictest rules of fiduciary duties. For example, an employee is not required to disclose his or her own breaches of contract.[32] Nor is the employee required invariably to place the interests of the employer above his own and to avoid even the appearance of a conflict of interest. The limits of the obligation of loyalty were explored in the case of the director of an *in vitro* fertilization clinic.[33] The director performed similar work abroad for his private income. On termination of the contract of employment, the employer established that the director had failed to obtain permission to perform this private work, which was a breach of the express terms of the contract. The employer failed, however, in a claim to recover the private income as a breach of a fiduciary duty that could be remedied by a duty to account for the 'secret profit'. The employee's liability was limited to the losses caused to the employer by the breach of contract, which, since the patients abroad would not have come to the British clinic, were nil. The director was liable, however, for the private income earned by his staff when they had been sent abroad by the director to perform procedures, since this practice had amounted to a breach of the duty of loyalty as there was a conflict of interest between the director's duty to direct those employees to work for the employer and his personal interest in profiting from their private work abroad.

An employee may also breach the duty of loyalty by taking preparatory steps for setting up a rival business to the employer. An employee might wish to notify potential customers of the intention to set up a rival business and may ask other employees to join the new venture. Although

---

[31] *Attorney General v. Blake* [2001] IRLR 36, HL.
[32] *Sybron Corp v. Rochem Ltd* [1983] ICR 801, CA.
[33] *Nottingham University v. Fishel* [2000] IRLR 471.

there is an element of disloyalty here, the need to encourage competition suggests that some latitude should be permitted. In the United States, the courts have permitted employees to take preparatory steps, but not to the extent of soliciting customers and other employees.[34] In Britain, the courts have issued 'spring-board' injunctions that prevent a former employee from using lists of customers that have been taken during the course of employment.[35] The objective of the injunction is not to prevent competition, but to provide an adequate remedy for the earlier breach of the duty of loyalty in taking the list of customers.

'NON-COMPETE' CLAUSES

The most controversial field in which competition law regulates the use of human capital concerns the right of an employee to leave a job and set up a rival business or work for a competitor employer. In general the common law respects a right of any person to use and exploit for the purpose of earning a living all the skill, knowledge, and experience that they have acquired during their education and working lives. Attempts to prevent an individual from entering a line of work are likely to be unlawful as a form of cartel or monopoly. Public policies permit some restrictions in order to protect the consumer, such as a requirement of relevant professional qualifications before holding oneself out to the public as a solicitor or a doctor. But attempts by a former employer to prevent its employees from working for rival businesses are closely controlled.

Former employers can prevent their employees from using intellectual property rights, such as patents, and confidential information. The scope of what may be regarded as confidential information is, however, uncertain. The information must be treated as a business secret by the employer and the employee must appreciate that it should be regarded as confidential. In practice this category is usually confined to 'trade secrets', such as technical information about designs for products, recipes, and chemical processes. In order to obtain wider protection against the use by former employees of the human capital they have acquired, in practice an employer must insist upon an express term or covenant in the contract of employment that will apply to activities following termination of the contract. Such 'non-compete' clauses fall under the scrutiny of the doctrine of restraint of trade.

The general principle applicable to non-compete clauses is that they

---

[34] *Jet Courier Service v. Mulei* 771 P. 2d 484 SCt Colorado (1989).
[35] *Roger Bullivant Ltd v. Ellis* [1987] ICR 464, CA.

will be regarded as invalid unless the term does no more than is reasonably necessary to provide adequate protection of an asset or a legitimate interest of the business. This principle attempts to draw a distinction between, on the one hand, the general human capital of the employee, and on the other, an advantage or asset inherent in the employer's business which can properly be regarded as, in a general sense, the employer's property, and which it would be unjust to allow the employee to appropriate for his own purposes even though the employee may have contributed to its creation.[36] Applying this principle in practice proves extremely troublesome and is the source of much litigation. Consider, for example, the case of clients or customers of the employer. The employer may regard its contacts with customers as constituting a valuable asset of the business, since the past pattern of dealing with these clients is likely to comprise part of the 'goodwill' of the business. On the other hand, former employees, who have no doubt formed these contacts with customers on a daily basis, will need to be able to contact these potential customers for their new work to be successful, and they may regard their knowledge of the market for the product as their most valuable asset. In a case concerning a temporary employment agency, for instance, some employees left the agency to set up their own business, for which purpose they wanted to contact clients of their former employer and temporary secretaries who had obtained posting through their former employer.[37] Was the knowledge about the names of clients and the pool of temporary secretaries a valuable asset of the business or part of the human capital of the employees? The answer is, of course, that it is both. The underlying problem here is that in many instances the most valuable asset of a business is the human capital of its employees.

To solve this conundrum, the courts apply the doctrine of restraint of trade to covenants not to compete by scrutinizing the scope of the covenant minutely to ensure that it provides the least restriction possible in order to protect the employer's interest. In the case of the temporary employment agency, for instance, the covenant forbade the former employees from setting up a rival business within a kilometre of their former office for six months. This clause was held to be invalid, because it provided more protection than was necessary. A different clause that prevented the former employees from contacting clients of the employer for a limited period of time would, however, have been regarded as

---

[36] *Stenhouse Ltd v. Phillips* [1974] AC 391, HL.
[37] *Office Angels Ltd v. Rainer-Thomas and O'Connor* [1991] IRLR 214, CA.

reasonable and valid. This practice of invalidating clauses that are drawn too widely has the effect of casting doubt on the effectives of any non-compete covenants, since it is often possible to imagine how the clause might have been drafted more narrowly yet still provide adequate protection for the employer's interests or assets.

To avoid the considerable uncertainty surrounding the validity of non-compete covenants, employers have also used what are commonly known as 'garden leave' clauses. Under these express terms of the contract, on termination of the contract by notice, during a long notice period the employee is required to stay at home on full pay and not work for anyone else. To achieve its objective, the employer will need to obtain an injunction that orders the employee to stay at home and not work for a competitor during the expiration of the notice period. Although the courts were at first disposed to enforce such express terms, it is now clear that they will be subject to similar scrutiny to that afforded by the restraint of trade doctrine.[38]

The doctrine of restraint of trade in its application to covenants against competition by former employees seems therefore founded on a distinction that is often incoherent, and which in practice creates considerable uncertainty in its application. There is a strong case for abandoning these subtle distinctions and instead forbidding any such covenants. The argument for permitting employers to try to protect themselves against competition by former employees is sometimes put as an incentive for employers to create jobs. If an employer, having taught a worker the business such as the job of being a solicitor in a small town, was then immediately vulnerable to the prospect of the trained employee setting up a rival business in the same town, it is suggested that the employer would forgo taking on the trainee in the first place. Although there may be instances of this kind, this argument is not ultimately compelling. The former employer can guard against this risk by paying the employee sufficiently to remove the incentive to set up a rival business. It should also be recognized that the employee may in effect have paid for the training by accepting reduced wages in the expectation of higher remuneration later once training has been completed,[39] so that the employee should be entitled to use this human capital elsewhere. In addition, the consumer benefits from the presence of rival businesses

---

[38] *William Hill Organisation Ltd v. Tucker* [1999] ICR 291, CA.

[39] P. H. Rubin and P. Shedd, 'Human Capital and Covenants Not to Compete' (1981) 10 *Journal of Legal Studies* 93.

by having a choice between businesses to be made on the basis of perception of relative skills and prices. Furthermore, it can be argued that the free movement of workers around different businesses, in the course of which they transfer skills and knowledge, and at the same time acquire new human capital, tends in the long run to enhance the competitiveness of business as a whole. In the Californian Silicone Valley, for instance, which has been the cradle of much innovation in computer technology, non-compete clauses are generally invalid, so that workers are free to move rapidly between firms and to set up their own businesses. It can be suggested that the invalidity of non-compete clauses in California provides the necessary legal setting for a high level of innovation in a knowledge-based economic sector. It is certainly worth considering whether, aside from specific technical information that the employer clearly marks as confidential and the value of which far exceeds any income that a former employee might obtain from a competitor, such as the formula for Coca-Cola, employers should be able through contract terms to limit their exposure to competition from former employees by non-compete clauses of any kind.

8

Discipline and Dismissal

Mr Madden claimed at his disciplinary hearing to be the victim of misfortune. He did not know it then, but his misfortune was only just beginning. His employers, a bank, suspected that he had committed a fraud against them. Mr Madden had worked for the bank with an unblemished record for more than 11 years. Three customers of the bank had discovered that their debit cards, which they were due to collect from their branches, had been misappropriated and used to purchase goods in shops. At about the same time, an unidentified bank employee had made unauthorized inquiries through the bank's computer system to check the financial status of these three customers' accounts. Mr Madden had been in the branches at the relevant time and had had access to the computer. The bank notified the police, who arrested Mr Madden and searched his home. But the police could not find any evidence to link him to the theft or fraudulent use of the debit cards, so he was released without charge. Mr Madden claimed that he knew nothing about it, and had merely been working as usual at the bank when the crime was committed. But the employer remained suspicious. Following an internal bank investigation, which demonstrated no more than that Mr Madden had probably had the opportunity to commit the crime, the bank held its disciplinary hearing that resulted in his summary dismissal.

Mr Madden brought a claim before an employment tribunal under his statutory right not to be dismissed unfairly.[1] The tribunal held that he had been unfairly dismissed. The tribunal noted that there was no firm evidence of the precise dates when the cards were taken, no direct evidence that Mr Madden had accessed the computer data, and no investigation of the personal financial affairs of other staff who might have taken the cards. Furthermore, the nature of the goods purchased with the cards did not seem to provide a motive for Mr Madden, for he had no reason to jeopardize his career and future employment prospects for such a paltry sum. The tribunal concluded that no

[1] Employment Rights Act 1996, s. 94.

reasonable employer could have dismissed an employee in such circumstances.

But Mr Madden's triumph was short-lived. The employer's appeal to the Court of Appeal was expedited by the court, because it was concerned that employment tribunals, which decide thousands of unfair dismissal cases every month, might have been stepping out of line. The Court of Appeal seized its chance. The employment tribunal's decision was reversed for an error of law.[2] It was held that no reasonable tribunal, properly applying the law, could have reached the conclusion that the dismissal was unfair. The tribunal, it was suggested, had made the mistake of reaching its own view on the merits of the dismissal decision. Instead, the tribunal should have merely asked itself whether the employer's decision to dismiss was within the band of reasonable responses available to an employer. Since the employer had carried out an investigation and developed on the basis of that investigation grounds for suspicion against the employee, that was sufficient for a reasonable employer to dismiss the employee. So Mr Madden's ultimate misfortune was not just that he lost his job and had his reputation damaged without any compensation, but that he became caught up in a battle in the courts, in which he was the hapless victim of the Court of Appeal's reassertion of its dominance and authority in the interpretation of the law of unfair dismissal. The message from the Court is that employers should be given a long leash: only if an employer has reached a decision to dismiss an employee that no reasonable employer could have reached should a tribunal conclude that the dismissal was unfair. The state should not meddle too closely with discipline in the workplace, for fear that the law might undermine the efficacy of dismissal as the employer's ultimate sanction that ensures the subordination of employees.

Discipline in the workplace is no doubt an unfortunate necessity. In the long run, discipline serves the interests of not only employers but also the workforce in ensuring the competitiveness of the business. To co-ordinate production efficiently, managers need to be able to secure compliance and co-operation from the workforce. Pay incentives and other rewards usually suffice for this purpose, but to counter serious disruption and inefficiency, an employing organization needs the power of discipline as a deterrent. Discipline may take many forms: deductions from pay, demotions, denial of discretionary benefits, and ultimately, dismissal or

---

[2] *Post Office v. Foley; HSBC v. Madden* [2000] ICR 1283, CA.

termination of employment. Survey evidence suggests that about 3.5 per cent of the workforce in the UK is disciplined each year.

To acknowledge the need for discipline in the workplace, however, is not the same as conceding to managers an unfettered power. Discipline can be exercised effectively whilst following just principles and fair procedures. Indeed, unless disciplinary power is exercised in ways that the workforce regard as fair, it is likely to prove counter-productive, by breeding resentment, inducing withdrawal of co-operation, and causing valuable workers to quit. Furthermore, discipline can be linked to corrective strategies, so that employees whose work is unsatisfactory can be detected and offered help such as training rather than simply being punished. In short, a fair system of discipline is conducive to competitiveness. The difficult question is what amounts to a just and fair disciplinary system in the workplace? And the question for the law is what contribution can it make to the construction and operation of a just and fair disciplinary system?

We can distinguish three broad answers to those questions in the history of employment law. The earliest legal response was to apply a contractual framework to questions of discipline. The express and implied obligations under a contract of employment determined the standards of fairness, and the legal remedy for breach of those obligations was the normal remedy for breach of contract. A second legal response was to recognize the justice and fairness of collective self-regulation of disciplinary arrangements. A collective agreement could establish rules and procedures for determining the justice of particular instances of discipline in the workplace. A third legal response, which today predominates in Europe, was to impose mandatory rules concerning standards and procedures for discipline on all employment relationships. As in Mr Madden's case, individuals subject to discipline in the workplace can enforce the legal standards and procedures by claims in specialized labour courts or tribunals. These three legal responses to the problem of ensuring fair and just discipline in the workplace are not necessarily mutually exclusive. In Britain all three may be available in a particular case. This chapter examines the strengths and weaknesses of these legal three techniques for regulating discipline and dismissal.

I. CONTRACTUAL PROTECTION

Once the employment relationship was analysed by lawyers as a contractual arrangement, the private law systems applied their normal

approach to disputes by insisting that the terms of the contract, supplemented by general principles of law, should determine the content of
the regulation of discipline. Until recently, however, contracts for the
performance of work rarely stated explicitly what disciplinary powers
were conferred on the employer and whether any limits applied. This
absence of express provision regarding discipline enabled the courts to
evolve default principles that could be inserted into every employment
relation. The content of these principles reveals common judicial perceptions of how much discretion should be granted to managers to use
disciplinary power to secure their aims.

DEFAULT PRINCIPLES

The general rules applied by the courts to disciplinary powers in
employment relationships conferred almost unrestricted power on
employers. In the common law, employers could withhold pay as a disciplinary sanction, either on the basis of an implied condition of the contract
that an employer could refuse to pay wages if the employee failed to
perform the assigned work, or by reference to terms implied by custom
about satisfactory standards of work. In defining the work required before
payment was due, it was possible for a court to interpret the contract to
place an obligation to complete the work before any payment fell due.
The famous case of *Cutter v. Powell* illustrates this doctrine of 'entire
obligations': the sailor had to complete a voyage before any wages were
payable, so his death at sea prevented his widow from recovering anything.[3] Even more significantly, the courts accepted the rule that an
employer could reject partial or unsatisfactory performance of the
assigned work by deeming it not to constitute any performance of
the work at all, so that all wages could be withheld.[4] It is only when the
employer accepts part performance of the contractual obligations that the
employer becomes liable to pay a proportionate part of the salary.[5] These
rules permit employers to withhold wages as a deterrent against informal
techniques of industrial action such as withdrawal of co-operation or
working to rule.

For the disciplinary sanction of dismissal, an interesting divergence
arose in the common law. In the United States, the courts developed the
default rule that contracts of employment could be terminated 'at will',

---

[3] (1795) 6 Term Rep 320, [1775–1802] All ER Rep 159.
[4] *Wiluszynski v. London Borough of Tower Hamlets* [1989] ICR 493, CA.
[5] *Miles v. Wakefield Borough Council* [1987] AC 539, HL.

that is for any reason at any time. It remains normal practice for American employers to dismiss employees peremptorily and to tell them to leave with their personal belongings immediately. Although English courts agreed that employers could terminate employment for any reason at any time, they also applied the normal rule for contracts of indefinite duration that such contracts contain an implied term that only permits unilateral termination on giving reasonable notice. The period of reasonable notice was usually assumed to be the period between payments, so that if the worker was paid by the day, the contract could be terminated lawfully by giving a day's notice. The remedy for the employee for breach of the implied term of reasonable notice was confined to a claim known as 'wrongful dismissal' for the net wages during the notice period. This amounts to a sum equivalent to wages during the notice period, minus the normal deductions such as taxation, and also subject to the employee's duty to mitigate loss. The implied term of reasonable notice thus places scant constraint upon an employer's power to terminate the contract at will.

Even this weak protection for economic security was subject to a further crucial limitation. If the employee had committed a fundamental breach of contract, an employer was permitted to terminate the contract unilaterally and summarily without payment for any notice period at all. Thus a claim for wages during the period of reasonable notice could be defeated by the employer showing that the employee's misconduct demonstrated an intention no longer to be bound by the contract.[6] Breach of the employee's implied obligations under the contract of employment, such as the duties of obedience and loyalty, provide evidence of such conduct, though an isolated instance of misconduct might not be regarded as amounting to a repudiation of the contract. In *Wilson v. Racher*,[7] a gardener was summarily dismissed following an argument with his employer, which became heated because the employee regarded the employer's criticisms of his work as unfair and unreasonable. The altercation terminated with the gardener walking away saying, 'Go and shit yourself'. Despite this bad language, the court upheld the claim for wages during the notice period, arguing that this isolated instance of misconduct did not indicate the employee's intention no longer to be bound by the contract.

---

[6] *Laws v. London Chronicle (Indicator Newspapers) Ltd* [1959] 1 WLR 698, [1959] 2 All ER 285, CA.

[7] [1974] ICR 428, CA.

Similar support for the employer's disciplinary power to terminate the contract of employment with or without notice applied in other legal systems. But during the twentieth century, most legal systems began to craft exceptions to this unconstrained disciplinary power. The exceptions could be based upon general principles of private law or implied terms. For instance, French courts could assert sometimes that an employer's exercise of the power of dismissal was an *abus du droit*, a misuse of the legal power in the circumstances. In the United States, some courts recognized that dismissal might in some circumstances be in breach of the implied term of performance in good faith. For example, a salesman paid in part by commission succeeded in a claim for a bad faith termination of the contract when he was dismissed for the purpose of denying the employee a lucrative commission bonus.[8] Another claim that was successful on similar grounds concerned a woman who alleged that she had been dismissed for refusing to date her foreman.[9] English law, however, has not followed this trend of crafting constraints on the unlimited disciplinary powers of employers through the general principles of the law of contract.

This issue came to a head in *Johnson v. Unisys Ltd*.[10] The employee had been dismissed summarily for unfounded reasons. The employee claimed substantial damages for breach of contract, because, following the dismissal, he suffered a nervous breakdown, which prevented him from obtaining another job. One way in which the claim was formulated was that the employer had broken an implied term of either performance in good faith or the duty not to act in a way calculated to destroy trust and confidence. The claim failed for three reasons. First, the court argued that such an implied term would be inconsistent with the express terms of the contract that permitted termination for any reason on the giving of reasonable notice. But there is no necessary contradiction here, for the express power to terminate on giving reasonable notice could be qualified by an implied term that the power should be exercised in good faith. Second, the court insisted that although the contract of employment may contain the suggested implied terms, those obligations do not apply to the manner of termination of the contract, but only to the performance of the contract. This argument relies upon the possibility of drawing a sharp distinction between actions connected to performance of the contract and

---

[8] *Fortune v. National Cash Register Co.* 364 NE 2d 1251 S Judicial Ct of Mass. (1977).
[9] *Monge v. Beebe Rubber Co.* 114 NH 130, 316 A 2d 549 S Ct New Hampshire (1974).
[10] [2001] ICR 480, HL.

actions connected to termination. This distinction is surely unworkable in practice. Is it possible to claim that an employer's breach of its own disciplinary code, which occurred in this case, is clearly only concerned with termination of the contract and not with its performance? Is a dismissal shortly before a bonus can be claimed an action concerned with performance or termination? The third reason given for rejecting the claim was the concern that such a development of the private law of contract would provide dismissed employees with an alternative to the statutory claim for unfair dismissal, but without the limitations and qualifications that Parliament had applied to the statutory claim. For instance, in this case the dismissed employee had succeeded in a statutory claim for unfair dismissal, but his compensation was severely limited by statute. His purpose in advancing a common law claim was to circumvent the upper limit on the statutory measure of compensation (at that time £11,500) with a view to obtaining an extra £400,000. The court was determined to block this route around the limits of the statutory claim, even at the expense of creating some unworkable and unpersuasive doctrinal distinctions.

This precedent may prevent the evolution in English common law of a claim for compensation for breach of an implied substantive limit on the power of an employer to terminate a contract of employment. It may be possible, however, to circumvent this decision in cases where the employee resigns in the face of unjust treatment by an employer. In *French v. Barclays Bank plc*,[11] for example, the employer withdrew a cheap loan facility at short notice causing the employee considerable financial loss and distress. Eventually the employee resigned. Although the withdrawal of the loan facility was not a breach of contract, the manner in which it was done was held to be a breach of the implied term of trust and confidence, so that the employee could claim substantial damages for this breach of contract. This decision produces the odd result that if the employee quickly resigns before he is dismissed, he may be in a stronger position to claim compensation for breach of an implied obligation of performance in good faith than if he waits to be dismissed. For the purpose of a claim at common law, in the face of intolerable treatment by an employer, the advice to employees must be to jump before they are pushed.

---

[11] [1998] IRLR 652, CA.

EXPRESS TERMS

The contractual approach to discipline permits the employer and employee to agree express provisions regarding discipline and termination of employment, which will be legally enforceable. The contract may provide for a disciplinary procedure and distinguish between types of misconduct and the appropriate penalty. If these rules are merely contained in staff handbooks or other presentations of organizational rules, however, as we have already noted, the courts may not view them as express terms of the contract, but merely exercises of the discretionary power of management that can be varied at will. That was the view taken of the employer's breach of its own disciplinary procedure in *Johnson v. Unysis Ltd*: the procedure was not contractually binding on the employer.

If a disciplinary code forms part of the express terms of the contract, the extent to which it constrains the power of the employer depends on its interpretation. English courts view express terms that confer protection against disciplinary power as somehow exceptional, so that the terms should be interpreted restrictively. In particular, judges view with scepticism any claim that employers have given up their implied power to terminate the contract for any reason on giving notice. These restrictive interpretations are often facilitated by apparent inconsistencies in the contracts themselves, which may both state that an employer can dismiss an employee on giving a period of notice and also state that disciplinary powers, including dismissal, should be exercised according to certain procedures and standards. For example, in *Taylor v. Secretary of State for Scotland*,[12] the contract of employment stated that the employee could be dismissed on giving three months' notice once he had reached the age of 55, but the contract also contained a provision that no one in the service should be discriminated against on the grounds of age. When the employer implemented a collectively agreed policy of compulsory retirement for all employees aged over 55, the employee claimed breach of the clause against age discrimination. The House of Lords rejected the claim, arguing that the age discrimination term was subject to the term permitting dismissal on giving three months' notice. The judicial committee managed to give some substance to the age discrimination term by saying that it prohibited the employer from discriminating between those employees aged over 55 on the ground of their age. In truth, the contract

---

[12] [2001] ICR 595, HL.

contained an internal contradiction, and the House of Lords gave priority to the term that facilitated the dismissal.

If an employee proves a breach of the express terms of the contract, the crucial question becomes whether the employee can obtain an effective remedy. In particular, can an employee achieve reinstatement in the job? Courts in common law jurisdictions have traditionally refused to grant orders of injunctions or specific performance amounting to reinstatement of the employee. It is said that just as a court will not order an employee to work for a particular employer, because that would involve too great an interference with individual liberty, so too an employer will not be forced to employ a worker. This argument is not wholly convincing, because the degree of interference with liberty involved in being required to employ someone is surely much less than a coercive order to work for a particular employer. A rather more persuasive reason given by the courts for refusing orders that effectively reinstate an employee is that the order will not prove practicable. Following a dismissal and hostile litigation, the likely breakdown of mutual trust and confidence will render it impossible to achieve the level of co-operation required in an employment relation. Yet these arguments do not necessarily rule out the possibility of specific relief in every case. If an employee merely seeks a court order that the employer should carry out the contractual disciplinary procedure, and that pending the outcome the employee will be suspended from work, the objection based upon the loss of mutual trust and confidence does not arise, and the interference with the employer's freedom is slight. As well as an order to comply with a disciplinary procedure during suspension from work, it may be possible in some cases to find some other practicable solution such as redeployment in another department of the employer's business pending the outcome of the disciplinary procedure.[13] But these are unusual cases. Normally a court refuses to order an injunction against dismissal, because it will not force an employer to continue to employ someone whom the employer wishes to exclude from the business.

In contrast, in civil law jurisdictions, it is possible to argue that a purported dismissal in breach of contract is invalid and should have no legal effect. If the dismissal is a legal nullity, technically the employee remains employed until the employer follows the terms of the contract correctly. In practice, however, it will be equally difficult for the employee to obtain reinstatement to the job if the employer resists this claim. Nevertheless, the continuation of the employment relation helps the

---

[13] *Irani v. Southampton and South West Hampshire Health Authority* [1985] ICR 590, Ch D.

employee to rely upon contractual rights and to insist upon full compensation. Although in general common law courts reject this notion of the nullity of dismissals, the argument has sometimes proved successful for senior public officials who are regarded as 'office-holders' rather than employees. In *Ridge v. Baldwin*,[14] a chief constable of a police authority had his dismissal 'quashed' on the ground of a breach of the rules of 'natural justice'. Ever since that exceptional case, however, the courts have insisted that most workers in the public sector are employed under contracts of employment and cannot raise issues of public law in connection with termination of that contract.[15]

If the dismissed employee is confined to a remedy in damages for breach of the express terms of the contract, the measure of compensation becomes the important issue. Here the award of damages is always severely limited by the operation of two principles. The first is that in the common law a dismissed worker is under a duty to mitigate loss, so that reasonable steps have to be taken to obtain alternative employment as soon as possible. The second limitation is that a court assumes that an employer would always choose to minimize liability, so that even where the dismissal was in breach of contract, if the employer had the power to terminate the contract lawfully, it is assumed that the employer has exercised that power, thus limiting liability under the contract. For example, if the employer breaches a contractual disciplinary procedure, damages are limited to the wages payable for the period of time that it would have taken to carry out the procedure correctly.[16] The effect of these limitations on the extent of an employer's liability is to prevent claims for compensation for long periods of unemployment following a dismissal. The courts have also rejected another possible basis for the measurement of compensation, namely the loss of the chance that if the correct disciplinary procedure had been followed the employee might have retained his job indefinitely.

These restrictions on the measure of damages can be criticized for not appreciating the significance of contractual disciplinary codes in the employment relation. An employer enters into a commitment to follow the disciplinary procedure in order to persuade employees that it intends to exercise its disciplinary powers fairly, so that they will be encouraged to give full co-operation and commitment to the employer's undertaking. By making the disciplinary procedure an enforceable contractual term, the employer makes this commitment more credible. But if the employer

---

[14] [1964] AC 40, HL.   [15] *McClaren v. The Home Office* [1990] IRLR 338, CA.
[16] *Gunton v. Richmond-upon-Thames London Borough Council* [1980] ICR 755, CA.

can dispense with the procedure at small cost, this commitment is substantially undermined. These rules governing the measure of compensation prevent an employer from making a credible legal commitment to protect employment security through binding disciplinary rules, which in turn discourages trust and commitment on the part of employees.

COMPULSORY TERMS

A closely connected regulatory strategy to the contractual model consists of the insertion by statute of some compulsory terms in contracts of employment, which may be enforced as if they were express terms of the agreement. This step was taken in the UK with respect to the period of notice required before termination. Legislation sets a minimum period of notice based upon length of service, which in effect provides determinate express rules on what amounts to reasonable notice.[17] The effect of this legislation was to increase substantially the length of notice required for weekly paid workers with many years of service. Another compulsory term requires the employer and employee to conform to some minimal procedural steps with respect to discipline and grievances.[18] In the case of discipline by the employer, the employer should normally give a written statement of the reasons for dismissal or other disciplinary action, hold a meeting with the employee to consider the matter prior to the disciplinary action taking effect, and make provision for an appeal against the decision. The effect of this compulsory term, together with similar provisions concerning grievances, seems to be that an employer or employee might be held to be in breach of contract for failure to follow the procedure, with the possible consequence of an award of compensatory damages. Although these compulsory terms clearly make the common law's protection of employees against unfair disciplinary action a little stronger, they do not undermine its basic stance that the courts will not review the substantive grounds for dismissal, no matter how arbitrary and unfair those grounds may prove.

2. COLLECTIVE SELF-REGULATION

The weak protection against unfair disciplinary action afforded to employees by the private law contractual model can be remedied through collective agreements. A recognized trade union can bargain for the employer to accept binding procedures and standards for disciplinary

---

[17] Employment Rights Act 1996, s. 86.   [18] Employment Act 2002, s. 30.

action. A collective agreement can fix longer periods of notice, establish disciplinary and grievance procedures, and constrain the grounds on which an employer may terminate the contract. In North America unions have developed this system through private arbitration, so that workers can challenge disciplinary action with the support of their union before an impartial arbitrator. These collective agreements usually provide a standard of 'just cause' for a dismissal, which the employer has to prove before the arbitrator endorses the disciplinary action. In effect, the arbitrator is empowered to develop a disciplinary 'law of the shop'.[19]

Three problems with this collective model for determining a fair disciplinary procedure constantly recur. First, it only ensures fair disciplinary procedures for those workers included in collective bargaining agreements, which may be only a small proportion of a nation's workforce. Second, the standards set by collective agreements depend on the bargaining power of the union, which, in periods of weakness, may not secure significant levels of protection for the workforce against unfair discipline. Third, the collective model is liable to place collective interests above the interests of an individual, so that a union may tolerate unfair discipline meted out to one worker for the sake of benefits either to the collective interests of the union or to shared interests between union and employer. This weakness of collective self-regulation was addressed by the American courts' development of a legal duty imposed on union officials to represent fairly all their members.[20]

Despite these problems with collective self-regulation of discipline, the inherent advantages of this method of regulation have led many to regret the failure of unions to develop such a system in the UK. An arbitration system has the potential to provide a quick and inexpensive method of dispute resolution, which is sensitive to the industrial relations context and the business needs of the employer. If the arbitration takes place speedily in the workplace, it is more likely that a successful claim could be remedied by reinstatement. An effective system of arbitration also provides employees with a credible commitment that the disciplinary system will be operated fairly, something that is very hard for the legal system, with its expense and delays, to achieve. In the UK, the government has introduced an arbitration system, but this is completely different in

---

[19] A. Cox, 'Reflections on Labor Arbitration' (1959) 72 *Harvard LR* 1482.
[20] C. W. Summers, 'The Individual Employee's Rights Under the Collective Agreement: What Constitutes Fair Representation?' (1977) 126 *University of Pennsylvania LR* 251.

nature.[21] It provides an alternative to litigation in the employment tribunals rather than being embedded in the collective self-regulation of a particular workplace. This arbitration alternative may attract some claimants, if it proves quicker than courts and tribunals, but for most employees the advantages afforded by the safeguards of a formal legal process should outweigh other considerations and lead them to reject this method of alternative dispute resolution.

3. MANDATORY REGULATION

In response to both the absence or weaknesses of collective self-regulation and the criticism that the default rules of judicial regulation scarcely provided any protection against unfair or unjust disciplinary action at all, national legislatures in Europe have intervened to impose mandatory legal rules against unfair dismissal. These statutes usually grant employees the right to contest the fairness of dismissal before an impartial forum such as a labour court or an employment tribunal. The standard of fairness depends not on any agreement between the parties, but on a legal conception of what fairness requires, with respect to both disciplinary procedures and substantive standards.

Mandatory regulation of dismissal has been almost completely rejected in the United States. It has been argued that regulation is unnecessary, because the parties can make effective provision through their contract. The fact that contracts of employment rarely constrain an employer's power to terminate the contract at will is explained by the willingness of employees to take the risk of unfair treatment, both because they can obtain higher pay in recompense, and because in any case employers are unlikely to act unfairly in general since that would damage their reputation and cause good workers to quit.[22] Yet these arguments against mandatory regulation seem unpersuasive. At the formation of an employment relation, the employee usually lacks detailed information about an employer's disciplinary practices, and indeed may be misled by vague promises of job security and fair treatment. The commencement of a new job is also an uncomfortable time for the employee to ask for information about rules governing misconduct or to bargain over their content. Regulation can respond to these difficulties by requiring mandatory disclosure

---

[21] TULR(C)A 1992, s. 212A; The ACAS Arbitration Scheme (England and Wales) Order 2001, SI 2001/1185.

[22] R. Epstein, 'In Defense of the Contract at Will' (1984) 57 *University of Chicago LR* 947.

of the employer's disciplinary code, but this information may not alter bargaining behaviour. Stronger regulation therefore applies a general standard of fairness on employers on the ground that the inequality of bargaining power of employees (in the form of information asymmetry) systematically prevents them from bargaining for an adequate level of protection against unfair discipline.[23] Under this justification, the mandatory regulation over discipline responds to a market failure in bargaining over discipline. If the objectors to mandatory regulation were correct, the enactment of a mandatory law should have no effect on the incidence of dismissals. But the statistical evidence points towards a reduction of dismissals following the enactment of protective legislation and comparatively lower rates of dismissal in regulated environments.[24] Another justification for mandatory regulation consists simply in the claim that the objective of the regulation is to require employers to respect the rights of employees as individuals: their right to be treated with concern and respect, their right to enjoy a measure of income and job security so that they can plan their lives, and their rights to privacy and liberty. Unfair disciplinary action may trespass on these rights when it becomes arbitrary, oppressive, or prejudiced. On this view, mandatory regulation of discipline in the workplace is an essential aspect of citizenship. This view is symbolized both by the UK's acceptance of the ILO Recommendation No. 119 on Termination of Employment,[25] and by the right to protection against unjustified dismissal in the Charter of Fundamental Rights of the European Union 2000.[26]

Mandatory regulation of discipline in the UK has used these two justifications both to impose requirements to disclose information and to insist upon substantive standards. The law has focused on the two most obvious disciplinary powers: deductions from pay and dismissal. Other forms of disciplinary action, such as suspension and demotion, can be challenged rather unsatisfactorily by the employee resigning and then claiming constructive unfair dismissal. In order to protect some especially

---

[23] G. Mundlak, 'Information-forcing and Cooperation-inducing Rules: Rethinking the Building Blocks of Labour Law', in G. de Geest, J. Siegers, and R. Van den Bergh, *Law and Economics and the Labour Market* (Cheltenham: Elgar, 1999), p. 55.

[24] For an assessment of the empirical evidence in the UK: H. Collins, *Justice in Dismissal* (Oxford: Oxford University Press, 1992), pp. 252–4; for country comparisons: C. F. Buechtmann, 'Introduction: Employment Security and Labor Markets', in C. F. Buechtmann (ed.), *Employment Security and Labor Market Behavior* (Ithaca, NY: ILR Press, 1993), pp. 3, 21.

[25] B. Napier, 'Dismissals: The New ILO Standards' (1983) 12 *Industrial LJ* 17.

[26] Art. 30.

important employment rights, such as the right to be a member of a trade union and the right to be treated without discrimination, employees can challenge directly action short of dismissal and other kinds of detriment. The level of protection afforded by this legislation seems to have been affected by three important variables: perceptions of the adequacy of information requirements to address problems of unfairness; the strength of non-legal sanctions available to the workforce to resist unfair disciplinary action; and concerns about the costs to employers of compliance with the legislation.

The significance of the first variable can be illustrated by the regulation of deductions from pay. Building on earlier legislation, the Truck Act 1896 applied criminal penalties against employers for deductions from pay under certain conditions. In part the legislation sought to address the problem of informational asymmetry by requiring the employer to post a notice in the workplace or have the employee sign a contract that specified the acts or omissions that might lead to deductions from pay or 'fines', and how the deductions would be calculated. Beyond this measure, however, the legislation established a substantive test that the deduction or 'fine' should have been fair and reasonable in all the circumstances of the case, and, if not, the employer could be fined and be forced to repay the worker. This substantive prohibition against unfair deductions was, however, repealed in 1986, leaving only a revised and abbreviated informational requirement.[27] An employer may make a deduction authorized by statute (such as taxation), by the terms of the contract of employment, or by any written consent given by the employee. The current legislation on deductions from pay therefore achieves scarcely more protection than the legal rights available under the ordinary law of contract, except that the worker may use the simpler procedure of an employment tribunal to recover the missing wages.

The justification proffered for the removal of the requirement of fairness, backed by criminal sanctions, was that this Victorian measure was no longer required. An informational requirement would provide adequate protection. The lack of current need for protection is always a bad argument against social legislation: the fact that an abuse no longer occurs is no reason to abolish the very legislation that may in fact be deterring it. In any case, the claim was patently false in view of the trickle of cases before the courts of harsh and unfair deductions, which indeed compelled the government to create an exception for workers in the retail

---

[27] Employment Rights Act 1996, s. 13.

trade, whose employers frequently deducted from pay the whole value of goods stolen by customers.[28] A more likely reason for the abandonment of mandatory standards of fairness was simply that the government was concerned to reduce costs to business and to give employers flexibility in how they constructed this aspect of their disciplinary procedures.

The second variable, namely the effectiveness of the workforce's non-legal sanctions, explains the origin of the statutory protection against unfair dismissal. The UK legislation was enacted in 1971, long after equivalent protections in most other European countries. Before 1970 the topic of dismissal was regarded in accordance with the philosophy of industrial pluralism as a matter for collective self-regulation. This view was abandoned, however, partly because effective collective bargaining on discipline had failed to evolve, and partly because, in the absence of collective procedures, the workforce tended to resort to unofficial strike action against perceived instances of unfair discipline. The legislation was therefore intended to provide a relatively informal legal mechanism for resolving disputes over dismissals that might avoid industrial disputes, and also to stimulate collective bargaining over disciplinary procedures. In short, the non-legal sanction against unfair dismissals was perceived to have become too powerful and disruptive, so that legislation was needed to provide procedures for dispute resolution.

The importance of the third variable, namely the cost to employers, has a persistent role in circumscribing the coverage of the statutory regulation of unfair dismissal. It explains, for instance, the use of a qualifying period, so that employees only become entitled to protection after a period of continuous employment with a particular employer. Until the qualifying period has been completed, which at present is set at one year, the employer can in most instances dismiss employees without incurring the costs of having to justify the decision. Similarly, the legislation is confined to employees with a contract of employment, so that other kinds of flexible working arrangements such as 'casual work as required' and consultancy in the form of independent contracting will not be covered. In some jurisdictions in Europe, small employers are excluded altogether from the legislation. Another common exclusion is employees over the age of retirement, a rule that is unlikely to persist once age discrimination laws have been implemented. The concern about the costs to employers also influences the judicial interpretation of the statutory provisions,

---

[28] Employment Rights Act 1996, ss. 17–22. T. Gorielly, 'Arbitrary Deductions from Pay and the Proposed Repeal of the Truck Acts' (1983) 12 *Industrial LJ* 236.

especially the standard of fairness. The courts frequently insist that employers should not be required to carry out disproportionately expensive procedures prior to dismissal, and should not be obstructed in the reasonable management of the business. The decision of the Court of Appeal in Mr Maddon's case revealed the implications of that insistence; it has a profound bearing on how the courts have interpreted the legal test of fairness or justice in dismissal.

4. THE STANDARD OF FAIRNESS

Although each legal system has its own particular formula for determining the justice and fairness of a dismissal, these abstract phrases such as 'socially justified', 'adequately justified', or, in the case of the UK, 'reasonable', all confront the courts with the same problem. The courts have to articulate a conception of fairness that establishes a balance between, on the one hand, the employer's interest in ensuring efficiency in production by the occasional use of disciplinary power, and on the other, the protection of the interests of employees, which include not only the economic interest in job security, but also, and perhaps more importantly, the interest in being treated with respect. The concern for the respect of individuals supports the need for fair procedures prior to a dismissal, and also insists that dismissals should not be for reasons that infringe basic rights of individuals, such as their right not to be discriminated against on the grounds of race and sex. The core issue for labour courts and employment tribunals is how the balance between these interests should be struck.

Although these tribunals are specially created for their expertise in industrial relations, there is noticeable reluctance to assume the role of being an appeal tribunal against every disciplinary decision. Wary of imposing too much cost on employers by excessive interference in managerial decisions, the courts in Britain have insisted that employers should be granted some latitude in their disciplinary decisions. As reaffirmed in Madden's case, the test is whether the employer's decision to dismiss was within a 'band of reasonable responses' to the employee's misconduct or other type of fault such as poor work. Provided that the employer acted in a way that other reasonable employers might in dismissing the employee, the fact that the tribunal believes that a dismissal was not justified in those circumstances is irrelevant. (The employer's decision may be wrong or harsh in the view of the tribunal, but nevertheless it must be upheld as fair if it falls within the range of reasonable responses of employers to the circumstances.)

Although this interpretation of the legislation does not prevent tribunals from intervening in cases where they feel that the employer has acted far too hastily, irrationally, or arbitrarily, it relieves employers from the prospect of meticulous scrutiny of the adequacy of their justifications for dismissal. In particular, the test of the band of reasonable responses prevents tribunals from intervening in cases where they feel that dismissal was too harsh a sanction for the misconduct, unless it can be argued that no reasonable employer would have dismissed an employee for such a minor infraction. What seems to be missing in this interpretation of the legislation is an assessment of proportionality as part of the balancing process. The relevant question perhaps should be whether the dismissal was required in pursuit of the employer's legitimate business interests, and whether this need was sufficient to justify the interference with the interests of the employee in job security and in being treated with respect. In the case of Mr Madden, for example, whilst no doubt a bank has a strong, legitimate interest in ensuring the honesty of its employees, did this need really justify a summary dismissal on the basis of a suspicion grounded in the purely circumstantial evidence that the employee had probably had the opportunity to commit the fraud, without the need to investigate the matter further to try to discover some better evidence of the employee's fault? The employment tribunal in that case clearly thought that a reasonable employer should have carried out further investigations in order to eliminate any other possible explanation of the theft of the debit cards. In the Court of Appeal's decision, there seems to be little appreciation that an employee of a bank who is dismissed for dishonesty is likely to suffer severe damage to his chances of future employment, and that such a serious charge against a person should require great care that the procedures should be fair.

This requirement that the employer's disciplinary procedure should be fair rests in part on a duty to respect employees as citizens. Just as the criminal law system insists upon a fair procedure prior to any punishment, so too before depriving a person of their livelihood and tarnishing them with a label of misconduct or incompetence an employer should follow a procedure that gives the employee a fair opportunity to defend himself. But a fair procedure can also be justified on the ground that it produces better decisions from the point of view of employers. It is wasteful for employers to dismiss good employees by mistake, and a fair procedure greatly reduces the chance of such mistakes. In their interpretations of the standard of fairness in dismissals, the tribunals in the UK have acknowledged the importance of fair disciplinary procedures. Yet they have tended to support their insistence on fair procedures on the ground of efficiency for the employer rather than respect for the basic rights of employees. As a consequence, tribunals permit employers to dispense with a fair procedure where the employer reasonably supposes that following a fair procedure would be a waste of time.

In many European jurisdictions, however, a fair procedure has been regarded as a basic right of employees, which must be observed in every case, even where the employee has been caught red-handed whilst committing a serious offence. Whilst not going so far, the UK legislation has been amended so that the failure of an employer to comply with the minimum steps of providing written reasons for the dismissal, holding a meeting with the employee, and giving a right to make an appeal against the decision, can be sanctioned by an increase in the compensation payable to the employee.[29] In addition, an employer's failure to follow an advisory Code of Practice promulgated by ACAS raises a presumption that the dismissal was carried out unfairly.[30] But it remains the case that the employer need not follow an elaborate procedure, if in the circumstances it was reasonable to think that such a procedure was unnecessary or wasteful.[31] Furthermore, when a tribunal considers that the employer should have followed a different procedure, if it also concludes that an appropriate procedure would not have affected the outcome of dismissal, the tribunal may rule that although the dismissal was unfair for an inadequate procedure, the employee should receive nil compensation in view of the substantial merits of the case.

The band of reasonable responses test not only allows employers considerable leeway in constructing a disciplinary procedure, but also grants them broad discretion in determining the kinds of reasons that may be used to justify a dismissal. If an employer promulgates a rule in the staff handbook against a certain type of conduct and explains that the penalty will be dismissal, a tribunal is likely to agree that breach of the rule is a fair reason for dismissal without closely inspecting the employer's need for such a strict rule in the circumstances. Thus in *Mathewson v. RB Wilson Dental Laboratory Ltd*[32] an employee was summarily dismissed when he returned late from his lunch-break in the park, where he had been arrested for possession of a small amount of cannabis. The employer

---

[29] Employment Act 2002, s. 31.
[30] *Code of Practice on Disciplinary and Grievance Procedures* (2000), issued under TULR(C)A 1992, s. 199.
[31] *Polkey v. AE Dayton Services Ltd* [1988] ICR 142, HL.
[32] [1988] IRLR 512, EAT.

relied upon its disciplinary policy of dismissal of employees convicted of criminal offences if their conduct raised doubts about their suitability, though this policy had not been communicated to the employee. The employer also stated its concern that the employee might be a bad influence on other members of staff. The tribunal upheld the fairness of the dismissal, even though the employers had not followed any kind of fair procedure at all and could not provide evidence to support their concerns that the employee might interfere with the business. A Scottish EAT dismissed the claimant's appeal, finding that the tribunal had interpreted the law correctly. 'The majority of the Industrial Tribunal came to the conclusion that it could not be said, on the information before the employers at the time of the dismissal, that their reaction in dismissing the appellant summarily, although harsh, was outwith the band of reasonable responses.'

In their concern to avoid imposing too much constraint and cost on employers, this tribunal's interpretation of the concept of unfairness in the statutory law of unfair dismissal provides weak protection for the interests of employees. The statutory question of whether the employer acted reasonably becomes transmuted into the looser test of whether the employer acted unreasonably. A reasonable employer might act harshly, without following a fair procedure, but this conduct evades the epithet of unreasonable if it was not perverse or irrational. Ironically, the common law contractual test can often provide better protection for employees, as for example in the case of *Mathewson*, where he would at least have been entitled to his wages for the period of notice unless the employer could have sustained the unlikely claim that, by his conduct of being late for work after lunch, the employee had evidenced an intention to repudiate the contract of employment. The underlying problem here is that in the assessment of the reasonableness of the dismissal, once the employer has put forward a substantial reason for the disciplinary action, the tribunal is likely to accept this justification as sufficient, without scrutinizing the justification closely under a test of proportionality in order to determine whether the infringement of the employee's interests in economic security and being treated with respect was a compelling need for the employer.

5. THE PROBLEM OF COMPLIANCE

As ever in employment law, the problem of securing compliance with regulation of discipline and dismissal raises difficulties. One potential advantage of collective self-regulation here, as elsewhere, is that it may secure high levels of compliance by the employer with the procedures and standards that have been collectively agreed. The private law model of individual enforcement that applies to the common law claim for wrongful dismissal and the statutory claim for unfair dismissal relies heavily on the risk that an employer will have to pay compensation to the dismissed worker. But an employer may rationally discount this risk in most instances, believing either that the employee will not have the resources and determination to mount a legal challenge or that the amount of compensation payable will be small. This is the problem of efficient breach of regulation that pervades employment law.

The introduction of cheap, informal legal avenues for redress plays an important role in helping to increase levels of compliance. Provided that dismissed employees can use a simple procedure, during which the legal system and the tribunals assist them to present their case, the chance of a successful claim will increase, with a commensurate stronger incentive for employers to comply with the required standards. In the UK, as elsewhere in Europe, the specialized system of labour courts or employment tribunals has undoubtedly helped the private law model of regulation to become more effective in the context of dismissals. Governments have become concerned, however, that the ease of access to justice for employees may be imposing too great a cost on employers, especially when they have to defend themselves against vexatious or meretricious claims. This concern has led to procedural measures that enable tribunals to filter out weak cases and to impose additional costs on employees who insist upon pursuing their claim even if it seems hopeless. The danger of these procedural devices is that discouraging claims will undermine the effectiveness of the legislation. Every lawyer knows that apparently hopeless cases sometimes turn out on closer inspection to be well founded. Although the proper examination of each claim by a tribunal certainly imposes costs both on employers and on the administration of justice, without ready access to justice the individualized claim for compensation technique of regulation is unlikely to achieve high levels of compliance with what have already been described as minimal levels of fairness in dismissal.

The other principal method for improving the effectiveness of this regulation is to increase levels of compensation, so that employers become more cautious when assessing the risk of a claim for unfair dismissal. The predominant outcome of a successful claim for unfair dismissal in the UK is an award of compensation equivalent to about three months of wages for the average worker. This award is comprised of a fixed element based upon years of service (the basic award) and a discretionary amount that the tribunal considers 'just and equitable' in the circumstances (the compensatory award). The amount of either award can be reduced by the tribunal, if it finds that the employee was to some extent culpable. Employers can therefore rely upon an argument concerning the employee's contributory fault to reduce compensation, even though the tribunal has already determined that this alleged fault was an inadequate justification for the dismissal. Given the low amount of average awards, together with various opportunities for employers to persuade the tribunal to reduce the amount of compensation, we can predict that, despite the frequent complaints voiced by employers about the costs of the law of unfair dismissal, in practice the regulation is unlikely to deter an employer which is determined to dismiss an employee even for no good reason at all.

The alternative possible remedy is reinstatement, that is an order to the employer to resume the employment relationship despite the dismissal. Many legal systems, including the UK, describe reinstatement as the primary remedy for unfair dismissal.[33] In practice, however, neither party to the employment relationship is likely to want this remedy once the case has reached a court or tribunal. The necessary element of trust and confidence between the parties will almost certainly have been undermined by the antagonistic postures adopted during the litigation. Thus it is unlikely that the tribunal will be asked for the remedy of reinstatement, and even when asked, it may regard such an order as impracticable. If the tribunal orders reinstatement, many employees will correctly judge that their long-term prospects are likely to be better secured by promptly seeking alternative employment. Although an order of reinstatement may be a blow to management reputation and authority, in truth it is often a cheap remedy in the sense that its financial costs to the employer may be small. As a consequence the financial incentives for compliance with the legislative standards may be lower than those provided by an award of compensation, which may in practice reduce levels of compliance. Greater use of the remedy of reinstatement therefore seems both impracticable and unlikely to improve levels of compliance.

Whilst an employer's disciplinary action will no doubt always provoke disputes that are hard to resolve, it seems possible to improve the degree of compliance with the legal standard of fairness by slightly more

---

[33] Employment Rights Act 1996, ss. 112, 113, 116.

elaborate regulatory techniques. One is to develop mandatory rules concerning the procedural steps required prior to a dismissal, which would be both necessary and sufficient in the sense that compliance with the rules would satisfy the test of fairness and breach of the rules would lead to an automatic finding of unfairness. This measure would not only help to resolve expeditiously a large proportion of cases, but also secure higher levels of compliance by providing employers with precise and binding guidance on what is required. Given the wide variety of reasons for dismissal and their varying significance in different workplaces, general rules about the adequacy of kinds of substantive reasons for dismissal are probably unworkable except to the extent that certain reasons such as discrimination on prohibited grounds can be ruled out altogether.[34] An alternative regulatory technique is to promote collective self-regulation of substantive standards within the workplace, through which employers could indicate more precisely their views about the relative gravity of disciplinary offences and employees could acquire a clearer sense of the boundaries. The legal system could provide an incentive for collective self-regulation by accepting a presumption that dismissal for a reason identified in the collectively agreed disciplinary code in the workplace should normally be regarded as an adequate justification. A variant on this approach used in some European countries is to use labour inspectors to scrutinize in advance an employer's disciplinary code, in order to ensure its fairness and to use deviations from an approved code as raising a presumption of unfairness. The point of these alternative regulatory techniques is to improve levels of compliance with the standard of fairness in ways that reduce costs in the long run for both employers and the administration of justice.

Although different techniques for securing compliance have been adopted in Europe, often with considerable weight being attached to the role of partnership institutions in supervising the exercise of managerial discretion, there is a shared model of mandatory standards governing disciplinary dismissals enforced by specialist labour courts and tribunals. The EC has the competence to legislate in this field, but only by a procedure that requires unanimous agreement. But the EC has already indirectly influenced the evolution of the law governing termination of employment through Directives on discrimination, fixed-term contracts,

---

[34] In the UK the category of 'automatically unfair dismissals' is used to protect social rights (see Chapter 11) and worker representatives in partnership institutions (see Chapter 6).

part-time workers, and the field of economic dismissals to be considered in the next chapter. Since measures requiring fair discipline at work can be justified both as contributing to competitiveness and as an aspect of a modern concept of citizenship, the topic is likely to prove one that the EC will embrace before long, at least to the extent of securing a uniform basic legal right to fair treatment.[35]

[35] B. Hepple, 'European Rules on Dismissal Law?' (1977) 18 *Comparative Labor LJ* 204.

9

Economic Security

Shortly before Mr Todd retired and sold his garage business at Deeping St James to new owners, without telling the purchasers he had increased the pay of some of his staff, including that of Mrs Woods his personal secretary for 28 years. The new owners had committed themselves to taking over the staff on the same terms, but they decided that Mrs Woods was rated too highly with her title of 'Chief Secretary and Accounts Clerk'. They tried to persuade her on several occasions to take less money, have a different job title, or work longer hours, but she refused. Much acrimony and friction arose between the parties, and only four months after the takeover Mrs Woods resigned and claimed constructive unfair dismissal. A tribunal decided that the employer, not having imposed changes to the terms of the contract unilaterally, had not repudiated it in a way that entitled the employee to resign. The Court of Appeal refused to interfere, even though Lord Denning MR accepted that 'all trust and confidence was lost on both sides'. Indeed, the Court of Appeal seemed to suggest paradoxically that the employee herself was in fundamental breach of the contract of employment by having insisted on retaining her existing terms and conditions.

> The obdurate refusal of the employee to accept conditions very properly and sensibly being sought to be imposed upon her was unreasonable. Employers must not, in my opinion, be put in a position where, through wrongful refusal of their employees to accept change, they are prevented from introducing improved business methods in furtherance of seeking success for their enterprise.[1]

Competitiveness implies economic insecurity for workers. As businesses respond to changing market conditions, new technologies, and other competitive pressures, they need frequently to restructure the organization of work. In essence, this restructuring requires new jobs to be created and old jobs to be eliminated. As the pace of technological and market change accelerates, to remain competitive and sometimes to stay

---

[1] Watkins LJ, *Woods v. WM Car Services (Peterborough) Ltd* [1982] ICR 693, CA.

in business at all, employers need to engage constantly in this kind of restructuring. Yet workers often demand that the law should help them to protect their jobs, to control the power of employers to engage in business reorganizations, and to ensure a high degree of economic security. Hiring workers when they are useful, and simply discarding them when no longer required, is tantamount to treating labour as a commodity. People cannot plan their lives and enter into worthwhile social arrangements, if they are vulnerable to a high degree of economic insecurity. Employment law has to address this tension between, on the one hand, the need of businesses to remain competitive, which apparently necessitates economic insecurity for workers, and on the other hand, the legitimate claim of workers to protect their interests in stability of employment and security of income.

This conflict of interest is not as sharp as it first appears. In order to encourage co-operation, loyalty, and commitment from the workforce, employers have an interest in assuring a degree of job security. Institutional arrangements for partnership through which the workforce can learn about and express their views about changes to the business can serve a similar purpose by reducing the fear of unheralded job losses. An employer's improvements to the human capital of the workforce in order to improve efficiency may also serve to enhance workers' employability, so that they can either perform new jobs with the same employer or find alternative employment more easily. Although the interests of employers and the workforce can overlap in these ways, nevertheless the moment frequently arises when an employer believes that economic reasons require a restructuring that necessitates dismissals.

As so often in employment law, a government is not a neutral observer of the conflict of interest over economic security. Governments no doubt wish to encourage the general enhancement of wealth that comes from improvements to competitiveness, which implies their general support for business restructuring. Yet they must also take account of the social costs of economic dismissals. To the extent that governments provide an economic safety net for the unemployed and their dependants, the cost of economic dismissals places a burden on public funds in providing social security benefits. High levels of unemployment, particularly if focused on a particular town or region, also present additional costs and problems for government, for mass dismissals may have a damaging effect on the whole local economy, and they may be associated with higher criminal justice and health care costs. Long-term unemployment is also one of the major causes of social exclusion. Governments therefore have to address their own policy dilemma that involves both support for restructuring as a necessary ingredient of a competitive economy and the need to minimize the social costs arising from economic dismissals.

Governments address this dilemma by using a wide range of measures that extend far beyond the concerns of employment law. Active manpower policies aim to help the unemployed find new jobs, either by providing assistance with job search and applications, or by offering training and education to enhance employability. Current schemes produced under the label 'welfare to work' tie the receipt of social security benefits to the active search for work, with the threat of the removal of economic support for failure to seek paid employment. A more difficult task for governments is to improve the supply side of the labour market. Governments need to ensure that workers have the skills required by employers in a rapidly changing economic environment, but governments do not have the requisite information about future requirements in the labour market to achieve this goal completely. Employers are better placed to organize appropriate training, but as we have seen often lack the necessary incentives. Although these social responses to economic insecurity are a vital element in helping to resolve the dilemma, it has to be appreciated that governments are relatively powerless in this field owing to the economic forces known as globalization.

The ease with which capital investments can be transferred from one country to another, often through the internal procedures of multinational enterprises, creates a competition between countries for capital investment. Many instances of restructuring are responses to these economic pressures. A factory may close in one country and open in another, where labour costs and taxation are much lower. More commonly perhaps, a business will 'outsource' components and services, taking advantage of lower labour costs elsewhere. A typical factory in Europe is often no more than a design and assembly plant, with all the components being manufactured elsewhere. Governments may wish to provide high levels of economic security for the working population, but the economic forces of global capitalism are likely to undermine these attempts at protecting jobs. Furthermore, governments fear that regulation designed to protect jobs will discourage capital investment in the first place. In the absence of international controls over capital movements, governments are wary of intensive regulation designed to protect economic security.

Nevertheless, some steps have been taken at a transnational level in the European Community and North America, which may place a brake on the speed of capital movement. In the EC these transnational measures are sometimes described as being intended to discourage 'social dump-ing', which in this context means the movement of businesses to other Member States with lower labour costs and inferior employment law rights. It is this concern that has led to the most intensive field of EC regulation in relation to employment. Though designed to slow down capital flight between Member States, this regulation has as an ingredient the provision of employment law rights. Although EC law does not pro-vide a comprehensive regime governing business reorganizations, three Directives concerning economic dismissals, sales of businesses, and insolvencies provide a skeleton for legal regulation. The study of these Directives reveals the complexity (and some might say the foolhardiness) of devising uniform laws for Member States with different traditions of industrial relations and diverse legal rules governing contracts of employment. Although the economic forces of globalizsation and the dangers of regulatory competition and social dumping pose a consider-able threat to economic security that can perhaps only be addressed by transnational regulation, the task of devising common labour standards even between relatively similar Member States of the EC proves almost impossible.

1 . CONTRACTUAL ALLOCATION OF RISK

Before examining these Directives, however, it is important to remem-ber that the contract of employment provides the basic framework for the allocation of risks connected with economic insecurity. Contracts implicitly allocate the risks of the absence of work or changes in the jobs required. For example, a contract that pays the worker on the basis of time in the workplace allocates to the employer, in the first instance, the risk of a shortage of work to be performed, though in the long run the employer can reallocate the risk by terminating the contract on notice or by using a contract of short, finite duration. In contrast, a contract that remunerates the worker on the basis of piecework or the completion of tasks, an arrangement that is often presented in the con-tractual form of an independent contractor rather than an employee, allocates the risk of a shortage of work to the worker directly. Casual work or 'zero hours contracts', in which the employee is used 'as required', and paid only for hours worked, also exemplifies the alloca-tion of the entire risk of the absence of work to workers. Contracts of employment may allocate the risk of the changing needs of employers for work of a particular kind to the employee by means of 'flexibility' clauses, which state as a term of employment that the worker should be willing to move jobs and location on the direction of the employer. The contractual framework of the employment relation permits the employer to exploit the opportunity provided by freedom of contract to allocate to the workers most risks connected with changing market conditions.

The common law was reluctant to interfere with this freedom of contract except for the limited qualifications of some implied terms, such as a requirement of reasonable notice prior to transfers in the location of work.[2] Present-day governments are also reluctant to interfere with this flexibility for fear that restrictions might damage the competitiveness of business. Nevertheless, some mandatory controls constrain the contractual pattern of risk allocation. Perhaps the most important of these, which we have already considered, is a mandatory notice period based upon periods of service.[3] An indirect restriction applies to fixed-term contracts. Although employers can offer fixed-term appointments, the expiration of the term without a renewal is deemed to count as a dismissal rather than an agreed termination.[4] Furthermore, EC law places a burden on employers to provide an objective business justification for the use of successive fixed-term contracts, rather than using contracts of indefinite duration.[5]

Aside from these sparse controls, an employee's only protection against adverse contractual allocations of risk is that the employer is bound by the express terms of the contract and cannot alter the fundamental terms without breaching the contract. In principle, such a fundamental breach of contract entitles the employee to resign and claim compensation for dismissal. As a remedy for economic insecurity, however, this voluntary leap into unemployment is scarcely attractive. When an employer unilaterally reduces hours of work, increases the tasks to be performed, requires a transfer to another workplace, or makes other major changes to the contract of employment that are not permitted by the ubiquitous flexibility clause, most employees will prefer to put up with the change rather than resign and seek the uncertain protection of a claim for constructive unfair dismissal. Anything short of a major breach of contract by the employer, as Mrs Woods learned to her cost, will not suffice.

---

[2] Above p. 107.   [3] ERA 1996, s. 86; above p. 167.   [4] ERA 1996, s. 95(1).
[5] Directive 99/7.

2. SAFEGUARDING DEFERRED PAY

Some important elements of the benefits received by an employee consist of forms of deferred pay. The most valuable provided by many employers is a pension scheme to which the employer makes regular contributions. These occupational pension schemes provide that on retirement the employee will receive either a lump sum or more commonly an annuity calculated as a proportion of the final salary. Though a valuable contribution to economic security, this contractual arrangement of a contributory pension scheme creates many risks for the employee. For example, the employer may fail to make its promised contribution, or decide to alter the benefits of the scheme, or in some other way reduce the value of this deferred remuneration at a time when it is too late for the employee to make adequate alternative provision for income during retirement. Some employee share schemes also contain an element of deferred remuneration to the extent that the employer subsidizes the acquisition of stock in the company.

In order to counter the risks inherent in deferred remuneration, it is possible to create a trust for the benefit of the workers. The trustees then hold the pension fund separately from the employer's property, so that they may require the employer to keep up its contributions and recognize that pensioners have an equitable proprietary interest in the fund. Although the law does not require a trust for the protection of employees, employers in Britain now invariably select this legal mechanism, because it is a condition of obtaining many taxation advantages which reduce the cost to the employer and improve the value of the pension to the employee. The trust device (combined with the ordinary law of theft and fraud) therefore addresses the risk that the employer will raid the pension funds or fail to comply with its contractual commitments. But the degree of protection afforded by the trust device depends heavily on the terms of the trust document and the discretion vested in the trustees. Since these arrangements are usually devised by the employer, who also appoints the trustees, there is plainly a residual danger for employees that the pension promise will not turn out as materially rewarding as expected. This risk has been addressed by a mandatory requirement that at least one-third of the trustees should be nominated by beneficiaries under the scheme,[6] and also by conditions attached to the tax relief for employers which require the benefits of the scheme to match the state earnings related pension

---

[6] Pensions Act 1995, Pt I.

scheme (SERPS) that applies in the absence of an occupational pension arrangement.[7] A Pensions Ombudsman also has extensive powers to investigate complaints about maladministration of an occupational pension scheme that has caused injustice to its members, and then make a legally binding instruction to the trustees to rectify a valid complaint.[8]

A similar reservation must be expressed about the protection afforded to deferred pay in the form of stock option plans. The employer may present the opportunity to acquire shares at a discounted price as a strong incentive to stay with the firm. But the offer is usually contractual in form, so the employer can devise the scheme in such a way as to reduce its commitment in the small print.

In both of these types of deferred remuneration, the problem that occurs is that the employee's expectations of deferred benefits are far greater than the employer's promise in fact, once the precise terms of the trust document or contractual scheme have been analysed carefully. The detailed provisions of these complex schemes can create unfairness in ways analogous to the small print in consumer standard-form contracts. To combat the misuse of small print in consumer contracts, legislation not only permits courts to invalidate unfair terms but also empowers official agencies and consumer groups to seek injunctions against the use of unfair terms. A similar collective remedial response as well as the official agency of an ombudsman may prove to be necessary to safeguard the interests and reasonable expectations of employees under these schemes for deferred pay. Governments should be cautious in regulating these schemes more rigidly, however, because employees usually obtain considerable economic security, and employers may react to costly regulatory requirements by reducing their commitment to helping employees to provide for old age and a reduction in the market for their skills.

3. ECONOMIC DISMISSALS

Most employment law systems recognize that economic dismissals require different rules from those applicable to individual disciplinary dismissals. An investigation of alleged fault of the employee is irrelevant when the employer's reason for a number of dismissals concerns market conditions, new technologies, and the expected efficiency gains from restructuring. Nor is the remedy of reinstatement likely to be favoured by

---

[7] Pensions Schemes Act 1993, ss. 13, 14.
[8] Pensions Schemes Act 1993, ss. 145–51A (as amended by Pensions Act 1995).

the law in cases of economic dismissals, for such a measure would block the competitive advantage that the employer hopes to achieve through restructuring. Instead, the regulation of economic dismissals can address three issues, the justification for the need to make dismissals, the selection process, and the provision of severance payments for those workers who lose their jobs.

JUSTIFICATION

The first issue is whether the business plans of the employer in fact necessitate economic dismissals as opposed to some other method of restructuring such as redeploying workers to other jobs, retraining, and changing hours of work, perhaps on a temporary basis. Some European legal systems have attempted to provide a judicial or administrative mechanism that requires an employer to justify to public authorities the need to make economic dismissals. Numerous problems have been encountered by such mechanisms, not the least being the difficulty for public officials of making the requisite business judgement about the requirements of the business and the options available. How can a judge, for instance, assess the validity of the employer's financial projections, assessment of the product market, and rejection of other alternatives? Even if a suitably qualified administrative body were established, it might not receive from the employer the detailed information needed to make a proper judgement, and employers might need to act more quickly than a complex administrative process permits. For these reasons, legal control over the substance of the decision that there is a need to make economic dismissals seems unworkable.

At best, a court or tribunal can investigate the veracity of the employer's claim that economic reasons motivated the dismissal. In some instances, economic considerations may be simply a pretext for dismissing an employee. This subterfuge may be revealed, for instance, if the employer subsequently hires another worker to perform the same job. More difficult is the case where the employer hires another employee who possesses different skills or attributes. In one English case, a new owner of the business dismissed a garage mechanic who had been engaged on the servicing of cars for 30 years, because the employee was unable to operate the new processes that had been introduced, including paperwork and the provision of estimates to customers.[9] The court found that this was not a dismissal for redundancy, no doubt being strongly influenced by the

---

[9] *North Riding Garages v. Butterwick* [1967] 2 QB 56, Div Ct.

consideration that the employer still required a worker, albeit one with different skills. It would make more sense, however, for such instances of replacement of workers with different skills and attributes to count as economic dismissals, which would then set in train appropriate procedural requirements.

These procedures imposed upon employers, whilst not involving a judicial determination of whether an economic dismissal was justified, can at least compel employers to consider alternative courses of action. At the level of an individual employee, the law can require the employer to go through a process of consultation with the employee and to consider whether redeployment may be possible. In the UK the tribunals have used the law of unfair dismissal for this purpose, so that where an employer dismisses a worker for economic reasons, though this would normally comprise a fair reason for dismissal, the employer may be liable to pay compensation for unfair dismissal, if either the employer has failed to consult the individual worker in advance, or it has failed to consider the possibility of offering suitable alternative employment. In addition, the employer is given an incentive to offer suitable alternative employment, for if the worker unreasonably refuses this offer, the employer is exempted from having to pay any compensation for dismissal including the redundancy or severance payment. It might assist both economic security and competitiveness if this exemption were extended to cases where employers offered jobs on the same wages but requiring new skills for which the employer offers to pay the cost of training.

Compulsory collective procedures are, however, much more likely to provide protection for workers against unnecessary economic dismissals. The leading model in this respect has been provided by German works councils. These councils have the right to be consulted prior to economic dismissals, and have the right to block such dismissals if they are not 'socially justified'. In practice employers have to try to seek the agreement of the works council to the need for restructuring and any consequent economic dismissals. Reaching such an agreement or 'social plan' may turn on the strength of the employer's case for restructuring, the compensation payable to dismissed workers, and the retraining opportunities provided to those who lose their jobs. If the employer fails to reach an agreement with the works council, it runs the risk that compulsory arbitration may impose a social plan and that in the meantime purported dismissals will not be legally effective. Some elements of this model have been enacted at EC level. The Directive on collective redundancies requires an employer who is contemplating dismissing 20 or more workers for economic reasons to inform and consult representatives of the workforce with a view to reaching an agreement concerning how economic dismissals might be avoided or reduced and concerning the possibilities for retraining and compensating dismissed employees.[10]

This model of information and consultation with a view to reaching an agreement presupposes the existence of partnership institutions, such as collective bargaining arrangements or works councils, which are accustomed to participate in economic planning. Where these are absent, which is more often the case in the UK, the philosophy of the Directive fits uneasily with the system of industrial relations. Employers often regard the decision in principle to make economic dismissals as part of an exclusive management prerogative, and are only willing to discuss with representatives of the workforce the consequences of their decision. On the other side, trade unions may be reluctant to agree to the necessity for economic dismissals, preferring instead to hold themselves out as protecting the jobs of their members or, as a last resort, to negotiate substantial severance benefits. But the EC Directive requires employers to inform and consult representatives of the workforce at an earlier stage, when economic dismissals are merely a possibility. Furthermore, the consultation is supposed to be about how to minimize economic insecurity through redeployment and retraining, not merely about the consequences of dismissals. The Directive also applies to businesses that do not recognize a trade union and lack any partnership institutions. In the absence of such institutions, the Directive requires employers to create them for the purpose of consultation by holding elections for representatives among the workforce. This creation of ad hoc institutions is surely unlikely to be effective or followed by employers, not least because the only sanction in UK law is modest supplementary compensation (the protective award) which dismissed workers can claim. The German model only makes sense and proves effective in the context of long-term partnership institutions, where the representatives of the workforce, perhaps advised by trade unions, can discuss the business plans and alternatives with employers.

SELECTION PROCESS

Assuming that economic dismissals become necessary, the question arises of who among the workforce should be dismissed, and who retained. Trade union representatives often propose the principle of 'last in, first

[10] Directive 98/59.

out', which protects economic security on the basis of length of service. This principle may correspond in a rough way to the potential economic losses associated with economic dismissals, for older workers may find it more difficult to find alternative employment and retrain for other types of work. Employers, however, have an interest in selecting for retention those workers who have the best skills or who are willing to acquire new skills. Even if the employer is prepared to negotiate criteria for selection with representatives of the workforce, their different interests may obstruct agreement.

In one of the most remarkable pieces of judicial creativity in English employment law, Lord Browne-Wilkinson, then president of the EAT, established a legal framework for fair selection for economic dismissals. The tribunal held that an employer would incur liability to pay compensation for unfair dismissal, if the employer used unfair criteria for selection for dismissal. In order to avoid paying this compensation, an employer is required to seek to agree with a recognized union the criteria to be applied, and to follow agreed criteria and allow the union to monitor their application. In the absence of such a collective agreement, the employer has to establish criteria for selection which so far as possible do not depend solely upon the opinion of the person making the selection but can be objectively checked against such things as attendance record, efficiency at the job, experience or length of service. In the case itself, *Williams v. Compare Maxam Ltd*,[11] following a dramatic decline in customers' orders, the employer asked departmental managers to 'pick a team' for their departments, so that the business could remain viable if those employees were retained, and the remainder were dismissed. The union was not consulted and there was a suspicion that departmental managers selected on the basis of personal preference. The EAT, overturning the decision of the tribunal, held that the dismissals were unfair because they had been carried out in blatant contravention of the standards of fair treatment generally accepted by fair employers.

Following this decision, employers have a strong incentive to adopt and follow objective criteria for selection for redundancy, and if possible reach agreement with a recognized union. The existence of these criteria, however, does not prevent bitter disputes arising about selection for economic dismissal. Workers who lose their jobs may feel that the criteria have not been correctly applied, or that the employer has manipulated the evaluation of vague criteria such 'capability' and 'motivation'. In such cases,

[11] [1982] ICR 156, EAT.

however, the courts impose substantial obstacles to employees who attempt to challenge the fairness of their dismissals. An employee has to be able to identify some particular instance that supports an allegation that the employer has unfairly applied the criteria before a tribunal will order the employer to disclose the details of the application of the assessment criteria to all workers. Provided the employer has adopted a justifiable set of criteria and there is no overt sign of deviation from this system, the tribunal will be reluctant to investigate the fairness of the dismissals any further. The Court of Appeal justifies this stance on the ground that to permit tribunals to scrutinize the selection process in any greater detail would undermine the legitimacy of this process and lead to protracted litigation.[12] To these points might be added the argument that provided partnership institutions can devise and monitor the criteria, this process is likely to ensure the most co-operative industrial relations and competitive business in the longer term.

REMEDIAL OPTIONS

For those workers who lose their jobs for economic reasons without any taint of unfairness in the procedures and grounds for selection, the question arises what remedy, if any, they might be accorded by employment law. Many legal systems, including that in the UK, require employers to provide a severance benefit to dismissed workers. Under the redundancy payments scheme of the UK, employees with at least two years of service are entitled to a payment calculated by reference to length of service, rate of pay, and age. This payment on dismissal provides a worker with a cushion against the economic insecurity arising from unemployment. This scheme may also be justified as forcing the employer to consider carefully whether or not economic dismissals are necessary, for the costs of redundancy payments may be greater than the marginal efficiency savings arising from workforce reductions.

The precise application of this scheme, however, raises the question of what should count as an economic dismissal or dismissal for redundancy. The hardest cases involve reorganizations of work that do not require a reduction in the size of the workforce but require employees to alter their times of work, duties, and job title, with a view to reducing labour costs and improving productivity. If an employee objects to such changes, unless the employer has the power to impose them under a flexibility clause, the insistence on unilateral variation may be regarded as a

---

[12] *British Aerospace Plc v. Green & Others* [1995] ICR 1006, CA.

constructive dismissal. But should the employee receive compensation, and if so, should this compensation be a redundancy payment or perhaps even the higher level of compensation for unfair dismissal? The fundamental question here is whether a system of compensation for economic dismissals is aimed at protecting job security or employment security. If the former, when an employer abolishes a particular job package and replaces it with another involving different times, duties, and responsibilities, an employee who is unwilling to accept the new package should receive compensation for the loss of the job. In contrast, if the aim of the law is merely to protect employment security, the fact that the employee is still required, albeit on different terms and conditions, shows that the employer has not interfered with employment security, so should not be liable to pay compensation in the event of the employee's resignation. Senior judges have persistently espoused the latter view. 'It is important that nothing should be done to impair the ability of employers to reorganise their workforce and their times and conditions of work so as to improve efficiency.'[13] To achieve that result the courts have declared that either the employee was not constructively dismissed in such circumstances, as in Mrs Woods' case, or if dismissed, the dismissal was not by reason of redundancy but for some other substantial reason, namely the unreasonable refusal of the employee to accept change, for which it was fair for the employer to dismiss the employee.[14] Such decisions in effect imply a flexibility clause into every contract of employment, whether or not the employer bargained for it in the first place.

Although it may be correct that in a long-term contract of employment the employee cannot have a reasonable expectation of job security in the sense of keeping exactly the same terms and conditions of employment, many proposed reorganizations of work go beyond changes to job packages because they reduce the income of the employee. Under the English statutory test for whether the reason for dismissal was redundancy, the question posed in such reorganizations of work is whether the employer has a continuing requirement for work of a particular kind.[15] A unilateral variation of terms therefore does not constitute a dismissal for redundancy, provided the employer still requires an employee to perform a similar job.[16] This test misses the point that some unilateral variations

[13] Lord Denning MR, *Lesney Products & Co v. Nolan* [1977] ICR 235, CA.
[14] *Hollister v. National Farmers' Union* [1979] ICR 542, CA.
[15] Employment Rights Act 1996, s. 81(2)(b).
[16] *Safeway Stores Plc v. Burrell* [1997] ICR 523, EAT; *Murray v. Foyle Meats Ltd* [1999] ICR 827, HL.

represent not merely a reorganization of work but a challenge to economic security, for they involve a reduction in pay and other benefits. If the aim of the legislation is to protect economic security by imposing a cost on employers as the price for measures that involve economic dismissals, it also makes sense to impose that cost in cases where the employer is unable to obtain the consent of the employer to a variation of the contract that entails a reduction in pay and benefits, for the resistance of these workers is motivated not by opposition to change in productive arrangements but in defence of their economic security.

In contrast to the system of mandatory severance payments in the UK, the remedial response adopted in other European legal systems places greater emphasis on the employer's co-operation with and funding of active steps to help the dismissed workers to find suitable alternative work. A social plan agreed with the workforce and a public authority might provide for the employer to assist with retraining, relocation, and job search. An employer can help both financially and by using its business contacts and knowledge about the employee to find a suitable route towards paid employment. The EC Directive on economic dismissals does not require an individual compensation remedy, but does envisage this kind of social plan both in its provisions about consultation and information with representatives of the workforce, and in its further requirement to give advance notification to public authorities about impending mass dismissals. This notification to a competent public authority must be given 30 days prior to economic dismissals, and during this period the public authority is under a duty to seek solutions to the problems raised by the projected collective redundancies. This model of close involvement in social plans by public authorities assumes a degree of public supervision of private businesses that fits uneasily into the British context. Although an employer commits a minor criminal offence under UK law if it fails to notify the central government,[17] there is no legal obligation placed upon the employer to co-operate further with public authorities, or, for that matter, for the central government to do anything at all.

In viewing these remedial options, governments are concerned, as we have noted, with their impact on capital investment and levels of employment. It is feared that the costs of economic dismissals may discourage capital investment and reduce business competitiveness. Many attempts have been made to try to ascertain the impact of different

---

[17] TULR(C)A 1992, ss. 193–4.

schemes of regulation of economic dismissals, without, however, much light being shed on the issue. The United States is widely regarded as the legal regime that accords employers the greatest discretion, with no requirements of either severance payments or social plans, and with only a limited duty to provide advance notification to the workforce in the event of plant closure or mass layoffs, which in effect amounts to a two-month notice period for the payment of wages that is subject to many exceptions.[18] This relatively unregulated regime can be compared to other legal systems, such as Germany with its model of inducing agreement with workforce representatives and the UK with its provision for severance benefits. But it is hard to detect any connection in practice between the differences among legal regimes and such measurable effects as levels of employment, the speed of adjustment to changing economic circumstances such as recessions, and the average length of job tenure. For example, it is suggested that large payments on termination of employment for economic reasons represent an additional cost that should depress demand and cause higher levels of unemployment. Yet though such correlation can be found in econometric studies for redundancy payments, the same statistics appear to reveal the opposite effect of lengthy notice requirements which amount to an equivalent cost. The claim that high levels of unemployment in Europe compared to North America are caused by 'Eurosclerosis', that is excessive regulation of business restructuring, seems to lack evidential support. Moreover, the view that UK law lacks equivalent protection for job security to that found in other EC Member States is equally difficult to support, for though the UK is only slowly beginning to learn the technique of devising social plans through partnership institutions, it has had the mandatory redundancy compensation system which is absent in other countries such as Germany.

The important question to be asked about the remedial system for economic dismissals is rather whether the law induces the employer to follow a transparent process of justification and selection for economic dismissals. Such a system provides workers with an assurance that their interest in economic security will be respected as much as possible in the context of competitive pressures that inevitably create conditions of economic insecurity. This assurance is vital both to counteract the market pressures that induce employers to treat labour like any factor of production to be dispensed with when not needed, and to help to establish the

---

[18] Worker Adjustment and Retraining Notification Act 1988, 29 USC s. 2101.

necessary co-operation for productive efficiency in the employment relation.

4. TRANSFERS OF BUSINESSES

The second EC Directive that affects business reorganizations concerns sales of businesses. The Acquired Rights Directive, as it is commonly known, applies when an employer sells all or part of a business. At its core the Directive announces the principle that such a transfer should not affect the employment security of the employees. The purchaser or transferee of the business has to continue the contracts of employment of all the existing employees. In addition, both seller and purchaser are under an obligation to inform and consult representatives of employees who may be affected by the transfer with a view to seeking agreement on any proposed measures that may affect employees. This latter obligation proves just as troublesome in the UK in the absence of partnership institutions as the equivalent consultation provisions for economic dismissals. In this instance, however, it has little impact, because the Directive does not apply to the sales of business through the mechanism of a transfer of shares, which is the most common method used in the UK. Nevertheless, the principle of automatic transfer of contracts of employment when the sale occurs other than by the mechanism of share transfer has presented complex issues for UK employment law and the laws of other Member States.

At the centre of the difficulties for the interpretation of the Acquired Rights Directive lies the central obligation in Article 4(1):

The transfer of the undertaking, business or part of the undertaking or business shall not in itself constitute grounds for dismissal by the transferor or the transferee. This provision shall not stand in the way of dismissals that may take place for economic, technical or organisational reasons entailing changes in the workforce.

It is hard to make sense of this provision in the context of the sale of a business. To maximize the value of the business for sale, the transferor will want to hand over the business as a going concern with only those employees that the transferee needs. The first sentence of Article 4(1) appears to say that it should be unlawful for the transferor or transferee to carry out economic dismissals in connection with the transfer. Yet the next sentence apparently contradicts this position by indicating that dismissals should be permitted for economic reasons. No doubt the obscurity is caused by the search for a formula acceptable to all Member States, but it leaves legislators and judges with the task of trying to implement an unclear requirement.

It is possible, though only with some invention, to attribute a coherent approach to dismissals in connection with transfers in the implementing law in the UK, the Transfer of Undertakings (Protection of Employment) Regulations 1981, often known as TUPE.[19] Because these Regulations are not integrated into the remaining domestic legislation and make no mention of such relevant matters as the employer's liability to make redundancy payments, the courts have had to evolve this integrated approach. In its bare bones, the interpretation of the Directive and Regulations that has emerged in the UK courts draws a distinction between the timing of dismissals. Dismissals made prior to the sale but in connection with the transfer are automatically unfair dismissals. Under the Regulations, this claim for unfair dismissal can be brought either against the transferor or more significantly against the transferee, so that the purchaser may be liable for considerable and indeterminate claims for compensation and even reinstatement. Concerns about the uncertain scope of such liabilities may deter purchasers, and reduce the sale price of the business. Dismissals made by the purchaser after the sale, however, are likely to be handled by the ordinary rules governing economic dismissals. Provided that the employer has an economic, technical, or organizational reason for reducing the size of the workforce, the new owner will be liable for redundancy payments on dismissing part of the workforce, but will only incur liability for unfair dismissal if an unfair process of selection for dismissal is adopted. The effect of these rules is strongly to discourage the previous practice of dismissing all or part of the workforce prior to a sale, and to protect employment security after the sale in the normal way of domestic law. Although this pattern contains a coherent and defensible interpretation of the Directive and TUPE, this regime remains highly controversial. The fundamental complaint, beyond the fact that the law is unclear and unpredictable, is that risk of indeterminate liability for compensatory awards for unfair dismissal prevents buyers of businesses from making a clear judgement about the value of the business.

A further complexity in these provisions arises in the common instance of the transferee's insistence upon variations in the terms of contracts of employment of the transferred employees. The transferee will often have

---

[19] SI 1981/1794.

to integrate its new workforce into its organization, which may involve the application of collective agreements and standard terms of employment. We considered above the difficulty of handling such cases where the employees regarded the imposed variation as a constructive dismissal. The Directive and Regulations have been interpreted to mean that, even if the employee agrees to work under different terms and conditions, this agreement has no effect if it is connected to the transfer, except to the extent that the terms benefit the employee.[20] The effect of this interpretation is again to discourage purchasers who may need to introduce variations in terms of employment in order to keep the business profitable and to eliminate anomalies in the terms applicable to the workforce. The courts have responded to this concern. Faced with a claim made months after a transfer for the higher wages paid by the transferor, even though the teachers concerned had ostensibly agreed to the new terms and conditions of the transferee in order to preserve their jobs, the courts found a route around the Directive by suggesting that the reason for the variation was not connected to the transfer but was rather a reorganization that the transferor would have also been compelled to carry out.[21] This loophole may enable purchasers to insist upon new terms and conditions of employment for the transferred employees. Without this route for business reorganization, the transfer could only happen with a subsequent variation of terms, by the transferor dismissing all the workforce prior to the sale, thereby rendering both seller and purchaser liable for the automatic unfair dismissal of all employees.

The most perplexing applications of the Acquired Rights Directive concern another form of business reorganization. During the 1980s it became a received wisdom in management circles that employers should concentrate on the core business and contract out or 'outsource' peripheral activities. The public sector imitated this practice by contracting aspects of public services to the private sector through a process of competitive tendering. Was this 'outsourcing' covered by the Directive? Its application to outsourcing was deeply contested by private business and the public sector. The cost savings achieved through outsourcing perhaps depended on numerous factors, but there was no doubt that the principal advantage was that the contractor enjoyed lower labour costs. The wages paid were typically lower, either because the workers were no longer covered by a relevant collective agreement, or because they fell outside

---

[20] *Credit Suisse Ltd v. Lister* [1999] ICR 794, CA.
[21] *Wilson v. St Helens Borough Council* [1998] ICR 1141, HL.

the good pay and conditions provided by a large firm or public authority. Workers who were effectively compelled to transfer to a contractor paying lower rates of pay tried with the support of unions to insist that as a result of the Directive they should continue to be employed on their former terms and conditions. The ECJ agreed that the Directive could apply to outsourcing, but only if the part of the business that was contracted out, 'the entity', retained its identity after the transfer. The idea behind this Delphic formula that the entity must retain its identity, now confirmed in the amended Directive,[22] is that a business comprises a combination of factors of production, such as machinery, workspace, and the labour force. Following a transfer, if these factors of production remain more or less the same, albeit with a new owner and employer, the entity has remained the same and the Directive applies. In contrast, if the new owner uses its own machinery and workplace, and hires new workers, the identity of the entity has changed. The fact that the work performed under the outsourcing contract is the same as that previously performed in-house is not sufficient for the Directive to apply.

Although the general idea behind this interpretation of the Directive is clear, its application to particular cases is far from predictable. Does the Directive apply to a case of outsourcing where the new employer takes on all or nearly all the previous staff, but uses its own equipment and machinery? Or does the Directive apply in the opposite case where the contractor buys the former employer's plant and machinery, but does not take on any of the previous staff? The Directive may not apply to either case, but the ECJ insists that the question has to be determined by examining all the factors of production and aspects of the business entity, in order to assess whether, looked at as a whole, the identity of the business (ignoring the change of employer) has remained the same. This unpredictable test can also be applied to second-generation outsourcing where an outside contractor loses the work to another contractor, with the effect that the new contractor may have to take on the existing workforce on the same terms and conditions or become liable for compensation for unfair dismissal.

In an effort to render the application of the Directive more predictable, the ECJ has suggested that where a business entity involves the use of plant and machinery, the absence of a transfer of these tangible assets to the new employer must lead to the conclusion that the entity has not retained its identity. In a case concerning the transfer of a franchise to run

---

[22] Art. 1(b), Directive 77/187 (as amended).

a bus service from one contractor to a new franchisee, the new operator used its own buses, and even though it hired the majority of drivers from the previous contractor, the ECJ held that the Directive did not apply.[23] Where the business entity involves few, if any, tangible assets, however, as in the case of providing a cleaning or catering service, the entity seems to be comprised of little more than its staff. In such a case, if the new contractor takes on a majority of the staff of the transferee, the Directive is likely to apply, with the consequence that the staff who are not offered jobs can claim unfair dismissal against the transferor and transferee, and the staff taken on can insist upon no adverse changes to their terms of employment.[24] Unsurprisingly, contractors, appreciating the potential costs of the application of the Directive, choose if at all possible in these labour-intensive industries not to hire any of the existing staff. Spotting that this device was an easy route to avoid the application of the Directive, however, the courts in the UK have developed a novel line of argument that the Directive applies, even if no staff are re-employed by the new contractor, when the purpose of the contractor in avoiding rehiring was to avoid the application of the Directive.[25] The result is almost surreal. A transfer of an undertaking can take place so that the entity retains its identity, even though the new employer has purchased no tangible property and taken on no staff from the previous contractor, but is merely performing much the same contract for services.

These twisting interpretations of the Directive reveal some of the complexities of transnational regulation in the EC.[26] The Directive imitated laws already present in France, Italy, and Germany, thus generalizing those rules at a transnational level as a brake on regulatory competition. In those countries, it is possible for a dismissal to be void, of no legal effect at all, until properly authorized by a court, so that the Directive could be understood to mean that dismissals on the sale of a business would be ineffective. In UK law, however, where unlawful dismissals are effective to terminate the contract of employment, there was no obvious solution for giving effect to the idea of dismissals on transfers being ineffective. The use of the law of unfair dismissal for this purpose, though the closest tool available, had the damaging effect for businesses that it

---

[23] Case C–172/99 *Oy Liikenne AB v. Liskojarvie and Juntunen* [2001] IRLR 171, ECJ.

[24] *Dines v. Initial Health Care Services Ltd and Pall Mall Services Group Ltd* [1994] IRLR 336, CA.

[25] *ECM (Vehicle Delivery Service) Ltd v. Cox* [1999] ICR 1162, CA.

[26] P. Davies, 'Transfers of Undertakings: Preliminary Remarks', in S. Sciarra, *Labour Law in the Courts* (Oxford: Hart, 2001), p. 131.

introduced great indeterminacy in the potential amount of compensation that might be payable, whereas in all other cases of economic dismissals under UK law the amount of compensation payable for redundancy payments is readily calculated. Here is an example of the transplant of a legal concept—a dismissal that is void—which cannot be made, so that a national legal system is forced to undermine its own coherent scheme for handling a particular problem.

Furthermore, the story of the Directive in relation to outsourcing reveals how uniform law merely results in the creation of new divergences.[27] In Germany and Italy, the courts had decided that their domestic legislation did not apply to outsourcing in labour-intensive service sectors. In France, the legislation was applied to such cases, though after the Directive had come into effect, the French courts reversed their position without reference to EC law. The ECJ, by applying the Directive to some instance of outsourcing in the service sector, cast doubt on the legal validity of these national laws, and the result of the references by national courts is the unclear compromise that in some instances the entity may retain its identity. In contrast to those jurisdictions, where the courts were perhaps reluctant to interfere with the cost savings to businesses achieved through outsourcing, the courts in the UK eventually interpreted the Directive in such a way as having almost been designed to prevent the reduction of labour costs through outsourcing. The outcome is that in applying the Directive, it is much more likely that a UK court will approve its application to contracting out of services with no transfer of other assets than any other national courts. The Directive has not harmonized the legal position, but merely created new differences.

5. CORPORATE INSOLVENCY

The third EC Directive concerns the economic security of employees in the event of their employer's insolvency.[28] The Directive requires Member States, subject to numerous qualifications, to provide a guarantee that outstanding wages are received by employees of an insolvent employer. In the UK, the relevant legislation, which preceded the Directive, provides that employees can claim from the social security system unpaid wages up to a limit of eight weeks and below an upper limit of £230 per week, restrictions which are permitted by the Directive. The Directive also

---

[27] G. Teubner, 'Legal Irritants: Good Faith in British Law or How Unifying Law Ends up in New Divergences' (1998) 61 *Modern Law Review* 11.

[28] Directive 80/987/EC.

requires Member States to guarantee payment of outstanding claims
resulting from contracts of employment, which has been applied in the
UK to additional claims for redundancy payments and other payments
due, but not to employer's contributions to occupational schemes, as
permitted by the Directive, and claims for compensatory awards for
unfair dismissal. These latter claims, which may prove substantial, are
not guaranteed, even though they seem to fall within the phrase of being
claims resulting from contracts of employment.

These guarantees of wages and other claims address most of the concerns about economic insecurity arising from the insolvency of the
employer, but they do not, of course, deal with the main concern, that of
future unemployment. In this respect, the best hope for the employees is
a corporate rescue, that is all or part of the business will be purchased and
run as a going concern, thereby preserving jobs. Although corporate
rescues often seem to provide the best chance for employees to obtain
economic security, supporting rescues through the legal framework for
insolvencies creates great tensions within the law governing business
restructuring. The purchaser of all or part of an insolvent company
would ideally prefer to take on the business without its outstanding liabilities, or if that is not possible, with those liabilities rendered limited and
predictable. Furthermore, if the purchaser is to run the business profit-
ably, it will almost certainly have to engage in restructuring involving
economic dismissals and variations in terms of employment of the
retained workforce. Unless the purchaser has a free hand in this way, it
may be reluctant to contemplate a rescue. But giving the purchaser a free
hand would, of course, pose a fundamental threat to all the laws that we
have considered so far in this chapter that protect economic security,
ranging from contractual rights of employees to their acquired rights on
transfers of undertakings.

The government is more than usually interested in the outcome in
cases of insolvency. For a start the government is often a major unpaid,
unsecured creditor with respect to taxes. If the social security system has
paid outstanding wages, the government is also entitled to claim those
sums from the insolvent business. As an unsecured creditor, the government may have little prospect of recovery of these sums unless the company is saved. In the UK the government is a 'preferred creditor' in
claims on insolvency, putting itself ahead of all other creditors except
those with fixed charges over assets, which is an advantage, but provides
no assurance of payment.

In some instances, it is possible that a corporate rescuer may be found who is willing to purchase the shares of the company and inject sufficient new capital to pay off all creditors including the workforce. But there is another route to corporate rescue that appears far more inviting for the purchaser. The rescuer can acquire the assets, both tangible and intangible, together with all or part of the workforce, as a purchase by a new corporate entity. By following this path the rescuer is not liable for the insolvent company's debts, and can effectively ignore the claims of unsecured creditors. This method of selling off part of the business as a going concern thus promises to be the most attractive to potential rescuers and therefore offers the liquidators of the insolvent company the best option for realizing the assets of the company.

Alert readers will notice, however, that the Acquired Rights Directive is likely to apply to this process of corporate rescue. After a while insolvency practitioners realized that the Directive could wreak havoc in their schemes for asset stripping of insolvent companies. Having acquired part of the business as a going concern, the purchaser might discover, first, that it could be liable under TUPE for claims for unfair dismissal from all workers who were not rehired, all outstanding claims under the contracts of employment of all employees of the insolvent company, the subrogated claims for wages paid by the government, and, second, that it might be unable perhaps to vary terms and conditions of the new employees without creating the risk of liability for constructive unfair dismissal. Even the former managers of the insolvent company, who are of course replaced in the rescue, could mount claims for unfair dismissal, since if the entity retained its identity, except for the change in ownership, their dismissal prior to the sale was automatically unfair. The Acquired Rights Directive, having been passed initially perhaps to place some brake on corporate restructuring and to remove an element of regulatory competition in capital markets, but then interpreted by the courts as part of an EC social policy to protect the rights of workers to economic security, became in the context of insolvency a major legal obstacle to corporate rescues, which themselves were highly desirable from the point of view of protecting the economic security of the workforce.

A satisfactory resolution of this conundrum is hard to find. One measure that might be taken is to prevent the government recouping the cost of payments out of the social security fund from a transferee of an insolvent undertaking. This prohibition would reduce, but not eliminate, the costs to the rescuer of meeting the outstanding claims for wages and dismissal of the employees of the insolvent company. The Acquired

Rights Directive has been amended to create other possible solutions.[29] It permits national legislation to exclude the liability of a transferee of an insolvent company's business for the debts arising from contracts of employment and payable before the transfer. It also permits national legislation to authorize representatives of the employees to agree alterations to the terms of employment with the purchaser with a view to ensuring the survival of all or part of the business. The absence of partnership institutions may render this second option rarely workable in the UK, though the principle of permitting collective adverse variations of terms of employment, as opposed to individual agreements to the detriment of the worker, provides a useful safeguard of collective strength for the worker in return for the flexibility that it affords the purchaser. The former option of giving the transferee an immunity would in effect cast the burden of outstanding wages on the social security system in many instances, and probably deprive employees dismissed prior to the transfer of any chance of obtaining a compensatory award for their automatically unfair dismissal. That outcome may appear tough on the taxpayers who have to foot the bill, and harsh on the workers who are unfairly dismissed but receive no compensatory award. But the taxpayers may in fact be benefiting from this arrangement, for an increase in corporate rescues reduces the social costs of unemployment caused by insolvencies. And the claim of the employees for a compensatory award for unfair dismissal has already been questioned as a rather artificial attempt to transplant a foreign legal concept into UK law, which already had in the redundancy payment system its own rather different response to the problems of economic insecurity arising from business restructuring.

[29] Art. 4a.

Part IV

Citizenship

10

Civil Liberties at Work

1. RIGHTS TALK

At the *Paradiso and Inferno* restaurant, not far from the London School of Economics in central London, the waiters complained that for many years in the 1980s they had not received their entitlement to a minimum wage. For workers in the catering trade at that time, a wages council fixed a minimum rate. The wages received by the waiters had exceeded that minimum, but only because the employer included within the pay a distribution of tips given by customers as an addition to a payment of the bill by credit card or cheque. The inclusion of the tips effectively doubled their wages. The waiters objected that these tips belonged to them already, as this was the intention of the customers, so that tips should not be counted as pay or remuneration by the employer. By a majority, the English Court of Appeal rejected this argument.[1] The employer could not be regarded as an agent of the customer or a trustee of those sums paid by cheque or credit card as part of the bill. Tips given in this way belonged to the employer, who then by contract apportioned the total according to a formula among the staff.

Dissatisfied with English justice, and having been refused leave to appeal to the House of Lords, the waiters boldly took their case to the European Court of Human Rights in Strasbourg. They claimed that the law of the UK violated Article 1 of Protocol No. 1 of the European Convention on Human Rights, which protects the right to the peaceful enjoyment of a person's possessions. By a majority, the Strasbourg Court rejected this claim.[2] The Court held that the decision of the English courts that the tips paid by credit card and cheque belonged to the employer was not arbitrary or manifestly unreasonable. It followed that by using the tips as part of the remuneration of the waiters, the employer had not interfered with the waiters' property. The dissenting opinion argued that the Convention right had been violated, since by permitting

---

[1] *Nerva v. R L &G Ltd* [1996] IRLR 461, CA.
[2] *Nerva v. United Kingdom* [2002] IRLR 815, ECHR.

these payments to satisfy the employer's debt to the waiters under the minimum wage legislation, the employer had enriched itself at the expense of its staff. Nevertheless, this odd claim for a minimum wage based upon a defence of the right to private property, though coming close to success, never quite gained its rosette.

All the preceding discussion of employment law could have been presented in terms of workers' rights. We could have examined the law as comprising a set of individual rights, such as the right not to be subjected to discrimination or the right not to be unfairly dismissed. There are many advantages in thinking about employment law through the prism of rights. The splicing together of the moral sense of rightness and the legal sense of entitlement enables the rhetoric of rights to provide a powerful and persuasive discourse. Furthermore, the assertion of a right tends to foreclose other policy arguments that may weaken employees' claims. Arguments about promoting competitiveness and fairness, for instance, tend to present a balance of policy considerations that propel the law towards measured interventions in the labour market. Once the language of rights is invoked, however, it tends to trump these other policy considerations. Employment lawyers appreciate some of these potential qualities of legal analyses framed in terms of individual rights, because they facilitate a strong emphasis on the interests and needs of workers for protective legislation. Nevertheless, employment lawyers have traditionally been wary of this way of presenting the logic of the law, and it has been avoided, at least till this point, in this book. It is worth considering why employment lawyers have tended to forgo the potential empowerment and persuasive force of rights talk.

The tradition of industrial pluralism caused employment lawyers to be initially suspicious of the rhetoric of individual rights. In a historical tradition where the protection of the interests of workers depended largely on the organizational strength of trade unions, the idea that individual legal rights might play a significant role in regulating employment seemed unlikely. On the contrary, the language of rights seemed to pose a threat to the industrial pluralist system in two ways. First, the typical list of rights embraced in liberal constitutions, such as rights to property and liberty, appeared to offer fundamental protections for the interests of employers whilst offering almost nothing to workers. In many cases employers have been able to invoke such constitutional declarations of rights for the purpose of both protecting their ownership of the means of production and all the rights associated with it, and protecting their freedom of contract against economic pressure from trade unions.

Hard-won immunities from legal action when pursuing industrial action turn out to be unconstitutional invasions of the employer's property and liberty rights. Constitutional rights have even been used at times to provide a legal basis for invalidating legislation designed to protect workers against harsh conditions on the ground that mandatory protective laws interfere with liberty or freedom of association—that is the freedom of the workers themselves. The second objection of industrial pluralists to the analysis in terms of individual rights suggests that ultimately the strength of workers necessitates their combining together as a collective entity, in solidarity. Their effectiveness depends upon leadership and discipline within the group, so that the collective force can be deployed to maximum effect. The danger presented by an exclusive focus on the protection of individual rights lies in the opportunity for individual members of the union to protest against the direction taken by the leadership. A worker who decides not to strike may try to invoke a 'right to work', and a worker who does not like the policy of the union can insist upon the basis of a right to freedom of association to leave the union and perhaps set up a rival. These individual rights, if vigorously protected by the law, are likely to weaken the collective strength of the union organization. Whereas employers as a single corporate entity can take full advantage of individual rights to protect their interests, organizations of workers can only be effective if the interests of individuals are to some extent sacrificed for the general good.[3] Industrial pluralists often regarded the danger of undermining collective action as too great a price to be paid for the admitted benefits of using the rhetoric of rights.

To a considerable extent these reservations about rights talk could be met by the extension of the range of rights. As an addition to the traditional protections afforded to the civil liberties of citizens against the misuse of state power, such as freedom of speech and the right to a fair trial, the law could recognize social and economic rights designed to protect workers against their employers. These rights might include the right to form trade unions, to engage in collective bargaining, to strike, and to be protected against unfair dismissal. Yet even with such an extensive list of social and economic rights, employment lawyers remained concerned about the implications of reducing the analysis to talk about rights. The problem arises that rights often conflict and need to be

[3] C. Offe, 'Two Logics of Collective Action', in C. Offe, *Disorganised Capitalism* (J. Keane ed.) (Cambridge: Polity, 1985), p. 170.

qualified and reconciled.[4] The task of interpreting the ambit of rights expressed in indeterminate language is vested usually in courts. The worry becomes that in balancing competing rights and interpreting their scope, the courts will display a lack of sympathy to collective organizations that interfere with property rights and freedom of contract. In short, the economic and social rights will turn out to be paper tigers when confronted with what lawyers regard usually as somehow more fundamental rights that protect the interests of employers. It has to be said that the history of employment law reveals many occasions when this fear turns out to be far from groundless.

Although rights talk can legitimately be accused of steering legal discourse in the direction of the three 'D's—'decontextualization, depoliticization, and decollectivization'—these failing grades have to balanced against the possible instrumental use of rights, as in the example of the waiters at the *Paradiso and Inferno* restaurant. The legal complexity of the argument in that case, with its investigation of equitable proprietary rights of the waiters to the sums representing tips, also illustrates how the instrumental use of rights talk necessarily commits the employment law to engaging with legalistic niceties rather than addressing the real policy issue of whether owners of restaurants should pay their staff so little that only the discretionary tips enable the staff to earn a living wage. In this and the next chapter, we consider the actual and potential impact of rights talk on employment law. The discussion follows the slightly artificial divide between rights concerned with traditional civil liberties, to be examined in this chapter, and economic and social rights considered in the next.

2. THE EUROPEAN CONVENTION ON HUMAN RIGHTS

The Human Rights Act 1998 incorporates the European Convention on Human Rights into UK law. It also requires UK courts to take into account the interpretations placed on the Convention by the European Court of Human Rights. Individuals such as the waiters can now assert their Convention rights against the government in a British court without the need to go to Strasbourg. At first sight, however, this legislation only provides a benefit to public sector employees, for only they can assert

---

[4] M. Koskenniemi, 'The Effect of Rights on Political Culture', in P. Alston (ed.), *The EU and Human Rights* (Oxford: Oxford University Press, 1999), p. 99.

against their employer, the state, that one of their Convention rights has been violated by the state. Even this protection remains unclear, for there is a view in UK law that public authorities are somehow acting in a private capacity when making contracts of employment, though the Strasbourg Court has never accepted such a restriction in assessing government actions under the Convention.[5] Nevertheless, the Human Rights Act is likely to present considerable potential for both private and public sector workers by means of its 'indirect effect' on UK law.[6] When interpreting national legislation, the courts are bound to try to apply an interpretation that respects Convention rights as far as possible. In the event that the court is unable to interpret the national legislation in a way that is consistent with a Convention right, it cannot invalidate primary legislation, but it can make a 'declaration of incompatibility', which is likely to compel any government to introduce amendments. With respect to the common law created by judges, the courts, as a public authority, are under a legal duty not to act in a way that is incompatible with a Convention right. This requirement is likely to be met by a reinterpretation of the precedents of earlier cases, in order to adjust the legal doctrine to the rights of the Convention.

The Convention rights are mainly directed towards the protection of the civil liberties of citizens against interference by the State. But many of these rights have a potential application in employment law issues. Article 6, the right to a fair trial, requires that in the determination of civil rights and obligations and criminal charges everyone is entitled to a fair and public hearing within a reasonable time by an independent and impartial tribunal. This right may place a limit on the extent to which a government can restrict or impede access to employment tribunals for workers seeking to vindicate their employment law rights. Article 8, the right to privacy, proclaims that everyone has the right to respect for his private and family life, his home, and his correspondence. Although plainly directed at intrusive state surveillance and invasions of privacy, this right may provide a ground for helping employees to protect their interests in the confidentiality of information held about by them by an employer, to place limits on surveillance in the workplace, and to restrict the grounds on which an employer may discipline an employee. Article 9 protects the right to freedom of thought, conscience, and religion. This article may

---

[5] G. Morris, 'The Human Rights Act and the Public/Private Divide in Employment Law (1998) 27 *Industrial LJ* 293.

[6] K. D. Ewing, 'The Human Rights Act and Labour Law' (1998) 27 *Industrial LJ* 275; K. D. Ewing (ed.), *Human Rights at Work* (London: Institute of Employment Rights, 2000).

Employment Law

enable workers to challenge employer's rules and practices that indirectly discriminate against members of religious minorities. Article 10 declares that everyone has the right to freedom of expression, and Article 11 protects freedom of peaceful assembly and freedom of association.

These rights are all limited, however, by the text of the Convention in ways that enable governments to restrict the exercise of rights by law on certain protected grounds such as national security, public safety, the protection of morals, to the extent necessary in a democratic society. Cases involving alleged violations of Convention rights thus typically pose two issues: whether the substance of the right has been violated, and whether the invasion is justifiable as necessary in a democratic society. Although a worker may be able to argue successfully, for instance, that a tribunal considering the question whether a dismissal was fair should pay respect to the worker's rights to privacy and freedom of expression, the protection afforded depends crucially on the extent to which the tribunal accepts that restrictions on these rights by employers is necessary in a democratic society for such purposes as the 'economic well-being of the country' (Article 8), and respect for the rights of others (Articles 8, 9, 10, and 11). The European Court of Human Rights typically uses a test of proportionality in order to determine whether the restriction on the right is justifiable. The Court has also granted states that are signatories to the Convention a 'margin of appreciation' in determining this question, so that for instance it tolerates differences between countries in the extent to which they restrict freedom of the press with respect to obscenity.

To the extent that these rights will have an impact on employment law, a recurrent issue will be whether the terms of contracts of employment can derogate from the Convention rights. Suppose that an employer insists as a term of the contract that employees should never speak to the press about the company without prior authorization; should this limit on freedom of expression be respected? It is tempting to take the moral high ground and assert that workers should never be permitted to contract out of their fundamental Convention rights. But this view, though attractive,[7] oversimplifies the problem. In entering such a contract, workers are exercising their right to freedom of association, so that we are encountering a problem of competition between Convention rights, which requires a balancing process to occur. Furthermore, some employers may be prevented from offering jobs at all without the assurance provided by the express terms of the contract, so that an insistence upon a Convention

---

[7] G. Morris, 'Fundamental Rights: Exclusion by Agreement?' (2001) 30 *Industrial LJ* 49.

right would not serve the interests of workers in the long term. A more nuanced approach to the protection of Convention rights against contractual terms therefore seems advisable.

Under a test of proportionality, for instance, it may be possible to forge a reconciliation between the legitimate business needs of the employer for the restriction and the interests of workers in enjoying unfettered rights. Consider, for instance, the problem raised in *Ahmed v. Inner London Education Authority*.[8] A full-time schoolteacher was refused permission by his employers to take off about 45 minutes every Friday afternoon, in order to comply with his duty as a Muslim to attend prayers at a nearby Mosque. The applicant argued in a claim for constructive unfair dismissal that his employers should have rearranged the timetable to enable him to exercise his freedom of religion. Although the case arose before the enactment of the Human Rights Act, the Court of Appeal considered its possible application. The majority of the court believed that the employer's refusal of time off was compatible with Article 9, because Mr Ahmed had agreed in his contract to those hours of work. Scarman LJ, dissenting, held that the education authority had to adjust its timetable to accommodate devout Muslims, even if this involved additional costs, for the authority was bound by national law, as interpreted by reference to Article 9, not to impede the religious worship of teachers.

When Mr Ahmed took his claim to Strasbourg, he failed at the first hurdle. At that time a Commission vetted cases for admissibility and prospects of success. This Commission accepted that the employer had interfered with the right to freedom of religion, but decided that the restriction was justified, so that the case should not proceed to a court hearing. The restriction was justified because the employee had had the opportunity to take a different job with hours that were compatible with religious observance, and indeed Mr Ahmed had subsequently obtained, at reduced pay, a four and a half-day job. Furthermore, the employers had not arbitrarily refused the request for time off, but had presented good organizational and economic reasons for the insistence on full-time work. This blunt view that, if a worker takes a job in which the terms of the contract restrict a Convention right, the worker cannot subsequently complain about the interference, is surely too strong. It provides an open invitation to employers to use standard-form contracts to eliminate Convention rights, and employees may feel compelled by economic necessity to accept such terms. Yet there are circumstances where the terms of the

---

[8] [1978] QB 36, CA.

contract impose a justifiable restriction on Convention rights, as in the case of a government intelligence officer who agrees to strict confidentiality of secret information. A better reconciliation between Convention rights and terms of contracts of employment would be to require the employer to justify the contractual restriction by reference to a test of proportionality, so that the employer would be required to demonstrate that the terms represented a business need of the employer that could not satisfactorily be met by any lesser restriction on the Convention right. If such a test had been applied in Mr Ahmed's case, his argument that a reorganization of the timetable or some unpaid time off would have met the employer's needs adequately without interfering with his Convention right might well have been successful. In the case of religious discrimination, such a test of proportionality for rules that indirectly discriminate is now required under the EC general framework Directive on equal opportunities in employment.[9] In the United States, learning from the excesses of the McCarthy era when public sector employment was conditioned on non-membership of the Communist party and oaths to that effect, the courts apply a balancing test to restrictions on the enjoyment of constitutional rights by public sector employees.[10]

Without attempting a comprehensive survey of the potential implications of Convention rights in employment law, it is worth investigating some especially controversial issues, where Convention rights may cause a significant adjustment to the legal position of employees. These issues concern the potential impact on employment law of two Convention rights, the right to privacy and the right to freedom of expression.

3. PRIVACY

The concept of privacy lacks any precise definition. One strand in its meaning is directed against intrusions into one's domestic and personal life, such as observation of what one does in one's own home or what is said in personal communications between friends. A related strand concerns the public exposure of personal details of one's life, or at least communication of these details to others without a person's consent. Although the constitutional protection of privacy is directed against the abuse of the state's monitoring powers over its citizens, that protection may also be afforded to individuals against unwanted press intrusions.

---

[9] EC Directive 2000/78.
[10] *Pickering v. Board of Education* 391 US 563 (1968).

With respect to employment, the right to privacy may place limits on monitoring in the workplace, and may control the extent to which employers can use a worker's outside activities as a justification for disciplinary action.

SURVEILLANCE

The invention of the factory enabled employers to obtain gains in productive efficiency through intensive surveillance of performance of work. The foreman could observe machine operatives and anyone noticed shirking, talking, or idle could be disciplined. Modern technology enables businesses to engage in constant surveillance, without the employees' knowledge, from a remote location through cameras, the monitoring of telephone conversations, and the reading of emails and other records held on computers. Although employers have a legitimate business interest in surveillance of performance of work, and they may also have valid concerns about security and compliance with regulatory standards, the legal question is whether there are any limits placed on the intrusiveness of workplace surveillance. It may be argued that, if an employee accepts a job, there is an implied consent to any kind of surveillance during the performance of work, since the employer has bought the employee's time. Against that view, it can be contended that there should be implicit limits on permissible surveillance, because the worker, as a person and not a commodity, deserves respect for some degree of privacy in their personal relations in the workplace. An employer may take the view that it needs to record conversations in the toilets to check that workers are not malingering there, but the employees who have a brief chat there, saying things that they would not say in front of their manager, may feel that the intrusive surveillance destroys any possibility for human or intimate relations in the workplace. Whether employers have a business interest in using all the modern technology of spying in the workplace must be doubted. A workforce subject to what are perceived as intrusive levels of surveillance is unlikely to respond with the type of co-operation that the employer needs. A chilling effect on personal relationships in the workplace may discourage co-operation and drive employees to look for jobs elsewhere.

In the UK, with one recent exception, there is no specific legal regulation of workplace surveillance. The starting point of the legal analysis is therefore that the employer can engage in any kind of surveillance that it wishes. The protection of the right to privacy in the European Convention on Human Rights raises the question whether this right might be available as a basis for challenges to certain forms of workplace surveillance. This issue was tested in *Halford v. UK*.[11] A senior policewoman brought a claim for sex discrimination because she believed that further promotion was being blocked. The dispute became especially bitter, because she believed that senior officers were conducting a campaign of vilification through the press and harassing her by bringing unwarranted disciplinary proceedings. The sex discrimination claim was eventually settled and she left the police service. But she brought proceedings against the police for an invasion of her privacy on the ground of telephone tapping. She claimed that her home telephone and a special line that she had obtained for her private calls at work had been tapped in order to obtain information to use against her in the sex discrimination case. She was unable to prove the tapping of the home phone, but she succeeded in her claim with respect to the private phone line in the workplace. The European Court of Human Rights held that her right to private life under Article 8 had been violated. Nor could the UK government justify this interference on the ground that the tapping was in accordance with the law, since the regulation of the public phone service did not cover the interception of telephone calls on the internal communication systems operated by public authorities.

Although this decision apparently places limits on the powers of the employer to engage in workplace surveillance, the protection afforded by the judgment for the privacy of workers is in reality threadbare. The point emphasized by the Court was that the police authority had encouraged the claimant to believe that her calls on her personal line at work would be private, the implication being that without that misleading impression having been given, the employer would have been entitled to monitor any calls without consent or notice. Furthermore, the Court also indicated that monitoring might be justified, if it was done in accordance with the law. The UK government responded to that possibility by enacting the Regulation of Investigatory Powers Act 2000. Although this legislation creates a civil wrong of intercepting telephone calls and other messaging systems such as email on private networks connected indirectly to the public telecommunications system without lawful authority, as is the case with the public telephone network, the protection of privacy is greatly diminished, because the employer enjoys lawful authority either if the sender of the communication has consented to the monitoring, or if the employer has a permitted reason. These permitted

[11] (1997) 24 EHRR 523, ECHR.

reasons include such broad categories as establishing the existence of facts relevant to the business, ascertaining compliance with regulation and quality controls, detecting crime, and detecting unauthorized use of the system. It seems improbable that an employer will not be able to bring itself within one of these categories, and in any case the employer can obtain a carte blanche for monitoring by securing the consent of an individual employee in a standard-form contract of employment. In effect, the legislative response to the *Halford* case has been an attempt to destroy any right to privacy of employees with respect to communication systems in the workplace.

That conclusion leaves open the possibility that other forms of surveillance such as video cameras may violate a right to privacy, but the prospects for relying on that right seem bleak. As long as the notion in *Halford* that consent by employees negatives any infringement of the right to privacy remains in place, employers can use their bargaining power to insist upon suitable contractual terms to authorize surveillance. It is possible that this view of the right to privacy may be reconsidered, for the European Court of Human Rights has acknowledged that privacy includes the right to establish and develop relationships with other human beings in the course of work,[12] but it is questionable whether this aspect of the right is infringed by the employer merely observing the behaviour with the ostensible consent of the workforce. It is also possible that the broad grounds for lawful authority for interceptions of communications granted by the UK legislation may be open to challenge on the ground that they represent disproportionate violations of the right to privacy in the pursuit of the legitimate interests of employers. But for the time being, the right to privacy appears to place no effective restriction on workplace surveillance.

CONFIDENTIAL RECORDS

In the course of employment, an employer is likely to acquire considerable information about employees. Much of this information, such as salary, medical history, and reports on performance, will be regarded by employees as confidential in the sense that they would not like it to be disclosed without their permission to anyone else. An unauthorized disclosure could be regarded as an invasion of privacy. On the other hand, an employer acquires and stores this information for business purposes,

---

[12] *Niemitz v. Germany* (1992) 16 EHHR 7, ECHR; M. Ford, 'Two Conceptions of Worker Privacy' (2002) 31 *Industrial LJ* 135.

and those purposes may involve disclosure, as for example in the case of writing a letter of recommendation. Although the disclosure of confidential information for such purposes may be unavoidable, an employee will still be concerned that the record is accurate and that no more information than is necessary is revealed.

The EC Data Protection Directive,[13] in pursuit of its avowed objective to protect an individual's right to privacy, concentrates on two key safeguards. The first protection applies the principle that the personal information should be collected for specified, explicit, and legitimate purposes, and then not used for other purposes. The second protection applies the principle that the individual should have a right of access to the data held about him, and for inaccurate or incomplete information to be rectified or erased. The form in which the data are collected does not matter. The information may be held on computer records, tapes, or documents. The protections apply whenever the data are organized so that specific information about a particular individual is accessible. The products of workplace surveillance, such as records of emails, may fall within these protections.

The key issue from the perspective of the right to privacy is whether the law prevents the employer from collecting certain kinds of information at all. The implementing legislation in the UK identifies a category of 'sensitive personal data',[14] which includes ethnic origins, political opinions, religious affiliation, trade union membership, health records, sexual activity, and criminal records. This information can only be collected (in summary) either with the explicit consent of the individual, or where necessary in connection with legal proceedings, or for the purpose of performing any legal right or obligation of the employer. There is a specific exemption for 'ethnic monitoring' for the purpose of ensuring equality of opportunity. The practical effect of these rules is unclear. Assuming that the employer can acquire this information without the consent of the employee, can the employer hold it and use it? The answer depends on the width of the exception concerning the legal obligations of the employer. An employer may be able to rely upon its obligations under employment laws, whether they be anti-discrimination laws, health and safety regulations, or the protections afforded to trade union members, to claim that the storage of the sensitive data is necessary for the employer to ensure compliance. With respect to other non-sensitive personal information held about employees by the employer, these data can be collected for

---

[13] EC Directive 95/46. [14] Data Protection Act 1998, s. 4(3), and Sched. 3.

the same reasons, but in addition the employer can invoke other grounds for keeping the record, including its necessity for the performance of the contract of employment. There is further a general ground for collecting data and revealing them to third parties, which permits the employer to rely upon its 'legitimate interests', except where this data collection is unwarranted 'by reason of prejudice to the rights and freedom or legitimate interests of the employee'. This vague balancing test effectively determines the legality of an employer's collection of general information about employees without their consent. What is clear about this data protection legislation is that privacy of personal information is not regarded as an inalienable right of employees, but can be relinquished by consent, and even in the absence of consent an employer may rely upon business purposes and legal obligations to justify its storage and use of confidential information.

Whether this elaborate data protection regime is ever likely to prove effective, even with these legal safeguards for privacy in place, seems doubtful. The remedial system is unusually powerful for employment law, though it studiously avoids any strict liability for breach of the rules. An individual employee can bring a legal action to order the employer to give access to data held, to prevent the use of that information if it is likely to cause distress or damage, and to have inaccurate information erased or rectified. The employee can also claim damages for breach of the rules governing data protection, though the employer has a defence that it had taken reasonable care to comply with the rules. There is also an independent Data Protection Commissioner whose tasks include the enforcement of the rules, with the prospect of obtaining a criminal penalty against an employer who has not used all due diligence to comply with an enforcement notice. But the effectiveness of the legislation must depend ultimately on the discovery by individuals that confidential information is being held without their consent or being used for unauthorized purposes, which may prove extremely difficult.

In a world linked by computer networks that can transfer vast quantities of information by a few keystrokes on a keyboard, it seems almost impossible to control the dissemination of confidential information about individual employees. Even though Europe has devised a transnational system, computerized information flows recognize no physical barriers, so that personal data can be stored in foreign locations where the regulations do not apply. Responding to this problem, the EC has agreed with the USA that European employers should only transmit personal data to the USA if the US company complies with the standards of the EC

Directive.[15] The weakness of this regime is that the US company can self-certify its observance of the data protection standards, and it is hard to see how this certification will ever be checked. In truth, new technologies render attempts to protect worker privacy through data protection laws always vulnerable to the unscrupulous.

TESTING

In the United States employers commonly use a wide variety of testing devices in order to vet potential employees. The polygraph or lie detector test can be used not only to explore the accuracy of job applicants' claims about skills and qualifications, but also to probe into the intimate details of the worker's personal life. Medical tests can not only supply information about current fitness for work but also in some kinds of testing, such as genetic testing, point to the long-term health prospects of a job applicant. Of course, an applicant for a job can always refuse to undergo such tests, but if they are used widely by employers, the applicant may be effectively excluded from the labour market. Employers have a legitimate interest in discovering information about a prospective employee's ability to perform the job. Employers may regard the personal life of an individual as relevant to that question and pose questions in the polygraph test such as: 'Are you happily married?' and: 'Do you ever get drunk?' By telling lies in answer to these questions, the job applicant may forfeit the chance of employment; but answering them truthfully may also undermine his job prospects. Respect for the Convention right to privacy may suggest that testing should be controlled, so that testing should only be lawful to the extent that it investigates personal matters that may have a significant impact on job performance.

In response to this concern for privacy, in the United States both federal and state laws regulate the use of polygraph testing. Federal law prohibits its use except for particular kinds of jobs, such as those involving national security and the handling of controlled substances.[16] But another large exception concerns an employer's testing as part of an internal investigation of economic loss to the employer's business, which is only permitted if the employer has a reasonable suspicion of the employee's involvement. Even where testing is permitted, the employee is entitled to certain procedural safeguards, such as the opportunity to see

---

[15] www.exports.gov/safeharbor; Q. Bargate and M. Shah, 'The EU/US Safe Harbor Data Protection Agreement—A Shotgun Marriage' (2000) 15(8) *Journal of International Banking Law* 177.

[16] Employee Polygraph Protection Act 1988, 29 USC s. 2001.

the questions in advance. Furthermore, questions concerning sexual behaviour, beliefs, and associations are not permitted. At the level of particular states, not only is there regulation of particular forms of testing, but state constitutions also sometimes provide for a right to privacy. This right may be used in some instances in a claim for compensation for dismissal contrary to public policy when an employee refuses to answer certain questions, but only if the employer cannot show that the questions have some bearing on job performance, a test that permits a wide range of topics involving private life that may influence an employee's motivation.[17] Similar elementary safeguards for the privacy of employees may have to be enacted in Europe, if testing becomes more common.

ACTIVITIES OUTSIDE THE WORKPLACE

What a worker does in his own time might be regarded as none of the employer's business. The exercise of sexual, cultural, and political preferences outside the workplace can be regarded as private matters, which have nothing to do with the contract of employment. Similarly, the people with whom a worker spends her spare time are private matters unless the activity involves assistance to a business competitor. Yet employers do not always respect such claims to privacy. They have a legitimate concern about the reputation of the business, which they fear might be damaged by an association through its employees with activities that receive public disapproval. Leaving aside religious and political activities, because they benefit from additional protections under the Convention, how might the right to privacy affect an employer's attempts to control other personal activities outside the workplace?

Although there is greater tolerance today, the sexual preferences of workers have sometimes been used by employers as grounds for discrimination. The EC framework Directive on equal opportunities in employment, when implemented, will provide workers with legal protection against less favourable treatment on the ground of sexual preference. But the Convention right to privacy will continue to provide an additional strand of legal protection. For instance, in answering the question whether a dismissal was fair when an employer used the employee's gay activities as the reason for dismissal, a tribunal would be bound to interpret the statutory test of the reasonableness of the dismissal in conformity with the Convention right to privacy. Respect for the Convention right should lead the tribunal to interpret the concept of reasonableness to

---

[17] *Cort v. Bristol-Myers Co.* 385 Mass 300, 431 NE 2d 908 S Ct of Mass. (1982).

exclude such discrimination, unless perhaps, applying a test of pro-portionality, the employer could point to serious damage to the business and the absence of alternatives to dismissal.

A more controversial application of the right to privacy concerns unlawful and criminal activities outside the workplace. Suppose that an employer learns that an employee has been arrested or convicted for a criminal offence committed outside the workplace, such as possession of prohibited drugs or shoplifting. Would a dismissal for such a reason amount to an interference with the right to privacy of the individual? An employer might argue that the criminal activity has undermined trust and confidence, and that in any case the involvement of public authorities removes the activity from the protected private sphere. Such arguments have generally prevailed in the tribunals in the UK. Recall the case of *Mathewson v. RB Wilson Dental Laboratory Ltd*,[18] where the arrest for possession of a small quantity of cannabis during the employee's lunch-time was held to be a reasonable ground for dismissal. Against that endorsement of an employer's disciplinary power extending to outside activities, an employee can assert that what he does in his own time, provided that it does not interfere with performance of work or substan-tially damage the reputation of the business, should not be any concern of the employer, and that the right to privacy is invaded by this monitoring of outside activities. Although the employer may understandably be unwilling to appear to condone the employee's unlawful activity, it is also important out of respect for the liberty and privacy of individuals to guard against the use of managerial disciplinary power to control how employees live outside the workplace. An individual's choice to take a particular job should not in general give the employer an indirect power to control that individual's choices with respect to other aspects of his or her own life.

DRESS CODES

One last illustration of the potential impact of respect for the right to privacy concerns employers' rules about clothing and grooming of hair at work. Employers justify these instructions on such grounds as satisfying customer preferences and enabling staff to be easily recognized for safety reasons. Rules that affect how a worker appears outside working hours, such as the requirement for men of a short haircut, certainly impinge on private life and may interfere with the right to privacy by constraining

---

[18] [1988] IRLR 512, EAT; above p. 175.

the life style and choices of an individual outside the workplace. Rules about dress codes in the workplace such as uniforms and bans on certain types of clothing limit the way in which workers may wish to present themselves as individuals to their co-workers.

Some indirect attacks on dress codes have been successful through applications of the sex discrimination laws. Employers have been unable to insist on bans on women wearing trousers, because tribunals are likely to find an unjustified disparate impact on women compared to men. But such claims are not invariably successful. For instance, a supermarket's ban on male workers having long hair was found not to amount to sex discrimination against men. The Court of Appeal held that different rules for men and women with respect to dress codes were not necessarily less favourable treatment for one sex, provided the rules applied conventional standards of dress.[19] Whether such a view can be maintained in the light of the Convention right to privacy is doubtful. The European Commission on Human Rights has accepted that an employer's prohibition on a male transvestite from wearing women's clothing in the workplace constituted an interference with the right to private life, though the prohibition was justified as a proportionate interference required by the employer's legitimate purposes.[20] If dress codes represent an interference with Convention rights, a male employee required to wear short hair, unlike female staff, must have suffered less favourable treatment, because an infringement of a right surely amounts to a detriment.

Although dress codes may be open to challenge directly or indirectly by reference to the right to privacy, or perhaps under the right to freedom of expression (to which we shortly turn), it seems likely that the employee's claim will ultimately prove unsuccessful. In the long run, whether framed in terms of discrimination or privacy, the issue is likely to turn on a proportionality test of justification for the employer's dress code. Courts seem unwilling to scrutinize carefully an employer's business justification for the rule. In an American case where uniformed policeman challenged rules requiring short hair and banning moustaches and beards, the Supreme Court accepted that there was an arguable interference with the right to liberty and privacy, but upheld the rules on the ground that they were not arbitrary.[21] The dissenting minority view was far more critical. Justice Marshall argued that 'an individual's personal

---

[19] *Smith v. Safeway plc* [1996] ICR 868, CA.
[20] *Kara v. United Kingdom*, No. 36528/97, 22 Oct. 1998.
[21] *Kelley v. Johnson*, 425 US 238 (1976).

appearance may reflect, sustain, and nourish his personality and may well be used as a means of expressing his attitude and lifestyle'. He doubted that the requirement of short hair for policemen in uniform either made it easier for the public to identify them or helped the police force's *esprit de corps*. The courts may be reluctant to become involved in supervising managerial decisions about dress codes, but if these rules interfere with Convention rights, the courts should at least require a rational relationship between the codes and the stated business purpose.

4. FREEDOM OF EXPRESSION

'Freedom of expression . . . constitutes one of the essential foundations of a democratic society and one of the basic conditions for its progress and for each individual's self-fulfilment.'[22] As this explanation of the right to freedom of expression suggests, the civil liberty is directed especially towards freedom of political discussion and freedom of the press on matters of public interest. In one case, for instance, it led to the invalidation of the conviction of French journalists, who had unlawfully obtained copies of the tax returns of the chief executive of Peugeot motor-car company. The journalists had revealed in their newspaper that, although the chief executive was bitterly resisting the workers' claim for a wage increase, he himself had recently been awarded a 40 per cent increase. But how does the right to freedom of expression apply to the workplace?

No one suggests that the right to freedom of expression should be unfettered in the workplace. An employer clearly has a legitimate interest in avoiding inefficiency and disruption of production arising from too much chat. Article 10(2) permits many kinds of justifications for interference with freedom of expression on the ground that they are necessary and proportionate restrictions in a democratic society for the protection of the rights of others. For example, racially abusive speech in the workplace would not receive any protection under the Convention right. It seems likely that an employer who uses its power under the contract of employment to forbid idle chatter in the workplace would be able to defend such a restriction as a justified interference. But can the employer rely upon the express and implied terms that construct the authority relation within employment to prevent at its discretion any kind of speech of the employee? There are limits to the employer's powers, though their scope remains unclear.

---

[22] *Lingens v. Austria* A.103 (1986) 8 EHRR 407, ECHR.

POLITICAL ACTIVITIES

Although an employer may be able in general to control how workers spend their time at the workplace, some employers try to control their employees' conduct outside the workplace. If an employer takes objection to an employee's political activities outside work, perhaps because they involve participation in a Communist or Fascist party, can the employer justify this interference with the Convention right to freedom of expression, which might perhaps be combined with the further right to freedom of belief and opinion? It is hard to see how such a restriction could be justified by private sector employers, since it is of the essence of a democratic society that political activities should not be restricted. In the UK, however, with the exception of Northern Ireland,[23] no legislation explicitly regulates political discrimination, so that employees seeking to contest employers' controls over their political activities outside work will have to rely on courts to interpret other laws, such as the law against unfair dismissal, in ways compatible with Convention rights. Public sector workers may more straightforwardly rely upon the Convention by using the Human Rights Act 1998, but here special considerations apply that may justify restrictions on their political activities.

Public officials such as civil servants, judges, police, and the armed services are usually forbidden to participate in political activities. Their neutrality, or at least apparent neutrality, is regarded as essential to the proper functioning of a democratic society, where the elected representatives of the people should be able to count on the impartial implementation of their political mandate. But should the restriction on political activities apply equally to all public sector workers? A German schoolteacher was dismissed from her position because she was an active member of the Communist party. She claimed that her rights to freedom of expression and freedom of belief had been violated.[24] Before the European Court of Human Rights, the German government sought to justify its interference with the teacher's freedom of expression on the ground that the legal constraint on public sector workers was necessary for the protection of a democratic society. Applying the test of whether the interference with freedom of expression was proportionate to the need to protect the democratic system of government, the Court concluded that the teacher's Convention rights had been violated. Although constraints

---

[23] Fair Employment and Treatment (Northern Ireland) Order 1998, SI 1998/3162 (N.I. 21).
[24] *Vogt v. Germany* (1996) 21 EHRR 205, ECHR.

on the political activities of some public officials were justifiable, the job of teaching in a secondary school did not fall into that category unless the teacher had attempted to indoctrinate pupils in anti-democratic views or perhaps had taken a public stance that involved or encouraged disobedience to the constitutional order. The implication of this decision is that a blanket prohibition on political activities imposed on all public sector workers violates the Convention rights. Although restrictions on senior civil servants, judges, the police, and the armed services are likely to be justifiable,[25] limits on the political activities of other public sector workers will be scrutinized carefully by the Strasbourg Court. For example, the British rules that restrict the political activities of local government officers,[26] in order to preserve their impartiality, were assessed carefully to test whether the rules were proportionate to the need to protect the impartiality of the service. These rules had prevented the officers from themselves standing for election or from giving active support to candidates. Upholding the rules, the European Court of Human Rights stressed that the constraints on political activities were proportionate because they only applied to about 2 per cent of local government employees whose duties involved the provision of advice to the elected councillors or the representation of the council in dealings with the media.[27]

WHISTLEBLOWING

What should an employee do if she suspects that some criminal, corrupt, or dangerous activity is taking place in the workplace? The obvious step to take is to report this suspicion to a manager, but employees may fear retaliation, especially if the manager appears to be implicated. Turning a blind eye is another option, but the employee may fear being caught up in the illegal activity or perhaps being put at risk by unsafe procedures. Should the employee speak out and tell someone outside the business? There is a public interest in helping employees trapped in such situations, for they may assist the detection of crime, reduce the level of mismanagement or corruption of businesses, and alert us to dangers for the safety of the workforce or the public. Yet employers have not always aligned themselves with this public interest.

Managers often regard workers who make repeated complaints about safety or allegations of managerial incompetence or corruption as the

---

[25] *Rekvenyi v. Hungary* (1999) 30 EHRR 519, ECHR (police officer).
[26] Local Government Officers (Political Restrictions) Regulations 1990, SI 1990/851.
[27] *Ahmed v. United Kingdom* (1998) 29 EHRR 29, ECHR.

source of dissension and the breakdown of discipline and co-operative work relations. Dismissal is a common response to employees who 'stir up trouble' or who tell outsiders including the press about their concerns. Employers have a good chance of justifying such a dismissal, because the employee may have broken an express term of confidentiality in the contract, or disobeyed an express instruction to refrain from making complaints, or the employer may be able to point to disruption to production or damage to the employer's business reputation. In dismissing such a worker, however, although managers may be acting in their own best interests, it is much less clear that the shareholders' interests are being served, let alone the broader public interest. Good communication in the workplace is, as we have seen, often a key to productive efficiency. For this reason, special protection against disciplinary action is afforded to the speech and conduct of worker representatives, such as trade union officials, safety representatives, works council representatives, and worker trustees of the pension fund, for without this safeguard these partnership institutions might not function satisfactorily.[28]

Given the potential chilling effect of the employer's disciplinary power, in order to promote the public interest and perhaps to protect shareholders against disloyal managers, many countries have enacted what are called 'whistleblowing' statutes, which seek to protect employees against retaliatory action. Many of these laws are restricted in various ways, such as being confined to the public sector and limited to disclosures of criminal activity to the relevant public authority. The law in the UK, however, provides a model for a comprehensive regulation of whistleblowing by applying to all sectors of employment and a wide range of issues.[29] Employees who make a 'protected disclosure' are entitled to compensation from their employer if they are subsequently victimized or dismissed. But employees are not entitled to speak about any of their concerns, to anyone, at any time. Their concerns have to relate to criminal offences, breaches of legal obligations, miscarriages of justice, the health and safety of any individual, and damage to the environment. This list is unlikely to include concerns about the employer's policies or how the business is run, unless the employee can point to breaches of the law including breaches of contracts of employment.[30]

The disclosure of a qualifying concern only receives protection if it is

---

[28] Employment Rights Act 1996, ss. 100, 102, 103.

[29] Employment Rights Act 1996, ss. 43A–L, 47B, 103A; D. Lewis, 'The Public Interest Disclosure Act 1998' (1998) 27 *Industrial LJ* 325.

[30] *Parkins v. Sodexho Ltd* [2002] IRLR 109, EAT.

made to the correct person. In general, the legislation provides that the correct person is either a person authorized by the employer to receive such disclosures of wrongdoing or a public official who is charged with enforcement of the relevant regulations. Employers can therefore conserve their power to discipline whistleblowers provided that they create a suitable reporting procedure to senior management. Employees can only disclose their concerns to others such as the press under highly restrictive conditions. One such instance of permitted whistleblowing is where the employee in good faith, and without any personal gain, and reasonably believing that their concerns are true, makes a disclosure to another person which is reasonable in all the circumstances in view of the seriousness of the matter; and in particular it is necessary either that the employee reasonably fears retaliation from disclosure to senior management of the employer, or that no public official has been prescribed to receive such a disclosure, or that the employee had previously made the disclosure to the correct person and that person had failed to take appropriate steps.

Without going further into the details of this legislation, it is apparent that an employee who reasonably fears that speaking about their concerns to their employer will provoke either retaliatory action or a cover-up, must find if at all possible the appropriate public official or watchdog, which assumes a knowledge of the internal workings of government that is likely to prove unrealistic. For example, where a charge nurse in a nursing home had raised with the manager concerns about physical and verbal abuse of elderly residents, and had received no response, the nurse reported these concerns to the local Social Services Inspectorate. The nurse was dismissed on the ground that he was 'not prepared to work with the company's basic interests in mind'. It turned out, however, that the nurse had disclosed his concerns to a body that was not the prescribed public authority. Fortunately, the tribunal upheld the claim for unfair dismissal on the ground that the employee's concerns were about a serious matter, were substantially true, and that the disclosure was reasonable in the circumstances following the inaction of the employer.[31]

The risk under the statute of high awards of compensation for dismissals for protected disclosures, which can include unlimited financial compensation and aggravated damages for injury to feelings, may alter employers' behaviour with respect to whistleblowers in the long run. But

---

[31] *Bladon v. ALM Medical Services Ltd*, unreported tribunal decision, discussed in C. Hobby, *Whistleblowing and the Public Interest Disclosure Act 1998* (London: Institute of Employment Rights, 2001), p. 22.

it must be observed that the most common reaction of senior management to whistleblowers seems to remain one of cover-up and victimization. Employees are still faced with the invidious choice of either keeping quiet or losing their jobs. Securing freedom of expression in the workplace even when important public interests are at stake seems to be beyond the capacity of legal regulation. Respect for the Convention right of freedom of expression may help to tip the balance in some instances in favour of a finding of reasonableness of the disclosure of a whistleblower, but it seems likely that the courts will regard the public interest disclosure laws as providing a fair and proportionate balance between the interests of employees in enjoying freedom of speech and those of employers in keeping their business confidential and restricting what employees may say. Similarly, the suspicion that the employer's motive for dismissal was to cover up corruption or wrongdoing may help to establish an employee's claim for compensation for unfair dismissal or breach of contract, but unless the courts support the possibility of substantial compensation, these remedies will not effectively deter such victimization.[32]

In the United States, where public sector employees can rely directly upon the constitutional protection for freedom of speech, the Supreme Court has limited the exercise of this right to speech on matters of 'public concern', and rejected the contention that complaints about mismanagement or poor policies count as matters of public concern for this purpose. Even if the speech is related to a matter of public concern, it can be restricted by the public authority when, because of the manner, time, and place of the speech, the employee's conduct disrupts the office and interferes with working relationships.[33] This stance of strong deference to the employer's judgement about the need to restrict freedom of speech in the workplace seems likely to be duplicated in any attempts to seek protection from the Convention right. But it can provide limited protection for those public sector workers who merely voice their concerns privately to their superiors, as in the case of the Greek army conscript who wrote to his commanding officer to complain that the army was a 'criminal and terrorist apparatus', for which he had been punished by three months' imprisonment.[34]

---

[32] E.g. *Foley v. Interactive Data Corporation* 47 Cal. 3d 654, 765 P. 2d 373, S. Ct. Cal. (1988).

[33] *Connick v. Myers* 461 US 138, 103 S. Ct 1684 (SCUS, 1983).

[34] *Grigoriades v. Greece* (1997) 27 EHRR 464, 1997-VII 2575.

PICKETING

There is an implicit recognition in the law governing picketing that the activity does raise issues concerning freedom of speech. 'It is lawful for a person in contemplation or furtherance of a trade dispute to attend . . . at or near his own place of work . . . for the purpose only of peacefully obtaining or communicating information, or peacefully persuading any person to work or abstain from working.'[35] Although there may be other aims, the purpose of pickets certainly includes the desire to inform everyone of the presence of official industrial action at a workplace and no doubt to persuade them peacefully not to do business with or work for the employer. If these purposes fall within the right to freedom of expression, any restrictions on picketing would need to be justified according to the proportionality test of the European Convention.

A comparison with the history of this issue in the United States is instructive. In 1940 the Supreme Court struck down a state law that prohibited all picketing on the ground that the law violated the First Amendment (freedom of speech). 'In the circumstances of our times the dissemination of information concerning the facts of a labor dispute must be regarded as within that area of free discussion that is guaranteed by the constitution.'[36] But the court gradually withdrew from that position, arguing that picketing, even if peaceful, was not just about the communication of ideas. The test became whether the restrictions on picketing were in pursuit of a valid state policy, such as to protect employers against economic torts and to keep the peace, and, if so, the restrictions were valid.[37] For a time the court questioned whether a state's protection of private property was a valid reason for always excluding picketing and leafleting from private property, especially where the private property was a shopping mall;[38] but the court eventually concluded that no constitutional question about freedom of speech arises without there being direct state action, which was not the case where an owner of private property sought to exclude pickets from it.[39]

This model may be followed in Europe under the Convention, though perhaps a stricter test of proportionality may have to be satisfied in order to justify restrictions on picketing. It has been acknowledged that picketing and other demonstrations may qualify for protection under the

---

[35] TULR(C)A 1992, s. 220(1).   [36] *Thornhill v. Alabama* 310 US 88 (1940).

[37] *Teamsters Local 695 v. Vogt, Inc* 354 US 284 (1957).

[38] *Amalgamated Food Employees Union v. Logan Valley Plaza* 391 US 308 (1968).

[39] *Hudgens v. NLRB* 424 US 507 (1976).

Convention right to freedom of speech,[40] and this protection may be extended by the right to freedom of assembly in Article 11. The police in the UK enjoy considerable discretionary powers in regulating picketing on the ground by using their powers to prevent a breach of the peace or an obstruction to the highway. These powers of a public authority have to be exercised in accordance with Convention rights, which suggests that the necessity or proportionality of the exercise of these powers may be subject to much closer inspection than hitherto. Even so, Europe may follow the US pattern of effectively permitting all legally mandated restraints on picketing on the ground that they are necessary to protect the rights and freedoms of others in a democratic society.

This conclusion about the scope for ensuring that workers enjoy the right to picket tends to confirm the suspicion of employment lawyers explained earlier that the protection of civil liberties often serves better the interests of employers than collective organizations of workers. Employers can rely on the protection of rights to property and liberty in order to delimit the scope for the exercise of employment law rights by trade unions. The question to which we now turn is whether the extension of rights talk to include social rights may improve the opportunities for employees to protect their interests through the law.

---

[40] *Steel v. UK* (1998) 28 EHRR 603, 1998-VII; *Middlebrook Mushrooms Ltd v. TGWU* [1993] ICR 612, CA.

Social Rights

In the middle of the twentieth century in Europe, various constitutions and charters began to include a wider range of rights than the traditional civil liberties discussed in the previous chapter. In France, for example, the Constitution of 1946 tried to express as basic rights of citizens both the principles of the Welfare State and the necessary protections for workers, such as rights to form trade unions and to take strike action. The Council of Europe not only agreed in 1950 the Convention on Human Rights but also added in 1961 a Social Charter. This Charter (in its current revised form of 1996)[1] augments the social and economic protections of the Welfare State by proclaiming, amongst many matters relevant to employment law, a right to just conditions of work, a right to safe and healthy working conditions, a right against discrimination, and rights connected to membership of trade unions, collective bargaining, and industrial action. In short, every aspect of employment law that we have considered is expressed in abstract terms as a basic right of workers in Europe. Most of these rights can also be discovered in international Conventions of the ILO and the Charter of Fundamental Rights of the European Union 2000.

The crucial difference between these international and transnational declarations of social rights and the protection of civil liberties discussed in the previous chapter is that the declarations of social rights are not directly legally enforceable by individuals. In the case of ILO Conventions, we have already noted that an independent committee of experts produces a report on the compliance by a state with a particular Convention, but this report only has political or moral force against a signatory to a Convention. A similar reporting mechanism applies to the European Social Charter, where the European Committee of Social Rights makes assessments of compliance with the general standards. Its reports put flesh on the general standards. For example, Article 4.4 gives the right to a reasonable period of notice for termination of employment, and the

---

[1] Signed but not yet ratified by the UK.

Committee has expressed the view that dismissal with less than one month's notice after a period of a year's employment with a particular employer is unreasonable,[2] though UK law only provides for a minimum of one week.[3] A recent additional Protocol of the European Social Charter establishes a novel enforcement technique. Representative national organizations of employers and trade unions can bring a complaint against their national government for failure to comply with the Charter, and if the Committee upholds the complaint, a Committee of Ministers of the Member States may recommend that the government subject to complaint should rectify the position, and that government can be required to report on the measures that it has taken.[4] This procedure harnesses the efforts of trade unions to police compliance with the Charter, though it does not alter the fundamental position that none of these international treaties provides individuals with directly enforceable legal rights.

Yet these declarations of social rights can have a significant impact on employment law. The rights set an agenda for employment law, strengthening calls for legislation or alternative regulatory techniques. For instance, the case for the introduction of minimum notice periods and the law of unfair dismissal in the UK was certainly assisted by the political pressure to conform to the ILO Convention on Termination of Employment and the European Social Charter. It is also possible for lawyers to try to persuade a court that its interpretation of national legislation should, if at all possible, conform to international Conventions. Although national courts rarely adopt that approach, at least for the purposes of EC law, the ECJ is required to respect the principles of the Charter of Fundamental Rights of the European Union 2000, which includes a wide range of social rights. Through these various routes, the tissue of 'soft law' tends to ossify over a period of time into new legislation or sympathetic judicial interpretations of existing legislation.

Consider, for instance, the legal protection for a worker's right to join a trade union. Under legislation in the UK, an employee has the legal right not to have action taken against him by the employer that prevents or deters him from joining or taking part in the activities of a trade union.[5] In effect, this law enshrines the right to be a member of a trade union and to take part in its activities. The question arose in *Associated Newspapers*

---

[2] Conclusions XIV–2, Vol. 1, p. 397.   [3] Employment Rights Act 1996, s. 86.

[4] H. Cullen, 'The Collective Complaints Mechanism of the European Social Charter' (2000) 25 *European Law Review*, Supp. (Human Rights Survey) 18.

[5] TULR(C)A 1992, s. 146.

Ltd v. Wilson[6] whether an employer had interfered with this right by offering to pay employees more on the condition that employees would ceased to authorize the trade union to bargain collectively on their behalf. A few employees declined and claimed that their legal rights had been violated. But the House of Lords denied their claim. One reason given was that the employer had not taken 'action' against the employee, but merely omitted to award a pay rise. This casuistry surely convinces no one. If an employer gives everyone else a pay rise except one employee because he wants to be a member of a union, this must be regarded as an action to the detriment of the employee just as much as if the employer had imposed a pay cut. The second reason given deserves closer attention. The House of Lords held that the action against the employees was not an attack on their membership of a trade union as such, but on their wish to have the union represent them for the purposes of collective bargaining. In other words, employees could remain members of the union without interference by the employer and take advantage of the services provided by the union except for the one concerning collective bargaining.

This argument relies on a possible reading of the statute, which only refers to membership and activities of a trade union, but it makes little sense from an industrial pluralist perspective. From that point of view, the main reason why people join trade unions and why that right needs to be protected is that they need the protection and greater bargaining power provided by collective bargaining. The judges chose not to accept that logic, no doubt being influenced by their respect for an employer's right to freedom of contract, which permits an employer to offer such terms of employment to each individual as it chooses. Nor is this a case drawn from the ancient past, when judges revealed a deep antipathy towards trade unions, but it was decided in the middle of the 1990s. This decision is an example of how employment law rights based upon traditional conceptions of civil liberties often do not provide the necessary guarantees for collective action that employees need for the purposes of effective union organization.

But in the context of a discussion of the potential implications of the soft law of social rights, the interesting part of this story is that this decision of the House of Lords was overturned in the European Court of Human Rights.[7] As we have seen, the European Convention on Human

---

[6] [1995] 2 AC 454, HL.

[7] *Wilson and National Union of Journalists v. United Kingdom* [2002] IRLR 568, ECHR.

Rights, enforced by the Strasbourg Court, does not embody social and economic rights, but rather a short list of traditional civil liberties. But in the *Wilson* case, the claimants could rely upon the right to freedom of association, which unusually includes elements of a social right by recognizing expressly an individual's 'right to form and to join trade unions for the protection of his interests'. The European Court of Human Rights interpreted the right to freedom of association to include elements of the social right to organize collectively.

It is of the essence of the right to join a trade union for the protection of their interests that employees should be free to instruct or permit the union to make representations to their employers or to take action in support of their interest on their behalf . . . It is the role of the State to ensure that trade union members are not prevented or restrained from using their union to represent them in attempts to regulate their relationship with their employers.

The claimants were awarded compensation for injury to feelings, and UK law, as interpreted by the House of Lords, was declared to be in violation of the civil liberty of freedom of association. In reaching its decision, the European Court of Human Rights paid close attention to the meaning of the right to organize in the European Social Charter and the equivalent and more detailed Conventions of the ILO. It noted that the expert committees under both the Charter and the ILO had expressed the view that UK law was incompatible with the right to organize. The decision illustrates, therefore, how social rights can have indirect legal effect by influencing the interpretation of legally enforceable rights, in this instance rights under the European Convention on Human Rights.

In this chapter, we consider the agenda set by these international declarations of social rights for employment law with a view both to completing this introduction to the concerns of employment law and as a way of pointing towards possible future developments. The protection of social rights through the law may provide a vital element in the evolving concept of citizenship.

I. HEALTH AND SAFETY

In earlier chapters we have observed the conflicts and struggles provoked by the wage labour system for the division of labour that evolved with industrialization. But even the most radical elements in that struggle, the Luddites, perhaps did not appreciate fully the latent risks to their lives presented by the techniques of factory production. Workers in the cotton mills suffered from 'strippers' and grinders' asthma', or byssinosis, which caused statistically high death rates. Although this occupational risk was recognized by doctors as early as 1831, no protective measures were taken until 1939, when sufferers and their dependants became entitled to meagre benefits under a statutory compensation scheme. Owing to difficulties in proving the occupational source of the illness and distinguishing it from exposure to general pollution and smoking, only a few claims for compensation proved successful. In the 1980s, using reports from Health and Safety inspectors that revealed that companies failed to use vacuum cleaners to contain the dust from cotton, workers, with the support of trade unions, began to bring successful claims for substantial compensation under the private law of tort.[8] In short, it was only when the cotton industry in Lancashire was in rapid decline under pressure of foreign competition and many companies were closing, that employers began to take adequate preventive measures and to pay realistic levels of compensation. One wonders whether the timing was mere coincidence.

The protection of the health and safety of workers has long been acknowledged as one of the fundamental social rights that should be safeguarded by law. In the European Community, a framework Directive establishes a duty on employers to ensure the safety and health of workers, and to inform and consult workers or their representatives on all questions relating to safety and health at work.[9] Through further detailed Directives and implementing national legislation, employers are required to comply with particular rules governing trades and business activities. These rules are enforced usually by inspectors who can prosecute employers for failure to comply. In addition, the employer is normally required to establish a partnership institution, such as the health and safety committees in the UK, where representatives of the workforce can raise health and safety issues and discuss solutions. A final strand in the EC legal framework requires employers to carry out formal risk assessments of every activity of the business and to communicate the results to the workforce, a process which is designed to alert the employer and employees to risks to personal safety and to induce preventive measures. Together these strands represent the most sophisticated regulatory strategy in employment law, with its combination of public standards and partnership self-regulation.

    [8] S. Bowden and G. Teedale, 'Poisoned by the Fluff: Compensation and Litigation for Byssinosis in the Lancashire Cotton Industry (2002) 29 *Journal of Law and Society* 560.
    [9] EC Directive 98/391.

In order to compensate individuals for breach of health and safety standards resulting in death, injuries, and occupational diseases, every legal system provides specialized systems aimed at ensuring that workers and their dependants receive compensation. Some of these schemes date back to the nineteenth century, when the rising incidence of accidents in the workplace associated with industrialization combined with a perception that society ought to help those who had fallen on hard times through no fault of their own contributed to the acceptance of the need for special regulation. At that time, private law systems provided an uncertain route for compensation for injured workers, because the law constrained such claims by such devices as requiring the employee to prove fault on the part of the employer, denying or restricting the vicarious liability of employers for the action of other workers that caused the injury, and exploiting the idea that liability was negatived by the worker's consent to the risk. The replacement German model involved a compulsory insurance system based upon contributions by employer and employee, from which the worker or dependants could draw an income in the event of a disabling accident.[10] In the United States, employers accepted under workers' compensation laws a system of prompt, no-fault liability for limited compensation, for which they had to take out insurance, in return for the elimination of private law claims based on negligence.[11] In Britain, after many twists and turns in legislative policy,[12] there are elements of both these approaches, leading to extraordinary complexity in the compensation system. The social security system provides through the state various potential benefits for those injured in the course of employment, including industrial injuries compensation and invalidity benefits. In addition, a statutory sick pay scheme requires employers to pay most employees who are off work through personal incapacity a low weekly amount (in 1996 set at £54.55) for a period up to 28 weeks.[13] But this legislation does not provide a basic employment right that ensures the continuation of a proportion of pay during sickness, for the purpose of the legislation was to transfer some of the costs to the social security system onto employers. As a result, the conditions of

---

[10] B. Hepple, 'Welfare Legislation and Wage-Labour', in B. Hepple (ed.), *The Making of Labour Law in Europe* (London: Mansell, 1986), ch. 3.

[11] A. Larson, 'The Nature and Origins of Workmen's Compensation' (1952) 37 *Cornell LQ* 206.

[12] P. W. J. Bartrip and S. B. Burman, *The Wounded Soldiers of Industry* (Oxford: Oxford University Press, 1983).

[13] Social Security Contributions and Benefits Act 1992, Pt XI, supplemented by Statutory Sick Pay (General) Regulations 1982, SI 1982/894.

eligibility for this statutory entitlement are extremely complicated, because they apply only when the employee would otherwise have enjoyed a claim against the state for some kind of income support.

Owing to the potential inadequacy of this state compensation scheme, however, the private law compensation system was never abolished, so that employees can bring claims in tort against their employer for negligence. These tort claims are sometimes effectively no fault claims if the employee can point to the breach of a particular statutory safety duty by the employer that caused the accident, and the court accepts that the breach of this particular statutory duty can be used as the basis of a private law claim. For example, if a failure by an employer to carry out a risk assessment is a contributory cause of an accident, breach of this regulatory requirement suffices to establish the employer's liability in damages for the injuries.[14] This system of private law claims was further strengthened by a mandatory requirement that employers should take out private liability insurance.

Private law claims remain a significant element in systems of compensation for injuries and diseases that fall outside the mandatory compensation arrangements, or where permitted as an alternative claim, as in Britain. In the United States, though workers are precluded from bringing claims for negligently caused injuries against their employer, in many instances, such as claims based on injury to health from asbestosis, they may bring claims for diseases linked to workplace conditions that fall outside the compulsory scheme or use product liability as an alternative to a claim in negligence.[15] Owing to the limitations of the statutory compensation scheme in the UK, particularly with respect to occupational diseases such as byssinosis, private law has been used to expand the range of protection against illness and disease in the workplace. For example, pressures on employees at work may lead to stress and prolonged psychiatric illness. Although such illness falls outside the statutory compensation schemes, under the private law of negligence an employer may be liable to pay compensation for psychiatric injury caused by stress arising from employment. The test is whether the employee's injury was reasonably foreseeable, whether the employer failed to take reasonable care to avert that injury, and whether such measures would have prevented the illness. Stress in the workplace is common,

---

[14] *Swain v. Denso Marston Ltd* [2000] ICR 1079, CA.
[15] E.g. *Mandolidis v. Elkins Industries, Inc.* 246 SE. 2d 907 (1978); *Porter v. American Optical Corp.* 641 F. 2d 1128, 5th Circ (1981).

and though employers must take the normal precautions such as permitting rest breaks and holidays, liability for psychiatric injuries resulting from stress depends upon the employer being alerted to the increased risk in the case of the claimant. For example, a claim by a schoolteacher for compensation for psychiatric illness induced by stress was defeated, because although teachers no doubt all suffer from stress, the psychiatric illness was not reasonably foreseeable by the employer as the teacher had a normal workload, and she had not complained to anyone about the stress she was suffering as a result of overwork.[16] It is plainly a mistake for employees to put up with stressful working conditions in silent fortitude.

This brief picture of the law governing health and safety at work reveals how it has been a concern of employment law for more than a century, but it also reveals the inadequacy of thinking about it exclusively in terms of social rights. Although the right to a safe place of work can be vindicated by a claim for compensation for injuries, the law increasingly takes as its priority the establishment of a safe workplace in which accidents and illnesses do not happen. To that end, employment law uses all the regulatory techniques with which we have become familiar. Even so, the law also recognizes that safety cannot be an absolute right. There are too many jobs such as those of firefighters and the police where absolute safety in the face of unforeseen contingencies proves impossible. Employment law insists instead that employers create systems of management, which through risk assessment procedures try as far as possible to anticipate dangers and to take measures that are designed to reduce or eliminate the risk. The compensation system reflects this acceptance that the right to a safe place of work cannot be absolute, by limiting the employer's strict liability to breach of rules that identify known hazards, and by applying negligence standards to the remaining causes of occupational injuries and diseases.

Yet the history of health and safety laws also reveals links to a broad conception of citizenship. The idea that compensation for occupational injuries and diseases should be secured through either compulsory social insurance or strict liability linked to private insurance represents an acknowledgement that society has a collective responsibility to protect its members from the hazards of work.

---

[16] *Hatton v. Sutherland* [2002] ICR 613, CA.

2. THE RIGHT TO ORGANIZE

As the *Wilson* case demonstrated, the right to join a trade union is both an aspect of the basic civil liberty of freedom of association and a social right. As a social right, however, the right has the more extensive meaning of the right to form organizations of workers for the purpose of bargaining with employers about terms of employment and workplace conditions. The right to organize implies a right to participate in the management of the enterprise through a variety of partnership institutions. The social right therefore expresses an ideal of citizenship in work, in which employees are not merely linked to the employer by contract, but also regarded as members of the organization, with rights to be informed and consulted about the plans and objectives of the business.

To fulfil such a role, trade unions need to be independent of the employer, and responsive to the interests and wishes of their members by means of governance through democratic participatory processes. As free associations of their members, unions are likely to fulfil these requirements, but the law can provide safeguards against manipulation of the trade union by employers, against oligarchical internal structures dominated by union officials, and against unfair treatment of individual members of the union. Yet the state must be careful not to regulate trade unions too closely, for such mandatory rules and structures may also undermine their independence, and may obstruct the union's need to be able to act effectively.

For the most part the common law courts restricted their regulation of trade unions to ensure compliance with the internal rules of the organization by treating those rules as terms of the contract of membership. But the courts could approach those rules in different ways. To justify non-intervention in a dispute inside the union, a court could argue that the internal remedies available under the rules of the union should be followed,[17] and that in any case a court should not intervene if the rules permitted some organ of the union to condone the alleged breach of the rules.[18] In contrast, the courts could intervene, should they so wish, in a particular dispute between a union and its members, by declaring the union to be in breach of implied terms in the contract of membership,[19] and by insisting that the proper interpretation of the rules was ultimately

---

[17] *Brown v. Amalgamated Union of Engineering Workers* [1976] ICR 147, Ch D.
[18] *Hodgson v. NALGO* [1972] 1 All ER 15, Ch D.
[19] *Radford v. NATSOPA* [1972] ICR 484, Ch D.

a question of law for courts.[20] This rather haphazard and unpredictable method of control exercised by the courts over the internal affairs of trade unions remains in place in the UK, but it has been largely superseded by a model of mandatory regulation, which was copied in part from the United States.

The American regulation was provoked amongst other reasons by a widespread suspicion that many unions had been taken over by organized crime. In Britain, however, there was no such problem, but there were allegations that militant union leaders were using their power to call industrial action for political purposes and against the wishes of their members. No doubt union leaders are from time to time out of touch with the wishes of their members or some section of the union, though the empirical studies suggest that the leadership is usually less militant than some sections of membership.[21] Even in the mineworkers union, where the leadership had a radical reputation, we find legal cases brought by members of the union aimed at restraining the leadership both in instances where the leaders were pressing for industrial action,[22] and in the opposite case where the leaders had agreed a settlement with the employers contrary to the wishes of some section of the union.[23] Despite this equivocal evidence in support of the claim that unions had to be 'given back to their members',[24] the UK now has extremely detailed mandatory legislation governing the internal affairs of unions and their relations with their members.

Financial propriety with the assets of the union is ensured by accounting and disclosure requirements.[25] The dangers of oligarchy are countered by a mandatory requirement to arrange for an independent scrutinizer to hold periodic secret ballots for the executive committee of the union and for the position of principal executive officer, usually known as the general secretary. No member of the union may be unreasonably excluded from standing as a candidate, and in general every member of the union should be entitled to vote in the election.[26] The risk of unfair treatment of an individual member of the union is countered by granting members the right not to be unjustifiably disciplined or expelled.

[20] *Edwards v. Halliwell* [1950] 2 All ER 1064, CA.
[21] R. Undy and R. Martin, *Ballots and Trade Union Democracy* (Oxford: Blackwell, 1984).
[22] *Taylor v. National Union of Mineworkers (Derbyshire Area) (No. 3)* [1985] IRLR 99, Ch D.
[23] *National Union of Mineworkers v. Gormley* (1977) *The Times*, 21 October.
[24] Green Paper, *Democracy in Trade Unions*, Cmnd. 8778, January 1983.
[25] TULR(C)A 1992, ss. 24–45D.   [26] TULR(C)A 1992, ss. 46–61.

This notion of unjustified discipline is defined further to include the case of discipline for the reason that the member failed to support industrial action.[27] Expulsion from the union is only permitted on certain grounds such as non-payment of dues in accordance with the rules of the union, and is not permitted for refusal to participate in industrial action or for having been or being a member of another union.[28] This regulation is rendered more effective by the presence of a public official, the Certification Officer, whose job includes investigation and adjudication over disputes about compliance with the rules. The whole legislative framework amounts to a steam hammer to crack a problem of internal union misgovernment that scarcely existed. It is unsurprising that the Committee of Experts of the ILO has concluded that the legislation and in particular the restrictions on a union's powers to discipline its members under its rules amount to excessive interference by public authorities in the internal affairs of trade unions.[29]

Although this regulation of the internal affairs of trade unions in Britain does not on its face directly interfere with the workers' right to organize, it should be appreciated that it subtly undermines the effectiveness of trade unions. The legislation imposes considerable costs on unions, particularly with the need to hold secret postal ballots both in the case of election of officials, and also in the case of industrial action discussed above.[30] The effectiveness of unions is even more crucially undermined by their inability to use discipline against their members in order to ensure their cohesion. If the leadership proposes a strike, which is endorsed by the overwhelming majority of its members in a secret ballot, a small group of members can ignore the strike call, set up a rival union, and bring litigation against the union that questions the legitimacy of the union's action, and then, possibly disastrously for the aims of the union, its officials are precluded from doing anything about that small group at all. It seems as if the UK law has matched the social right to organize with an opposed right to disorganize.

That is not to say that the right to organize should entitle a union and its members to force other workers to join or stay in a particular union. The question of whether a worker can be required to be a member of a particular union if the worker wants to be employed with a particular employer or in a particular craft raises the question of the legitimacy of a

---

[27] TULR(C)A 1992, ss. 64–7.   [28] TULR(C)A 1992, ss. 174–7.

[29] ILO, International Labour Conference, 87th Session, 1999, *Report of the Committee of Experts on the Application of Conventions and Recommendations*, Report III (Part IA).

[30] Chapter 7.

'closed shop'. If an employer agrees that only members of that particular union should be employed in particular jobs, the organizational and bargaining position of a union is enhanced. Many countries including the United States permit such closed shop agreements to be binding, because they promote the social right to organize, and often they prevent industrial disruption arising from competition between unions or disagreements between members and their leaders. To counter the risk that the interests of some members will not be adequately represented by the leadership, the law, as in the United States, can impose on union officials a duty to represent its members fairly. But in view of the difficulty of adjudicating between the competing interests of sections of the union's membership, the courts have confined their interventions to cases of arbitrary, discriminatory, or bad faith failures to represent members.[31] From the perspective of the civil liberty of freedom of association, a closed shop that limits job opportunities to union members interferes with the freedom not to belong to a particular trade union or any trade union at all. This interference with the civil liberty of freedom of association has been grounds for the European Court of Human Rights to declare that closed shops are usually contrary to the Convention right: the right to freedom of association in Article 11 also included the negative right to dissociate.[32] UK law now conforms to this civil liberties standard. Although closed shop agreements are not unlawful in themselves, any action taken by an employer to compel union membership will be regarded as unlawful discrimination resulting in liability for substantial levels of compensation to a worker who has been denied a job, put at a disadvantage, or dismissed on the ground of non-membership of a particular union.[33] If the union tries to induce an employer to enforce a closed shop agreement, the union can be joined as a party to the proceedings and required to pay a just and equitable contribution to the compensation, which may amount to all of it. Unions in Britain have therefore ceased to try to bargain for a closed shop agreement.

This brief survey of the law governing the relation between trade unions and their members reveals a pattern of intensive mandatory regulation. The propriety of this degree of state interference in organizations of workers is constantly challenged by reference to the standard of the social right to organize. No doubt it is right to be concerned about state

[31] *Vaca v. Sipes* 386 US. 171 (1967).

[32] *Young, James and Webster v. United Kingdom* (1982) 4 EHRR 38, [1981] IRLR 408, ECHR; M. Forde, 'The "Closed Shop" Case' (1982) 11 *Industrial LJ* 1.

[33] TULR(C)A 1992, ss. 137, 146, 152.

interference, for totalitarian governments use such techniques to control workers' movements and to stifle the potential input of trade unions as representative institutions to broader political debate. Although this historical perspective explains the misgivings about state controls over trade unions, it can be suggested that if organizations of workers are to be recognized as vital ingredients in a new conception of citizenship, these organizations must accept the discipline of public accountability, transparency, and democracy. Instead of union autonomy being sacrosanct, what is more important is that workers' organizations can claim the authority derived from high standards of good internal governance, so that they can claim to be the legitimate representatives in the various mechanisms for setting labour standards at different levels of governance. In other words, an expanded notion of citizenship implies that representative institutions that engage with the broader issues involved should conform to public standards. In so far as mandatory regulation guarantees those standards, it should not be criticized simply because it involves state interference with trade unions. On the other hand, if state interference imposes considerable costs on unions and in other ways obstructs their attempts to evolve effective organizations, one must question whether this legislation is inspired by a search for a broader conception of citizenship that embraces the Webbs' ideal of industrial democracy based upon voluntary membership of self-governing trade unions.[34]

3. THE RIGHT TO STRIKE

The right of workers to take industrial action is also protected by the European Social Charter and ILO Convention 87 (1944). The right to strike is regarded as a fundamental social right because without the right workers will not be able to use their collective strength to improve their working conditions. It is central to the industrial pluralist ideal of joint regulation of the workplace. It is less clearly an essential ingredient of modern notions of occupational citizenship, but certainly the workers involved in partnership institutions must be able to make credible threats of withdrawal of co-operation unless the employer participates fully. The right to strike is not expressly protected by the European Convention on Human Rights, but in the *Wilson* case the Strasbourg Court recognized that unless trade unions could threaten industrial action in connection with their representation of their members, their ability to provide

---

[34] S. and B. Webb, *Industrial Democracy* (London: Longmans, 1897).

effective representation would be gravely weakened, thereby undermining their members' right to freedom of association.

Protection of the right to strike requires as a first step an immunity for the trade union and its officials against civil and criminal actions for organizing strike action. We examined this aspect of the law above,[35] where we noted that in the UK the intricacies of the legal immunities combined with the procedural requirements of balloting tended to place serious obstacles in the way of trade unions seeking to organize industrial action. Although the requirement that a union should hold a ballot to approve industrial action fits into a notion of trade unions having to observe high standards of internal governance, some of the detailed requirements of the procedure seem excessive, such as the requirement that the union should notify the employer seven days in advance when the industrial action is to start, who will be involved, and whether it will be continuous or discontinuous.[36]

But the underlying problem with the adequacy of protection of trade unions and their officials in connection with the right to strike in UK law is the uncertainty caused by the fluidity and indeterminacy of the economic torts created by the judges during interim proceedings. In a case we considered earlier concerning UNISON's campaign against a private finance initiative for a new hospital, the trade union unsuccessfully sought a declaration that the complex restrictions on industrial action in UK law were contrary to the right to freedom of association. The European Court of Human Rights accepted that the right to freedom of association included the right of trade unions to protect the occupational interests of their members through industrial action. Nevertheless, the right to strike could be restricted within the margin of appreciation of states in a proportionate way in order to protect the rights of others, which include the rights of the employer to carry out its functions effectively and to enjoy freedom of contract. In effect, the Court upheld the 'trade dispute' limitation on lawful industrial action as necessary in a democratic society for the protection of the rights of others.[37]

Protection of the right to strike also implies an immunity for an individual worker who obeys a strike call. Under the private law of contract, industrial action will almost certainly amount to a breach of contract by an employee. A refusal to work would also normally be sufficient to justify a dismissal. If the right to strike is to be guaranteed, therefore, the

---

[35] Chapter 7.   [36] TULR(C)A 1992, s. 234A.
[37] *UNISON v. United Kingdom* [2002] IRLR 497, ECHR.

individual worker needs to be protected against dismissal or a claim for breach of contract. Most industrial countries have recognized this requirement of the right to strike by protecting employees against dismissal in response to strike action. In civil law systems it is common for the law to insist that during strike action the contract is suspended, but can be resumed once the industrial action is over. Without a similar concept of suspension, in common law systems an employer's dismissal of strikers is regarded as being effective to terminate the employment relation. Protection of the right to strike can therefore only be achieved by giving the worker the right to be reinstated on the conclusion of the strike. Unions usually bargain for this arrangement as part of the settlement of the strike, but if the employer adamantly refuses to take back the workers who went on strike, the only option left for the law is to award the dismissed strikers substantial compensation. After unfavourable criticism by the ILO and the European Social Rights Committee over many years, UK law recently introduced significant though limited legal protection for individual workers dismissed for taking part in a strike. If an employee is dismissed during the first eight weeks of an official strike, that is a strike authorized by a trade union after a ballot and within the union's statutory immunity, the dismissal is automatically unfair.[38] But if the strike action falls outside this protection by being an unofficial strike or lasting longer than eight weeks, a dismissed employee has no claim for compensation at all.[39] Thus if a union makes a mistake in following the mandatory procedures concerning balloting and notification, it exposes all its striking members to dismissal without compensation. If a union organizes a strike to protest against dismissals of unofficial strikers, it has no immunity, so it cannot protect its members by any means from its own mistake.[40] An adequate protection of the social right to strike should require that an employer, if it chooses to use its ultimate economic weapon of dismissing all strikers permanently, should pay the normal compensation for economic dismissals or redundancies.

One final immunity has also been suggested as necessary to complete the legal protection of the right to strike. Under most social security systems, a worker is excluded from benefits relating to unemployment for a certain period of time, if the worker leaves a job voluntarily or is dismissed for misconduct. Should this exclusion apply to strikers? Since the

---

[38] TULR(C)A 1992, s. 238A.
[39] Subject to an exception for selective dismissals: TULR(C)A 1992, s. 238.
[40] TULR(C)A 1992, s. 223.

days of the poor laws in the nineteenth century, in Britain persons who are not working owing to strike action and are directly interested in the dispute have been disqualified.[41] Notice that this exclusion is not confined to strikers, but also applies to those who are laid off as a result of industrial action and who might benefit from the result of the strikers' claim. Nor does the exclusion distinguish between strikes and lock-outs by employers. The main justification for this complete exclusion of strikers from social security payments is that the state wishes to remain neutral in industrial disputes. Payments to strikers might be regarded as providing financial support for them against the employer. Only in cases of hardship after all sources of income for the family including union strike payments have been considered will the state provide income support to strikers' dependants, but never to the strikers themselves.[42] These disqualifications are harsher than those applicable to employees who are dismissed for severe misconduct. The question can be asked whether this stance in relation to social security payments is genuinely neutral or whether it tends to favour the employer by reducing as much as possible the income to the strikers' family. Other legal systems take a more even-handed approach, preventing, for example, claims for unemployment benefits for the first eight weeks of the strike action, which in effect treats strikers as if they had been dismissed for misconduct.

Most legal systems create some exceptions to the right to strike. Formulations of the social right usually admit two kinds of exception. The first concerns collective agreements. If a union calls a strike in violation of a binding collective agreement, in many jurisdictions the strike becomes unlawful. In the United States, for instance, a court will issue an injunction that compels the union to take the issue to binding arbitration, as agreed under the collective agreement. Rather unusually, in UK law there is no such exception, since the collective agreement is not usually regarded as legally binding in itself. The appropriate terms of the collective agreement are likely to be incorporated into individual contracts of employment, thereby becoming enforceable by employees against the employer. But the employer cannot usually enforce the collective agreement against the union by obtaining a court order to desist from breach of the collective agreement.[43]

A second exception to the social right to strike concerns certain classes

[41] Jobseekers Act 1995, s. 14.
[42] Social Security Contributions and Benefits Act 1992, s. 126.
[43] TULR(C)A 1992, ss. 179, 180.

of workers, such as the military and the police, who are forbidden by law to take strike action.[44] But how far should this exclusion extend? It is sometimes suggested that all workers who perform 'essential public services' should be excluded from the right to strike. Yet this formulation might apply to all workers in the public sector—prison warders, the fire service, the health sector, and transport, power, water, and perhaps even communications workers. It might be possible to persuade the workers in these sectors to refrain from industrial action, but only if they received a reliable guarantee that their wages and other conditions would be set by some independent process, free of the employer's dominating influence. Such a guarantee is probably impossible on economic grounds for any state to give except perhaps in wartime. The right to strike even for workers in most essential public services has to be accepted, and the best solution is for the state to provide an independent mediation and arbitration service that is likely to enjoy the confidence of the parties.

Although most of these workers in the public sector retain the right to strike, their actions may be restricted by further civil and criminal controls over their conduct. In UK law it is a criminal offence for an employee to break the contract of employment with reasonable cause to believe that the consequence will be to endanger human life or expose valuable property to destruction. As we have seen, many other minor criminal offences may be committed during industrial action involving picketing, such as the quaint Victorian offence of 'watching and besetting' the home or workplace of another person. These criminal offences have no exceptions for official strike action, so that when the police authorities are so minded or instructed by government, they can arrest strikers under these vague offences and effectively stop industrial action in its tracks. Similarly in France, the right to strike is qualified by an exclusion of strikes where there is 'faute lourde', though the meaning of 'heavy fault' is left to the courts to determine.

In these and similar legal measures we can detect a reluctance on the part of modern states ever to take the idea of the social right to strike so seriously that they relinquish the power, should governments so wish, to take decisive action through force to break a strike. The right to strike is always contingent on the state's ultimate monopoly of force.

---

[44] Incitement to Disaffection Act 1934; Police Act 1996, s. 91.

4. RIGHTS AND CITIZENSHIP

Despite the misgivings expressed above about the potential disadvantages of employment law becoming embroiled in the intricacies of rights talk, it is also apparent from this brief examination of the evolution of civil liberties and social rights in connection with employment that the law about rights can have a profound impact on nearly every aspect of legal regulation. To the extent that the soft law of social rights becomes imbricated in the legally enforceable tradition of civil liberties, the tendency of rights talk to favour individual interests over the necessarily collective interests of groups of workers may be abated.

In the European Union, the ambitious declaration of the Charter of Fundamental Rights of the European Union 2002 merges civil liberties with a wide range of social rights. Even if this declaration does not form part of a future constitutional settlement for the 25 Member States of Europe, it may exercise a profound influence on how the European Court of Justice develops the principles of EC employment law. The Charter embraces a conception of citizenship that not only protects civil liberties and equality but also views workers as having fundamental entitlements to fair and just working conditions, to social inclusion through work, and to the right to be consulted about the plans of their employers. Such rights will not guarantee a paradise in the workplace, but they will certainly dampen the fires of the inferno.

12

Shelf-life

Short books should whet the appetite. Unlike the first book published in this series, *The Concept of Law*, in which H. L. A. Hart presented a timeless concept of a national legal system, I have never had much confidence in reaching a final conclusion on a comparable concept of employment law. As I remarked in the opening chapter, employment law, with its focus on a pivotal mechanism of a market society for constructing social integration and the distribution of wealth and power, must always remain controversial and provisional, as it responds and adapts to changes in the division of labour and shifts in political values. Even so, one interpretation of the particular historical conjuncture at the beginning of the twenty-first century encourages me to believe that this brief account of a concept of employment law may have the shelf-life of a fine aperitif rather than that of a canapé.

The historical moment that suggests we may have reached a degree of permanence in employment law is the consolidation of the economic and political bloc of the European Community. This political project, which draws 25 Member States into an ever closer union, entails not only the establishment of a huge labour market, but also a set of common political and legal principles for the governance of employment relations. The principles of this European model, I have suggested, embrace the three central themes around which my account has been organized: social inclusion, competitiveness, and citizenship. These themes have become central to the European model, because they serve to justify this system of supranational government. Social inclusion promises that every citizen of the European Community will benefit from the enlargement of the economic and political sphere of governance in both material and non-material ways, which is necessary to establish and protect social cohesion. Competitiveness in the economic system is vital for delivering the improved standard of living promised to all citizens as the potential result of transnational co-operation and regulation. Citizenship represents a guarantee of the protection of civil liberties and social rights, an affirmation that is so necessary after a century in Europe when abuse of state power pervaded the history of so many Nation States.

Of course, these thematic priorities in Europe do not determine the details of employment law. They suggest principles to be adopted, but also establish fundamental tensions between rights that need to be resolved. Nor do these thematic priorities determine at what level of governance the principles should be implemented. Although the European Community has a vital role in articulating the broad reach of these principles, their detailed implementation can be achieved through a variety of methods and levels of governance. For employment relations the regulatory methods include, in addition to standard form of mandatory legislative instruments, the special techniques of collective self-regulation that can be adopted at a variety of levels from the particular enterprise to the supranational Social Dialogue. Since every employment law system in Europe represents a series of historical compromises forged as a result of political and sometimes industrial conflict within each country, the imposition of uniform transnational laws encounters enormous difficulties in articulating precise standards whilst at the same time permitting each state to implement the standards by regulatory techniques that honour past political settlements and reflect the particular circumstances of local labour markets and industrial structures. To be reflexive and thereby achieve high levels of compliance, transnational employment regulation has to respect the varieties of capitalism.[1] Employment law in Europe can be harmonized around common supranational principles, though in the medium term at least, it cannot easily be unified or denationalized.[2] The achievement of a common European model will rely rather on processes and dialogue, on partnership institutions, on techniques of 'soft law', and on the mutual observation of the Open Method of Co-ordination between Member States.[3] Some areas of employment law, particularly those concerning the sensitive political compromises representing the consolidation of the industrial pluralist model at the beginning of the twentieth century, may remain indefinitely outside the competence of the EC, and be subject only to the broad parameters of fundamental

---

[1] P. A. Hall and D. Soskice (eds), *Varieties of Capitalism: The Institutional Foundations of Comparative Advantage* (Oxford: Oxford University Press, 2001).

[2] C. Kilpatrick, 'Emancipation through Law or the Emasculation of Law? The Nation-State, the EU, and Gender Equality at Work', in J. Conaghan, R. M. Fischl, and K. Klare, *Labour Law in an Era of Globalization* (Oxford: Oxford University Press, 2002), p. 489.

[3] S. Sciarra (ed.), *Labour Law in the Courts* (Oxford: Hart, 2001); C. Barnard, 'The Social Partners and the Governance Agenda' (2002) 8 *European LJ* 80.

social rights for which each state is awarded a wide margin of discretion. But the remainder of employment law, particularly those parts that are perceived to constitute essential ingredients in the themes of social inclusion, competitiveness, and citizenship, seem destined to become subject to processes and dialogue at a European level with a view to the creation of common minimum standards.

This broad historical interpretation of the course of employment law helps to situate the particular position of the United Kingdom today. For most of the twentieth century the story of British employment law can be crudely summarized as an unceasing struggle between the liberal vision of freedom of contract and the industrial pluralist ideal of power-sharing between capital and labour. Although the elements of this struggle can be found in the history of all industrialized countries, the British perception of the problem and how it might be resolved was perhaps most clearly akin to the solutions found in North America.[4] The legal foundation of employment relations provided by the common law was an intensely private, individualized contractual relationship, which created few expectations of long-term diffuse obligations of fair treatment and mutual assistance. Under pressure from organized labour, this legal scheme was adjusted to permit, and to a limited extent to promote, a narrow version of industrial pluralism through which labour unions could bargain collectively with employers over terms and conditions of employment. The legal framework that created this space for collective self-regulation, though differing in its detailed formulations between the UK and America, was in both countries assiduously policed by the courts,[5] so that the exception to free market competition was confined and never permitted to spill over into a broader agenda of power-sharing between capital and labour. Regardless of whether liberal freedom of contract or industrial pluralist policies prevailed at any given time, employment relations were regarded as essentially an activity of private ordering, with only the basic ground rules of the operation of the labour market regulated by the state.

Although the historical influence of American law and the shared common law heritage retain a significant presence in British employment law, the interpretation of the present trajectory of UK employment law

---

[4] D. C. Bok, 'Reflections on the Distinctive Character of American Labor Laws' (1971) 84 *Harvard LR* 1394.

[5] Lord Wedderburn, *The Worker and the Law*, 3rd edn (London: Sweet & Maxwell, 1986), ch. 1; K. Klare, 'Judicial Deradicalization of the Wagner Act and the Origins of Modern Legal Consciousness, 1937–1941' (1978) 62 *Minnesota LR* 265.

articulated in this book suggests that the tectonic plate that binds Britain to continental Europe now exerts a far greater influence than hitherto. That European tradition, led by France and Germany, conceives of employment law as part of a broader set of social policies, through which the state secures the welfare of its citizens. How employment relations are conducted and how businesses are managed are subjects of public interest, not merely private agreement. The agenda of social law, of which employment law constitutes a vital part, is to provide a much deeper and more encompassing resolution of the paradox examined at the outset of this work that 'labour is not a commodity'. Employment law fits into European Social Policy, not merely transnational labour market regulation and employment policy. Workers and employers are not merely private actors in the labour market, but also participants in processes of governance that reconcile the needs of social cohesion and a broad notion of citizenship with the pressing requirement constantly to improve the competitiveness of the relations of production.

I am not suggesting that some invisible hand of economic imperative or destiny will bind Britain to a European model of employment law. The construction and agreement upon the evolution of that model remains a political task, subject as ever in employment law to pragmatic compromise and changes of mind. Even less am I suggesting that the American influence in the global economic system and in particular its distinctive approach to employment law will cease to put its mark on how the law evolves in Britain and Europe. The relative likely influences of the American and continental European traditions have guided my selection of comparative legal material. Nevertheless, it seems to me at the beginning of the twenty-first century that we have passed some kind of watershed in Europe, where we have committed ourselves through such documents as the Charter of Fundamental Rights of the European Union 2000 to a distinctive and separate model for employment law. The details of this model of course remain uncertain, and many variations are possible and have been proposed.[6] Catchy labels such as 'The Third Way', or even 'New Labour Law', are often misleading, but they do help, I suggest, in grasping some dimensions of the new perception of employment law that is emerging as a surprisingly broad consensus across the European

---

[6] E.g. B. Bercusson, S. Deakin, P. Koistinen, Y. Kravaritou, U. Muckenberger, A. Supiot, and B. Veneziana, 'A Manifesto for Social Europe', (1997) 3 *European LJ* 189; K. Ewing (ed.), *Working Life: A New Perspective on Labour Law* (London: Institute of Employment Rights, 1996).

Community.[7] What I have attempted to achieve in this work is a sketch of the principal elements of a concept of employment law and how they are interrelated. No doubt this rough draft is inaccurate and incomplete; others will improve upon it by detecting a clearer structure in the architecture of employment law in Europe as it constantly evolves. This task is as much art as social science. But whatever configuration of the themes of social inclusion, competitiveness, and citizenship emerges, the future vitality of British employment law seems destined to be determined by the position of these islands on the European continental shelf.

[7] A. Giddens, *The Third Way* (Cambridge: Polity, 1998); A. Giddens (ed.), *The Global Third Way Debate* (Cambridge: Polity, 2001).

Index

Advisory, Conciliation and Arbitration
   Service (ACAS)
   establishment of 20
agency workers
   contractual relationship 41–2
   regulation applying to 42
association, freedom of
   exercise of 212
   right not to join union 243
   trade union, right to join 235

business
   market conditions, response to 181
   outsourcing by 183
   restructuring 181–2
   social dumping 184

capital investments
   transfer between countries 183
casual worker
   protection of employment law rights,
     exclusion from 40
   unfair dismissal, no protection from 172
catering trade
   minimum wage, tips included in 207
child labour
   eradication, attempted 48
childcare
   availability of 95–6
children
   work hours, limitation of 16
citizenship
   anti-discrimination laws 54
   civil liberties, protection of 24
   employment law, theme of 24–5
   social rights 24–5 see also social rights
civil rights see also rights; social rights
   citizenship, as part of 24–5
collective agreement
   disciplinary provisions 159
collective bargaining
   bargaining unit, scope of 122
   binding disciplinary procedures and
     standards, for 167–9
   collective self-regulation, as 30–1

developments, minimum wages
   impeding 81–3
duty to bargain 124–5
legal intervention, techniques of 120–1
mechanisms for 120
obstacles, removal of 18
partnership institution, as 125
procedural regulation, as 30
promotion of 19–20, 120–6
reform 20
right of 116
scope of topics 126
Trade Boards, by 20
trade union recognition 122–4
weaknesses 31–2
workers obtaining gains from 42
combination
   criminal conspiracy, as 18
company
   European Company Statute 131
   organization of 130
   ownership 130
competition law
   contractual restraints on competition
     freedom to work, on 150–1
     loyalty, obligation of 151–3
     non-compete clauses 153–6
   employment law, and 136
   human capital, application to 150–1
   industrial action, and 140–50 see also
     industrial action
   maxims of 135
   migration of workers 136–9
   state aid 139–40
competitiveness
   employment law, theme of 23–4
compliance with employment law
   breach, right to pursue claim for 29
   collective self-regulation 30–1
   employees, incentives for 29
   inspectors, system of 29
   minimum wage 84
   minorities, interests of 32
   policing of standards 29
   procedural regulation techniques 30

compliance with employment law *cont.*
  securing, difficulties of 28
  soft law initiatives 32
  weaknesses 30
confidential records
  data protection 218–19
  privacy, right to 217–20
  unauthorized disclosure 217
consultation with employees
  arrangements for 127
  Directives 126–7
  economic dismissals, proposals for 128
  European Works Councils 128–9
  legal institutions for 128–9
  legal provisions requiring 129
  legal regulation, contribution of 128
  mechanisms for 126–30
  statutory framework 126
  topics for 129
contract
  consumer 8
  employment *see* contract of employment
  freedom of 14–17
  short term 8
contract of employment
  authority structure 10–11
  breach
    damages, remedy in 166
    employer's business, obstruction of
      99
    express terms, of 164–7
    fundamental 161
    industrial action, by 145
    purported dismissal, validity of 165
    statutory immunity 145–7
    work to rule, by 99
  compulsory terms 167
  conflict, management and resolution of 9
  consensual relation between parties, as 6
  disciplinary provisions *see* discipline
  discretionary power under 103–4
  disputes arising during 8–9
  diversity of arrangements 37
  entire obligations, doctrine of 160
  exchange of work for pay, as 100
  express terms 33–4
  fair treatment under 115
  formality 107–8
  formation, rules for 6
  freedom of contract, principle of 14–17
  freedom to offer terms 102
  grievances, provision for dealing with
    109–10

implied terms
  adaptation 106–7
  breach of 161
  customs and conventions, insertion of
    36
  day-to-day managerial behaviour,
    controlling 105
  elements of 102–3
  express terms overriding 104
  express terms, relationship with 36
  general principles of private law, and
    36
  legal obligations, defining 34
  loyalty, of 151–3
  mutual trust and confidence 103–6
  nature of 34
  regulation by 35
incompleteness 10–12
indefinite duration, of 38–9
indeterminacy 10
inequality of bargaining power 6–7
labour, acquisition of 37
legal framework 103
long-term nature of 8–9
negotiation 14
obligation to provide work 113
ordinary contract law, inadequacy of
  13
package 100
performance of 12
performance of work, for 37
refusal of employee to accept conditions
  imposed 181
regulation 5
  implied terms, by 34–7
  legal analysis, starting point 33
  rule-books 33–4
  special characteristics 33
  termination, relating to 35
remuneration under 108
repudiation 176
risk, allocation of 184–5
standard-form, use of 44
statutory rights, excluding 45
take it or leave it basis, on 6–8
training and educational opportunities,
  provision for 112
variation of obligations under 106–7
  transfer of business, after 197–8
  unilateral 193–4
work to rule, whether breached by 99
worker's needs, balancing 12
working relation, patterns of 37

Council of Europe
  Social Charter 232

data protection
  remedial system 219
  safeguards 218
  sensitive personal data 218
  transfer of data outside EC 219–20
disability discrimination
  disabled persons, definition 71
  justification 71–2
  reasonable adjustments, duty to make
    71–2
  structure of law 71
discipline
  binding procedures and standards for
    167–9
  collective self-regulation 167–9
  compliance with regulation, securing
    176–80
  construction of procedures 175
  contractual framework 159
  contractual protection
    common law rule 160–1
    compulsory terms 167
    default principles 160–3
    express provision, absence of 159–60
    express terms 164–7
    general rules 160
  corrective strategies, linked with 159
  effective exercise of 159
  fair procedure, requirement of 174–5
  forms of 158
  mandatory regulation 169–73
  mandatory rules 159
  need for 158–9
discrimination *see also* disability
    discrimination; race discrimination;
    sex discrimination
  age 73, 164
  application of laws 41
  best practice, adoption of 74
  business-to-business contracts, laws not
    covering 41
  but for test 57
  circumstantial evidence of 57–9
  Codes of Practice 73
  considerably smaller proportion of
    disfavoured group, against 59–62
  covert 58
  enforcement 73–4
  equal opportunities monitoring 59
  eradicating 73–5

indirect 59–62
justification
  business interests, serving 69
  customer preference 63–4
  differences between groups,
    accommodating 65
  disability, accommodating 71–3
  ethnic minorities, in favour of 64
  foreign nationals, against 63
  formal qualification, need for 68
  grounds for 62
  occupational qualifications 63–4
  policy ambitions, balancing 68
  positive discrimination 64–7
  proportionality, test of 65–71
  real need 67
  underlying principle 62–3
laws prohibiting
  competitiveness, serving economic
    goal of 54
  cultural prejudices, not changing 55
  framework of 54
  justification 54
  labour market, effect in 56
  requirements of 55–6
  social inclusion, not ensuring 55
legal regulation, evolution of 56
participatory self-regulation 75
past, reversing effects of 65
positive
  European law 65–6
  justification 64–7
  past discrimination, reversing effects
    of 65
  proportionality, test of 65–6
  UK law 67
  US law 66
protected groups 56
proving 56–62
religious 93
selection for redundancy, in 60–1
sexual orientation, on grounds of 57
sexual preference, based on 221
unconscious 58
unequal treatment, principle against
  54–5
dismissal
  compliance with regulation, securing
    176–80
  constructive 105
  contract of employment, repudiation of
    176
  costs of 173

dismissal *cont.*
  criminal offence outside workplace, for
    222
  economic
    alternative courses of action,
      consideration of 189
    circumstances counting as 192–3
    collective compulsory procedures
      189–90
    costs, effects of 194
    different skills, requiring workers
      with 188–9
    justification 188–90
    reasons, investigation of 188
    remedial options 192–6
    rules for 187–8
    schemes of regulation, impact of
      194–5
    selection process 190–2
    social plan, agreement of 194
  fairness, standard of 173–6
  procedural steps prior to 179
  proportionality, assessment of 174
  redress, avenues for 177
  social rights 233
  striking, for 246
  substantive reasons, adequacy of 179
  transfer of business, effect of *see* transfer
    of business
  unfair *see* unfair dismissal
  whistleblowing, for 227
  wrongful, common law claim 177
distributive justice
  questions of 13–14
dress code
  right to privacy, and 222–4
  sex discrimination, as 223

economic security
  competitiveness, effect of 181–2
  conflict of interest 182
  corporate insolvency 201–4
  deferred pay, safeguarding 186–7
  Directives 184
  dismissals
    alternative courses of action,
      consideration of 189
    circumstances counting as 192–3
    collective compulsory procedures
      189–90
    costs, effects of 194
    different skills, requiring workers
      with 188–9

    justification 188–90
    reasons, investigation of 188
    remedial options 192–6
    rules for 187–8
    schemes of regulation, impact of
      194–5
    selection process 190–2
    social plan, agreement of 194
  government, role of 182–3
  length of service, based on 191
  reorganizations of work affecting 193–4
  risk, allocation of 184–5
  transfer of business, effect of *see* transfer
    of business
employee
  human capital benefits 110
  loyalty, obligation of 151–3
  rival business, setting up 152–3
employee share ownership schemes
  incentives 32
employer
  exercise of discretion, monitoring 11
employment law
  additional cost of production, imposing
    15
  aim of 5
  balance in 5
  citizenship, theme of 24–5
  competition law, and 136
  competitiveness, theme of 23–4
  compliance *see* compliance with
    · employment law
  conflicting frameworks 21
  controversial and provisional, remaining
    250
  conventional structure for exposition,
    lack of 25
  current position 252
  distinct character of 31
  employment relations
    regulating 5, 13
    stabilizing and regulating 14
  Europe, priorities in 250–1
  European Community, themes in 21
  European influence 253–4
  European legal systems, in 19
  globalization, effect of 45–50
  implementation, difficulties of 27
  industrial pluralist model 17–20
  institutional framework for workplace, as
    23
  legal scholarship, as subject of 5
  liberal paradigm 16–17

mandatory rules and procedures 11
objectives of
  freedom of contract 14–17
  industrial pluralism 17–20
  shifting 14–20
  whether achieving 15
reflexivity, need for 37
regulatory competition 45
rigidities 15
social inclusion, theme of 22–3
social regulation, objection to 15
starting presumption 40
employment regulation
  acceptance of changes, effect on 44
  contracts to which law applying 38,
    41
  mandatory, case for 42–5
  problems for 37
  scope of 37–42
  state, role of 95–6
equal pay
  equal value, work of 88
  individual employees, claims by 90
  job evaluation 88
  material factor, difference due to
    88–9
  national legislation 87
  need for 86–7
  occupational segregation, differences
    due to 87–9
  principle of 87
  similar value, work of 87
  women's work, perception of 89
  work and life, effect of balancing 86
European Community
  agreement to proposals, securing 46–7
  anti-discrimination laws 54
  economic and political bloc,
    consolidation of 250
  employment law, themes driving 21
  employment law traditions, differences
    in 47
  movement of capital, Directives on
    46
  principles, implementation of 251
  social regulation, enactment of 47
  uniform minimum labour standards,
    rejection of 46
European Convention on Human Rights
  Human Rights Act, incorporated in
    210
  national legislation, interpretation of
    211

public authorities, duties of 210–11
rights under
  assertion of 210
  employment law, impact on 212
  fair trial, to 211
  interference by State, protection
    against 211
  privacy, to 211, 215 *see also* privacy
  proportionality, test of 213
  restriction of exercise of 212
  terms of contract restricting 213–14
  violation, issues of 212
European Works Councils
  introduction of 128
  regulation 129
expression, freedom of
  dress codes, challenge to 223
  fundamental right, as 224
  scope of 224
  workplace, in
    generally 25, 224
    picketing 230–1
    political activities 225–6
    whistleblowing 226–9

factories
  inspectors 29
  women and children, hours of 16
free movement of workers
  Bosman ruling 138
  EC law 138–9
  foreign workers, entry of 137
  migration 136–9
  qualifications, recognition of 137–8
freedom of contract
  flexibility and fairness, allowing 114–15
  labour, acquisition of 37
  principle of 14–17

globalization
  levels of regulation, and 45–50
  phenomenon of 45
grievances
  settlement of 109–10

health and safety
  compensation
    complexity of system 237
    private law claims 238
    psychiatric injuries, for 238–9
    specialized schemes 237
    tort law, under 236, 238
  Directives 236

health and safety *cont.*
  employment law, as concern of 239
  occupational risks 236
  origins of law 235–6
  risk assessment 239
  social right, protection as 236
homeworkers
  laws applying to 38
household
  division of labour in 77
human capital
  benefits 110
  competition law, application of
    150–1
  innovation 113–14
  investment in 110
  training 111–13
  work experience 112

income
  work producing 3–4
industrial action
  balloting 149–50
  competition law, and 140–50
  criminal offence, as 18
  economic torts 143–5
  immunity 141, 145–7, 209
  injunction against 141–3
  interference with employers' business
    144
  peaceful picketing 148
  procedural restraints 149–50
  right to take 244–8
  secondary 147–9
  strikes *see* strikes
  trade dispute, in contemplation or
    furtherance of 145–6
industrial conflict
  effect of 17
  parties to, compulsory mediation or
    arbitration 143
  political conflict, separation from
    116
  political revolution, prevention of
    escalation into 19
  relative isolation, in 19
  threat of 116
industrial democracy
  analogies 132–3
  arguments for 132–3
  notion of 132
  public sector, in 133
  structures 133

industrial relations
  collective co-operation, securing
    117
  inherent problems of 116–17
  juridification 9
industrialization
  effects of 76–7
  geography of 77
injunction
  balance of convenience test 141–2
  disobedience to 142
  strike, against 135, 141–3
innovation
  facilitation of 113–14
  profit-sharing 114
insolvency
  corporate
    economic security of employees
      201–4
    government interest in 202
    guarantees 201–2
    rescue of company 202–3
    unpaid wages, claiming 201–2
    transfer of business 203–4
intellectual property rights
  preventing use by employee 153
International Labour Organization
  labour standards, promulgation of
    48
  motto of 3

Jockey Club
  women, exclusionary rule against
    53

Kahn-Freund, Otto 6, 13

labour
  buying 3
  commodity, not 3, 13
  household, in 77
  intensive division of 4
  sexual division 77–8
  social division 76, 94
  state, role of 95–6
  supply, control of 17
labour standards
  deregulatory strategy 43
  disobedience, incentives for 28
  European Community, in 46–8
  flouting 49
  inefficient 28
  international agreement on 48–9

mandatory regulation, effect of 42–5
negotiation of 47
regulatory competition 45
securing compliance, difficulty of 28
United Nations, promotion by 48
Luddites
attacks by 76–7
meaning 76

Marx, Karl 3, 5
maternity leave
right to 92
maternity pay
subsidized 96
minimum wage
catering trade, in 207
complexity of regime 85–6
compliance with legislation 84
contingent payment schemes 85
contracts to which law applying 38
development of collective bargaining,
effect on 81–3
disadvantage arising from 43
disobedience, incentives for 28
employment effects 80–1
enactment of 42
fixing 80
inspectorate 84
mandatory law 79
objections to enactment 86
supply and demand, effect on 81
UK legislation 80
workers not receiving 27

partnership
co-operation through 117
collective bargaining *see* collective
bargaining
conflicts of interest, presupposition of
118
consultation mechanisms 126–30
institutional arrangements 118, 182
institutional structure 119
legal regulation 118
promotion of 118
Rover, example of 118–19
patents
profit-sharing 114
paternity leave
right to 92
pension schemes
occupational, maladministration of 187
safeguarding 186–7

picketing
expression, freedom of 230–1
political activities
expression, freedom of 225–6
local government officers, by 226
public officials, by 225
privacy
activities outside workplace, as to 221–2
concept of 214
confidential records 217–20
data protection 218–19
dress codes, and 222–4
employment, relating to 24–5, 215
European Convention on Human Rights,
under 211
strands of 214
surveillance, use of 215–17
testing 220–1
production
co-operation 10

race discrimination
ethnic minorities, in favour of 64
first prohibition of 53
statutory provisions 56
redundancy
circumstances counting as 192–3
collective compulsory procedures 189–
90
information and consultation on 189–90
justification 188–90
payments 192, 201
selection process 190–2
restraint of trade
application of doctrine 154
garden leave clauses 155
non-compete clauses 153–6
right to work
origin of 53
rights
assertion of 208
collective entity, of 209
conflict of 209–10
employer's, invasions of 209
European Convention *see* European
Convention on Human Rights
extension of range of 209
individual, rhetoric of 208
instrumental use of 210
proportionality, test of 213
social *see* social rights
wider range, extension to 232
workers, of 208–9

self-employment
  attractions of 39
  contractual relationship, features of
    40
  increase in 39
sex discrimination
  considerably smaller proportion of
    disfavoured group, against 59–62
  dress codes, and 223
  Equal Opportunities Commission
    formal investigation of employer,
      carrying out 74
    litigation, assistance with 90
    standing of 73–4
  full-time work, insistence on 92–3
  Jockey Club, by 53
  privacy and decency, to protect 64
  statutory provisions 56
Smith, Adam 7
social inclusion
  employment law, theme of 22–3
  protected group, of 55
  regulation 22
social regulation
  objection to 15
social rights
  association, freedom of 235
  citizenship, and 24–5, 249
  civil liberties, and 232
    merger with 249
  declarations of 232
  employment law, impact on 233
  health and safety 235–9 *see also* health
    and safety
  organize, right to 240–4 *see also* trade
    union
  reporting mechanism 232
  Social Charter 232–3
  soft law, implications of 234
  strike, to 244–8 *see also* strikes
  trade union, right to join 233–4
social seclusion
  unemployment, effect of 182
stakeholder organizations
  management 131
  model of 130
  representation, effect of 131
state aid
  competition law provisions 139–40
statutory sick pay
  entitlement to 237
stock options
  deferred pay, as 187

strikes
  dismissal during 246
  essential public workers, by 248
  individual workers, immunity 245–6
  injunction against 135, 141–3
  right to strike 244–8
    exceptions 247–8
  social security benefits during 246–7
  trade unions and officials, protection of
    245
surveillance
  work, at 215–17

telecommunications
  surveillance 216
temporary workers
  contractual relationship 41–2
  regulation applying to 42
termination of employment
  common law rule 160–1
  compulsory terms 167
  default principles 160–3
  disciplinary power 160–3
  evolution of law, EC influence
    179–80
  express terms 164–7
  fundamental breach of contract, for
    161
  implied substantive limit, compensation
    for breach of 163
  limitations on 22
  manner of 162
  pay in lieu of notice 113
  reasonable notice, period of 161
  regulation of 35
thought, conscience and religion, freedom
  of
  right to 93, 211–13
tips
  remuneration, as 207
tort
  economic 143–5
trade secrets
  protection of 153
trade union
  activities, limits on 116
  assets, financial propriety 241
  balloting procedures 149–50
  closed shop, legitimacy of 242–3
  competition law, immunity from 143
  criminal conspiracy, as 18
  effectiveness, regulation undermining
    242

expulsion from 242
immunity 141, 145–7
independence, need for 240
internal rules, treatment of 240
mandatory regulation 241, 243–4
members, fair treatment of 241,
   243
minorities, interests of 32
organize, right to 240–4
political activities 18
recognition 122–4
right to join 233–4, 240
state control 244
United States, regulation in 241
training
   appropriate skills, in 183
   human capital, investment in 111
   legal rights to 112
   provision of 100
   skills, acquisition of 111
   subsidies for 111–12
transfer of business
   Acquired Rights Directive 196–201
   dismissals
      coherent approach to 197
      grounds for 196
      sale, after 197
   employment security, effect on 196
   franchise, of 199–200
   identity, remaining same 199
   insolvency, following 203–4
   outsourcing 198–9
   transnational regulation 200–1
   TUPE Regulations 197
   variation in contract terms following
      197–8

unemployment
   government, cost to 182
   long-term, effect of 182
   manpower policies 183
unfair dismissal
   compensation
      awards 178
      levels of 177
   concept of unfairness, interpretation of
      176
   fairness, standard of 173–6
   mandatory law of 37
   merits of dismissal decision, view of
      tribunal on 158
   proportionality, assessment of 174
   reasonableness of decision 158

reinstatement, remedy of 178
statutory protection
   age of retirement, employees over
      172
   origin of 172
   qualifying period 172
   suspicion of fraud, on 157–8
   unemployment effects 43

vocational training
   right of access to 25

wages
   deductions from 171
   deferred pay, safeguarding 186–7
   distribution of wealth by 3
   fixing rates of 20
   gender effect 86–7
   low pay, problem of 79
   minimum *see* minimum wage
   payment mechanisms 100
   payment schemes 108
   sweated trades, in 82
Wages Councils
   abolition 82–3
   creation of 82
   effects of 82
   low minima, establishing 83
   orders, failure to comply with 85
welfare system
   income from 79–80
   types of benefits 80
whistleblowing
   cover-up 229
   expression, freedom of 226–9
   protected disclosures 25, 227–9
   statutes 227
   United States, in 229
   victimization 229
women
   work hours, limitation of 16
work
   economic model 78–9
   inducements for 100
   life, division with 78–9
   stream of income, providing 78
worker
   freedom of 3
   partnership institutions 24
   person, as 3
   protection of employment law rights,
      exclusion from 40
   system of production, compliance with 4

workforce
  co-operation, securing 117
  partnership *see* partnership
working time
  balance of 91
  Directive 91
  industrialization, at time of 77
  long-hours culture 90
  longer working week, agreement to
    44
  part-time 90, 92, 94
  regulation of 91

religious observances, right to 93
right to choose 94
time off, rights to 92
upper limit 91
work/life balance, addressing 79
workplace governance
  flexible model 101–2
  Fordist system 100
  Japanese system 101
  mixture of models 102
works rules
  issue of 100